My Years with the British Red Cross

My Years with the British Red Cross

A Chief Executive Reflects

Sir Nick Young

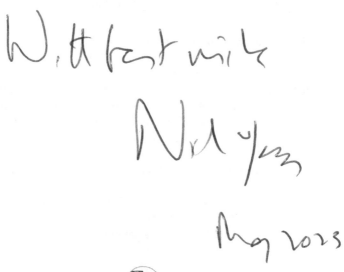

With best wish

Nick Young

May 2023

PEN & SWORD
HISTORY

First published in Great Britain in 2022 by
Pen & Sword History
An imprint of
Pen & Sword Books Ltd
Yorkshire – Philadelphia

ISBN 978 1 39906 700 3

Typeset by Mac Style
Printed in the UK by CPI Group (UK) Ltd, Croydon, CR0 4YY.

Pen & Sword Books Limited incorporates the imprints of Atlas,
Archaeology, Aviation, Discovery, Family History, Fiction, History,
Maritime, Military, Military Classics, Politics, Select, Transport,
True Crime, Air World, Frontline Publishing, Leo Cooper, Remember
When, Seaforth Publishing, The Praetorian Press, Wharncliffe
Local History, Wharncliffe Transport, Wharncliffe True Crime
and White Owl.

For a complete list of Pen & Sword titles please contact

PEN & SWORD BOOKS LIMITED
47 Church Street, Barnsley, South Yorkshire, S70 2AS, England
E-mail: enquiries@pen-and-sword.co.uk
Website: www.pen-and-sword.co.uk

Or

PEN AND SWORD BOOKS
1950 Lawrence Rd, Havertown, PA 19083, USA
E-mail: Uspen-and-sword@casematepublishers.com
Website: www.penandswordbooks.com

This book is dedicated to the volunteers and staff of the British Red Cross who, day in day out, across the world and around the corner, do everything they can to meet the needs of vulnerable people in time of crisis – and, in particular, to the members of my management team, who became great friends as well as great colleagues, and to Sheila Ashbourn and Paula Collier, my PAs during this period, who had to put up with so much!

Contents

Abbreviations

8NS – organizational development exercise in which four national societies from 'developed' countries worked closely and cooperatively with four national society partners from 'developing' countries, learning lessons together

AIDS – acquired immune deficiency syndrome, caused by damage to the immune system by the HIV virus

ATV – all-terrain vehicle

BA – British Airways

BBC – British Broadcasting Corporation

CBDP – community-based disaster preparedness

CCTV – closed circuit television

CEO – chief executive officer

CESG – cost and effectiveness steering group, a joint working group of trustees and senior staff set up to identify cost savings and efficiencies

COBRA – Cabinet Office Briefing Rooms

DC – Detective Constable

DEC – Disasters Emergency Committee, a joint venture of the UK's leading aid agencies which launches fundraising appeals for major disasters and distributes the funds according to each agency's capacity to respond

DFID – Department for International Development (now part of the Foreign, Commonwealth and Development Office)

DPRK – Democratic People's Republic of Korea (North Korea)

ECOMOG – Economic Community of West African States Monitoring Group, a West African multilateral armed force

ERU – Emergency Response Unit

EU – European Union

FAO – Food and Agriculture Organization of the UN

FCO – Foreign and Commonwealth Office

Federation – the International Federation of Red Cross and Red Crescent Societies, currently comprising 192 member national societies. Its offices are in Geneva.

G24 – grouping of twenty-four national societies from rich and industrialized countries

GDPR – General Data Protection Regulation, made under the Data Protection Act 2018 which created strict rules governing the use of personal data

HIV – human immunodeficiency virus, which attacks the body's immune system and, if not treated, can lead to AIDS

HMG – Her Majesty's Government

HRH – His/Her Royal Highness

ICRC – International Committee of the Red Cross, an impartial, neutral and independent organization whose exclusively humanitarian mission is to protect the lives and dignity of victims of armed conflict and other situations of violence, and to provide them with assistance. Based in Geneva.

IDF – Israel Defence Forces

IDP – internally displaced person

IHL – International Humanitarian Law, a set of rules which seek, for humanitarian purposes, to limit the effects of armed conflict

IOC – International Olympic Committee

IRA – Irish Republican Army

IT – information technology

ITN – Independent Television News

ITV – Independent television

KFOR – the Kosovo Force, a NATO-led peacekeeping force in Kosovo

KLA – the Kosovo Liberation Army

KPMG – an accountancy firm established in 1987, when Klynveld Main Goerdeler merged with Peat Marwick

LRC – Liberian Red Cross

MDA – Magen David Adom, the Red Shield (or Star) of David, Israel's national medical emergency, disaster, ambulance and blood service, recognized by the ICRC as the national aid society of Israel and a member of the International Federation of Red Cross and Red Crescent Societies.

MI6 – Military Intelligence, Section 6, formally the Secret Intelligence Service, the British Government agency responsible for foreign intelligence.

MOU – Memorandum of Understanding, a document which outlines the broad outlines of an agreement reached by two or more parties

MP – Member of Parliament

NATO – North Atlantic Treaty Organization, a collective defence grouping of countries from Europe and North America

NDMA – Pakistan's National Disaster Management Agency

NEPARC – the New Partnership for African Red Cross and Red Crescent Societies

NGO – non-governmental organization, a non-profit entity that operates independently of government

NHQ – national headquarters

NHS – the National Health Service

NK – the disputed territory of Nagorno-Karabakh

O2 – entertainment arena in Greenwich, formerly known as 'The Dome'

OIC – the Organization of Islamic Cooperation, an international organization with fifty-seven member states, most of them Muslim-majority countries

ONS – Operating National Society, a national Red Cross or Red Crescent Society from a 'developing' country

ORHA – the Office of Reconstruction and Humanitarian Assistance, set up by the US government to act as a caretaker administration in Iraq

PMI – Pelang Merah Indonesia, the Indonesian Red Cross

PNS – Participating National Society, a national Red Cross or Red Crescent Society from a 'developed' country

PRCS – Palestine Red Crescent Society

PST – Psychological Support Team, a team of volunteers set up by the British Red Cross under a contractual agreement with the FCDO to provide psychosocial support to people affected by crisis situations outside the UK as part of the FCDO Rapid Deployment Teams

RAF – the Royal Air Force

RC – the UN resident coordinator

RNID – the Royal National Institute for Deaf People

RNLI – the Royal National Lifeboat Institution

SARC – Syrian Arab Red Crescent

SARCS – South African Red Cross Society

SMT – senior management team

STD – sexually-transmitted disease

TB – tuberculosis

UAE – the United Arab Emirates

UK Ops – the UK operations division of the British Red Cross

UKO – UK Office

UN – the United Nations

UNHCR – the United Nations High Commissioner for Refugees

UNICEF – the United Nations Children's Fund

UNOCHA – the United Nations Office for the Coordination of Humanitarian Affairs

WAAF – the Women's Auxiliary Air Force

WFP – the United Nations World Food Programme

WHO – the United Nations World Health Organization

Acknowledgements

This is very much a personal memoir. It is not a formal or official history of the British Red Cross. The views expressed do not necessarily reflect the views of the British Red Cross, or of any other Red Cross or Red Crescent organization. I have written what I personally recall about the events and situations I witnessed. Inevitably, therefore, other people's memories of those events may differ, and they may take a different view of their importance or significance. I am sure I have omitted to mention events or activities that others may feel should have been included. I can only offer my apologies to anyone who is disappointed.

I am enormously indebted to the five chairs of the British Red Cross board of trustees with whom I worked, Lady Limerick, Professor John McClure, James Cochrane, Lord Allen, and David Bernstein, for their support and encouragement at the time, and for agreeing to read through 'their' section of the manuscript, offering helpful advice and comment and correcting some of my howlers. Lady Limerick also generously sent me numerous interesting papers from her own substantial archive.

Former colleagues Martin Farrell, Mike Adamson, Roger Smith, Jean Henderson, Mark Astarita and Alexander Matheou also kindly read through the draft manuscript and gave me helpful suggestions and ideas. Mary Mawhinney, and Michael Meyer at the British Red Cross also generously helped and advised in various ways, including the correction of errors and misconceptions. Julia Mackenzie, a friend from another charity, also gave me the benefit of her considerable editing experience.

Sir Stephen and Lady Lamport, both close friends and former colleagues, have also been enormously generous with their ideas and encouragement, as ever.

At Pen & Sword, everyone has been as helpful and friendly as ever. Henry Wilson has been brilliant throughout the process, Jon Wilkinson has designed a beautiful cover, Matt Jones has been a great and patient production manager, and George Chamier has been a marvellous editor.

All the opinions expressed in the book are my own, as are any remaining mistakes – for which I apologize unreservedly. Where possible and feasible, I have sought permission from all individuals featured in images, and from those who took the original photographs. I would like to thank everyone who has consented, and to apologize most sincerely to anyone whom I have not been able to contact or whom I have accidentally omitted.

I am very grateful to the British Red Cross and the Ministry of Defence for authorization to use the Red Cross designation and emblem on the jacket of the book, as are the publishers.

Finally, I must thank my darling wife Helen and my sons Edward, Alex and Tom, for their constant loving support and encouragement throughout my time at the Red Cross, even though the work took me away from home far too often. No one could ask for a more wonderful family.

Introduction

The question that popped up again and again when I was chief executive of the British Red Cross was a simple one: 'Yes, but what do you actually do?'

The question was simple but surprising because, to me at least, the answer seemed so obvious, and I used to wonder, slightly indignantly, if my counterparts in commercial companies or the public sector were ever faced with similar queries.

And yet, it's relatively easy to understand why the question needed to be asked.

To many people, the way charities actually work is a bit of a mystery. As charities have become, over the last forty years or so, more professionally run, images of Victorian-style philanthropy and 'do-gooding' have begun to dissipate – and yet they linger on and cause confusion in the minds of those who have little experience of 'charity' beyond an ad on the TV, an encounter with a collector on the street, a spot of local volunteering, or as a recipient of charitable services.

Furthermore, the Red Cross itself, once described as the UK's 'best known but least understood' charity, is a strange mix of domestic and international activity; of homespun local volunteering and the global politics of conflict and disaster; of passionate humanitarian impulses and careful government-focussed diplomacy. It is an organization with an extraordinarily powerful reputation and brand but often without (except in times of relatively rare conflict and disaster) a regular or constant high-profile presence in the minds or experience of the general public.

In this book I have tried to explain the job by describing some of the hundreds of issues and events that I had to deal with during my thirteen years at the Red Cross, and to show how I responded and why.

I loved my job. Every day, every hour of every day, was different. Sometimes it was difficult, hard, scary even. More often it was exhilarating, inspiring and incredibly, deeply moving. I worked with so many able, committed and energetic colleagues and friends, volunteers and staff alike; and met so many people, often in the direst distress or at the worst time of their lives, whose courage and determination to survive and succeed was little short of miraculous. I was privileged to have the chance to serve with them and for them, and lucky to have been given the opportunity to make, sometimes, a difference in their lives.

What was my contribution as chief executive? Well, I used to joke that what I did mostly was make a lot of noise and wave my arms about. And looking back, I can see some truth in that. I wasn't an 'expert' or specialist and I relied a great deal on members of my team to deploy the skills they had in such abundance with what (I hope) was relatively little distracting interference from me.

I felt that my main task was to enthuse, to encourage, to praise and appreciate, in an organization that was sometimes pretty hard on itself in its drive to live up to the 'Red Cross ideal'; doing work that, for all our efforts, sometimes seemed barely to scratch the surface of need; and in an environment that was increasingly critical of charities and demanding (rightly) of rigorous accountability.

At the same time, of course, I had to give a lead on strategic planning, budget preparation and monitoring, good volunteer and staff relations and management, organizational design, and so on. This stuff is all available in books and courses, and many of them are excellent. There is lots you can learn from others, as you watch and wait for your turn to lead; and if you are lucky you will know some 'wise old foxes' who, in their various fields, have seen it all and done it all and are happy to share their experience with you.

But I do see leadership itself as an intensely personal thing that you have to feel your way into – slowly, cautiously, humbly and with some trepidation – testing the ground as you move forward, but being ever prepared to seize opportunities, as they arise, to make your mark.

As a young commercial lawyer at a big City of London law firm, and subsequently as junior partner in a well-established firm in East Anglia, I had little opportunity to lead, but I did see leaders in action, amongst both my fellow lawyers and my clients, and the ones that impressed me did so with their personalities and their capacity to communicate and inspire, rather than with their technical knowledge of the law or commerce. Personally, I felt constrained and frustrated by law, bored with its restricting detail, though admiring of those who had mastered its intricacies and were at home in a world of paper, rules and precedent, willing to sublimate their own ideas and ambitions in favour of facilitating those of their clients. I found 'helping big companies get bigger' increasingly unsatisfactory as a life's work, and dreamt of getting out.

I wanted to find a job where I could make a real difference in people's lives, and felt called towards the voluntary sector, though I had little idea, in the early 1980s, whether that was a viable option, financially, for someone with three children under six and a large mortgage. My first attempts to find out were met with blank rejection ('We're not looking for any lawyers today, thanks') or, in the case of one recruitment agency which claimed to specialize in the voluntary sector, total astonishment that I should even think of giving up a flourishing career in the law for such a fanciful whim ('Oh no, dear boy, you can't possibly do that. We'll find you a couple of trusteeships, but you mustn't give up your legal career.')

I was lucky. On the spur of the moment one afternoon, I rang up the charity nearest to where we lived in Ipswich, the Sue Ryder Foundation, wanting to find someone in the world of charities who could tell me what it would be like to work for one. Somewhat to my surprise, I was put straight through to Lady Ryder herself. She listened to my tale and then said, 'Well, you'd better come and see me – what are you doing tomorrow?'

The next day, I was in her tiny office listening to this fragile, bird like colossus of the voluntary sector talking about her work in Eastern Germany and Poland after the war with victims of the Nazi concentration camps, and her subsequent efforts to set up a string of nursing homes for people with cancer, multiple sclerosis and other chronic conditions in the UK and overseas. She was unsettling but inspiring, and I had the feeling, as I drove home four hours later through Suffolk fields of ripening corn and under a huge setting sun, that I was somehow being picked up and put down in the right place.

Nearly a year later, and after months of personal soul-searching, debates with my ever-encouraging wife Helen, agonized financial calculations (since making the move would involve a very significant salary sacrifice) and conversations with Sue Ryder and her war-hero husband Leonard Cheshire, himself one of the great philanthropists and charity pioneers of our time, I handed in my notice to my astonished fellow lawyers and set out to help Sue Ryder build new nursing homes.

I was hooked from the start. Working with architects, builders, local health authorities, medical and nursing specialists, and teams of local volunteers raising money and eventually taking over the running of each Home for themselves, I had the chance, at a local level, to lead projects of my own. We turned beautiful but often crumbling historic houses into living, breathing homes for people who could no longer manage life on their own, our entire focus being to create a top-quality caring environment in a building known and loved for generations by local people.

This was my first opportunity to lead and, in doing so, to make a difference in people's lives, and I knew from the very first day that it was, indeed, where I was meant to be. 'SR', as Sue Ryder was known to all, was by no means easy to work for, living as she did a life of relentless schedules, self-sacrifice and service to others, from five or earlier in the morning till late at night, seven days a week, but she taught me everything there was to know about passion, commitment and the way to inspire others by example, and with a vision of what could be – in the words of her favourite poem, by George Linnaeus Banks:

> *For the cause that lacks assistance,*
> *For the wrong that needs resistance,*
> *For the future in the distance,*
> *And the good that I can do.*

Sue Ryder had been clever enough to surround herself with 'wise old foxes', men and women at the top of their professional trees, who guided Foundation policy and advised on key aspects of the way the Homes were run. I sat at their feet, metaphorically, and lapped up all their wise counsel and fascinating stories.

But at the end of the day, when you're in the hot seat yourself, and all eyes turn to you and people ask, 'Well, now what do we do?', you have to find the answer within yourself; and for me that meant relying upon four key aspects of leadership that I tried my best to exhibit.

First was to demonstrate the passion and compassion that I saw reflected day after day in the volunteers and staff I led. Listening to someone just back from a mission to a disaster area overseas, or to a volunteer who had just saved a life with her first-aid skills, or to a new recruit dazzled by the prospect of joining 'the Red Cross' always generated the kind of atmosphere that you just wanted to bottle, so that you could spread it around and dip into it when times were hard. That passion was why many of us had joined the voluntary sector in the first place and what kept us going – and what, as chief executive, I had to encourage, nurture and channel in the right directions. It demanded a degree of compassion, too, not only for those we were seeking to help, but for the volunteers and staff themselves as well, because burnout was a danger – and the compassion had to be balanced with the requirement sometimes to make decisions in the interests of the organization that may well have seemed less than compassionate to those affected by them.

Second was the task of communicating a powerful and inspiring vision for the organization that was ambitious and uplifting, but also reasonably realistic and achievable. 'Where there is no vision, the people perish' says the Book of Proverbs, and that is as true for a charity as it was on the way to the Promised Land. One of the challenges in a charity like the Red Cross is that each volunteer and staff member can have their own vision for what's needed and, as chief executive, you have to be prepared to step in at some point and say, 'This is where we're going' – and then communicate that vision over and over again, and with enormous enthusiasm and optimism (ad nauseam sometimes) until that magical day when, unasked and unprompted, people start reciting it back to you.

Third comes emotional intelligence. I guess there was a time in my life when, like most people, I imagined that a chief executive spent most of his or her time deciding things, and telling people to get on and do them. But of course, it isn't like that, or shouldn't be. I knew that the way to get the best out of people was to get close to them, to try and see things through their eyes, to work with them to find a way through, to be sensitive, flexible and encouraging, and to suggest solutions rather than try and impose them. It takes time, but in the end it's quicker, and infinitely more satisfying.

Finally, for me, it was all about trust and confidence. I wanted to trust and to be trusted; to allow colleagues the space to make decisions for themselves, either singly or in small groups, whilst being trusted enough myself to be able to step in and make a final decision if necessary, knowing that that would be respected. This is the ultimate right of the chief executive, the right to make the final call and to accept the responsibility that goes with it. Do it too soon and you're simply joining in the argument, too late and you risk looking, and being, indecisive and weak. I made mistakes – we all do – but if you trust yourself and your team enough, and if you have earned their trust in return, the risk will be small.

And that's where confidence comes in. You can't know everything, or be everywhere, but you have to be confident that you know enough and that, if you don't, someone in your team will. Leadership is all about people: you have to know and understand them, to trust and have confidence in them; and they need to feel the same about you.

What follows is in no way a handbook on leadership and management. I'm not qualified to write such a thing even if I wanted to; nor is it intended to be an exhaustive or objective history of the British Red Cross, and the international movement of which it is a part, during my years of service, 1990–1995 and 2001–2014.

I did not keep a daily diary; it's just what I remember or recorded in the few notes or personal papers I kept, and my take on the things I worked on, some of the places I visited and some of the people I met and worked with. I have tried to describe what struck me at the time, how I responded and why; and I hope that in so doing an answer to the question, 'What did you actually do as chief executive?' will become a little clearer.

I am conscious, as I re-read this book that, although I divided my time more or less equally between our work in the UK and internationally, it is my stories from overseas that stand out most clearly. On long drives to remote disaster areas, or returning home, usually by overnight flight, from a visit to one of our partner national societies, I often had time to scribble a few personal reflections and memories, and these I have kept and used in the writing of this book. I regret now that I did not try to do the same on my frequent visits around the UK, where our volunteers and staff were no less dedicated and hard-working and often had to deal with very similar issues and personal tragedies to their colleagues working internationally. I apologize for this imbalance and hope that my friends and former colleagues in the UK will forgive me – and at least find some interest in learning more about what we were doing across the world, whilst they were working so hard around the corner.

One thing needs to be borne in mind. None of the successes or achievements described were mine alone or even in significant part. The Red Cross was, and remains, full of the most incredibly passionate, inspired, able and committed volunteers and staff, and it is to each and every one of them that credit must be given. I beg their forgiveness for any mistakes, misapprehensions or misunderstandings on my part that appear in these pages, and for my failures to cover adequately all that they did.

Above all, I offer my humble thanks to them, and particularly to all the members of my management team, who accepted me as their leader, put up with my shortcomings, and allowed me to make a lot of noise and wave my arms about as their chief executive. I loved every minute of it.

Chapter 1

Director of UK Operations, 1990–1995

*War in the Gulf and the Simple Truth Appeal – The National Strategy
and the branches – Focus on emergencies – The structure – International
affairs and the Movement – 125th Anniversary – Time to move on*

I felt very strange, and rather lonely, as I made my way up four flights
of stairs to my office tucked away in 'the attic' on the top floor of
labyrinthine nineteenth-century offices in Grosvenor Crescent,
Belgravia – the national headquarters of the British Red Cross, one of
the 190 national societies that formed part of the international Red Cross
Red Crescent Movement at that time.

Strange because I had got up at 5.00a.m. to catch the first train
from Ipswich to London and was feeling strained, scratchy-eyed and
insubstantial as a result; lonely because, apart from the uniformed
receptionist, I appeared to be the only person alive in the gloomy, fusty
old building. Everyone else was hidden away behind dark-stained fire-
doors leading off dingy, airless corridors.

The recruitment process had not been encouraging. For some reason,
the name of the employer was kept secret until after the first meeting with
the head-hunters; and the second encounter, which was more like a pre-
membership grilling for a London club than an interview for the world's
leading emergency response organization, left me equally mystified and
confused. All I knew on that first day, 3 September 1990, was that I was
part of a new management team being brought in to modernize the Red
Cross. I was the second recruit.

Finding my office eventually, I met for the first time, my wonderful
personal assistant Sheila (who, poor thing, was destined to work with me
for another twenty years), but I could not help wondering if I had made
the right decision, leaving the Sue Ryder Foundation to join what was
beginning to seem quite an old-fashioned institution.

My job was 'Director of the Home Division', which meant 'assisting and advising' ninety independent county branches in the UK in the delivery of Red Cross peacetime services and in implementing Red Cross Council policy. These county branches were formed by and accountable to the Society's Council (or board of trustees), but they were all separately registered as charities, with their own trustees, volunteers and staff.

Whilst the chief executive (then called Director General) or I could encourage and advise them, it soon became clear that we had very little power to tell them what to do or how to do it. Some of them were excellent, but the picture was very mixed, and the challenge was to some extent compounded by the fact that the Council itself was composed almost entirely of 'Branch Presidents', who were at times understandably hesitant to decide upon remedial action if they thought it might be unpopular amongst their volunteers, or their peers.

This structure contributed significantly to the administrative and other problems facing the Red Cross in the UK at that time. Through two world wars, in fulfilment of its role as one of three officially-designated 'voluntary aid societies' (the others being St John Ambulance and St Andrew's Ambulance), it deployed thousands of volunteer nurses to the battlefield and sent millions of life-saving Red Cross food parcels and other comforts to prisoners of war and the wounded: it was, as a result, easily the best known and most respected charity in the country. By the end of the Second World War, its branches were running large numbers of nursing and residential homes, hundreds of ambulances, a wide range of community nursing and welfare services, and parts of the blood transfusion service.

With the establishment of the National Health Service and the welfare state in 1948, however, much of that changed. Many of these activities were subsumed into the NHS, and the branches of the British Red Cross were left trying to fill gaps in services to vulnerable groups in the community (such as the frail elderly, and children and adults with disabilities). They ran a few residential homes, provided some auxiliary services in hospitals and developed training courses for the public in first aid, basic nursing and welfare skills. They also provided first aid cover at events. But for the next forty years or so the organization as a whole struggled to find and promote a really clear role for itself at home.

Overseas, the British Red Cross continued to give strong support to international relief efforts during times of conflict and natural or man-made disaster, providing funding, delegates to work overseas and its valued 'tracing and message' service which aimed to link up individuals separated from their families as a result of war or forced migration. But the branches, in working to identify 'gaps' in local state service provision and then fill them, were sometimes so creative in inventing new services that, by the 1990s, it was no longer possible to describe in a simple sentence what the Red Cross did in the UK. Even the powerful unifying image of the Red Cross as a leading emergency response and first aid organization had become diluted over time (despite magnificent responses to incidents like the sinking of the *Herald of Free Enterprise* at Zeebrugge and the bombing of Pan Am Flight 103 over Lockerbie).

The decentralized structure, with some fiercely independent county branches, exacerbated this problem, as several counties 'did their own thing', often at very small scale and with scant reference to the national headquarters' attempts to impose unifying strategies and priorities, common standards or economies of scale. A few branches actively ignored the national headquarters, seeing it as an 'ivory tower'; and, in some quarters at least, the feelings of antipathy seemed to be mutual.

Sylvia, Lady Limerick, the hard-working and hugely dedicated 'chairman' of the organization's governing Council at that time, with years of personal experience of the Red Cross at all levels, summed up branch resistance for me perfectly in my first formal meeting with her.

'You will find, Mr Young,' she said, 'that if you want to change things in the Red Cross, it will take five years. If you want to change them quickly, it will take ten.'

As I returned to my attic office and started chewing this over with the members of my management team, I could see that we were in for interesting times, if the stated goal of modernizing the Red Cross was to be achieved. I was excited but somewhat daunted by the challenge, which seemed so much bigger and more complicated than my previous job of setting up new Sue Ryder homes.

Meanwhile, the task of recruiting my fellow directors continued, with the arrival on 1 January 1991 of the new Director General, Mike Whitlam, an experienced and well-respected voluntary sector leader. Mike was ambitious, determined and energetic, and he quickly set about creating a management team to match.

We barely had time to draw breath. In mid-January 1991 the Americans (at the head of an international coalition) launched Operation Desert Storm with a massive bombing attack on Iraq designed to force President Saddam Hussein into withdrawing his forces from Kuwait, which he had invaded in August the previous year, intending to use its oil to help finance Iraq's war with Iran. The US bombing attack was followed five weeks later by an overwhelming ground assault on the Iraqi troops in Kuwait and then the invasion of Iraq itself.

Whenever there is a major international armed conflict, the Red Cross comes into its own, its wartime mandate being exercised primarily through the International Committee of the Red Cross (ICRC), a Swiss organization based in Geneva which was founded in 1863 by the Swiss businessman-turned-humanitarian Henri Dunant, after a life-changing personal experience helping the wounded on the battlefield of Solferino in Italy.

The ICRC is an independent, neutral organization whose internationally recognized role is to gain access to and ensure humanitarian protection and assistance for victims of armed conflict and other forms of violence. It acts both in response to emergencies and, more routinely, to promote respect for international humanitarian law (IHL) and its implementation in national law. Its mandate is based on the Geneva Conventions of 1949 and their additional protocols.

For their part, national Red Cross (or Red Crescent) Societies, such as the British Red Cross, have a wartime mandate under the rules of IHL to act as 'voluntary aid societies', auxiliaries to the medical services of their country's armed forces, helping to provide care for sick and wounded service personnel, for example. Additionally, working with and through the ICRC, National Societies do what they can to assist the victims of armed conflict, either directly by providing expertise, trained staff or materials, or indirectly, with a fundraising appeal, for example. As the national Red Cross Society for one of the partner countries in the Coalition, we immediately started discussions with the Ministry of Defence about how best we might help.

To my astonishment at the time, I soon found myself setting up a 24-hour helpline to answer calls from the worried families of British people living in Kuwait or Iraq. A little later, I was tasked with designing 'comforts packages' to be transported into Iraq from Jordan, for several hundred British civilian hostages who had been captured in Kuwait and then taken to Iraq to be held by Saddam at strategic locations as 'human shields'. The packages included food treats, souvenirs from home and things to help pass the time – and in a nice link back to the wartime era, we designed them exactly to the specifications of the Red Cross parcels that had brought such comfort to prisoners of war five decades earlier.

We also started working with another recognized 'voluntary aid society', St John Ambulance, to prepare for the possibility of large numbers of military casualties coming back to the UK, in which case we expected to be helping to provide ambulance transport from airfields to one of the few remaining military hospitals, and nursing and welfare volunteers to help in the hospitals themselves and with affected families.

Weeks later, after the Iraqi Army had been defeated by the Coalition, another international crisis came to the fore, involving Saddam's brutal treatment of the largely Kurdish population of northern Iraq, following an uprising against his regime. The US Air Force imposed a no-fly zone over northern Iraq, but not before hundreds of thousands of Kurds had fled their homes and were camped out in appalling conditions in mountain areas on the borders with Turkey and Iran.

Late one Friday afternoon, we got a message from the Conservative politician Jeffrey Archer asking for a discussion about the possibility of launching a fundraising appeal for the Kurds. I was the only director in the building and was about to head off to the Red Cross Training Centre near Guildford for a conference, so I asked one of my senior managers to investigate, with a colleague from the International Division. He came back somewhat shaken by Archer's forthright style, but also excited by his apparent determination that a fundraising appeal bigger than *Live Aid* was needed and that he should lead it with support from the Red Cross.

Mike Whitlam and our new fundraising director, a sparky Welshman called John Gray, seized on this idea as an opportunity to put what they saw as the sleepy Red Cross 'on the map' in fundraising terms and to build its public profile as an international player. A consultant's report about the organization, entitled *Best Known Least Understood*, which we received about this time, gave added impetus to the plan, and Mike was also keen to use the appeal, which was called *The Simple Truth*, as a chance to engage Princess Diana (then 'Patron of British Red Cross Youth') as a more active participant in the charity's work.

Weeks of whirlwind activity followed, particularly for Gray, organizing fundraising in the UK, and by other Red Cross Societies in their own countries; and for our new Finance Director Stephen Brooker, negotiating contracts for a spectacular global TV event featuring simultaneous concerts round the world. Our own event featured MC Hammer, Chris de Burgh, Tom Jones and others in a sell-out concert at Wembley Arena, attended by Princess Diana, the Prime Minister and many other VIPs – and produced yards of free media publicity for the Red Cross. Meanwhile, Archer was busy persuading governments to pledge more support to the Kurds, with the result that, in the early summer, Whitlam felt able to claim that an astonishing £57m had been raised worldwide (nearly £10m more than *Live Aid*) – a claim that was to come back to haunt me ten years later.

But it was very exciting to be at the centre of all this global humanitarian activity; and when, a few weeks later, our offices in Grosvenor Crescent were occupied for a day by Kurdish refugees in the UK noisily protesting about the treatment of some of their brethren being held captive in Turkey, our sense that the Red Cross was a significant player on the world stage was brought to life for the new team. Work came to a standstill, and staff could only get in and out via a back door into the mews behind. After a tense negotiation the protesters were eventually persuaded to leave, upon our promise to relay their concerns to HMG.

This early involvement for the new management team in high-profile global issues, and the breathtaking pace at which events unfolded, was a huge learning experience at a time when, as a team, we were ill-prepared for it. There was considerable debate within the organization, for example, about whether it was in accordance with the fundamental Red Cross principle of impartiality to focus an appeal on one particular group (i.e. the Kurds) at a time when other groups in the area were also being persecuted, or had similar needs. We made mistakes, there is no doubt, but we also developed a level of confidence for the work ahead.

In the midst of all this drama and international excitement, the new management team was engaged with what seemed at the time to be the monumental task of modernizing the Red Cross. We felt that the potential for turning this 'sleeping giant' into a dynamic and powerful force for good, nationally and internationally, was enormous. With tens of thousands of loyal volunteers at work in local communities, a great brand and an extraordinary and proud wartime reputation, it was impossible not to feel excited at the prospect.

But there was a lot that needed to change. There were no detailed plans or standards for developing many of the services being offered at local level, and no funds for doing so anyway; there were very few experienced fundraisers or communicators either at national or local level; some local staff were operating out of small centres, temporary huts or ageing and unsuitable properties, mostly in poor condition, expensive to maintain and unsuitably located; local activities were under the control of county committees of trustees, some of whom had little or no experience of running local community services, insufficient funds to recruit high calibre staff and little interest in following what were seen by some as the irrelevant diktats of an out-of-touch national headquarters ... and so the list went on.

But all was not lost. In 1990 the national Council, chaired by Lady Limerick, had passed a new strategy focussed on emergency response, building on a previous strategy exercise in the mid-1980s. This 'National Strategy' adopted the new mission of giving 'skilled and impartial care to people in need and crisis', predicated upon providing 'nation-wide a limited number of services common to all branches and comparable in scale and quality throughout the country'. In deciding whether to initiate or develop any service, the branches were to be 'guided by the principle that Red Cross action should be concerned with the emergencies which arise in the lives of individuals, families and communities, and to which volunteers can make a significant response'.

Wisely anticipating that the appetite for yet another 'strategy' exercise would be limited, to say the least, and recognizing the risks of further organizational drift, Whitlam decided to adopt the 1990 National Strategy wholesale, and to task his divisional directors with producing detailed plans for operationalizing its 'Care in Crisis' message as 'One Society', by enhancing the number and calibre of staff and volunteers, dramatically increasing income (then at around £42m per annum) and expanding service provision 'in a business-like manner'.

These divisional plans, which contained the hooks and hints for everything we wanted to do over the next few years, were then amalgamated into the 'Five Year Plan 1992–1996' that, once approved by the Council, became our agenda for action. The launch of the Plan was celebrated in November 1992 with a splendid gala for 10,000 Red Cross volunteers at the Royal Albert Hall (donated free for the night), under the banner *Play Your Part* and attended by Princess Diana. Movingly, the Chairman of the BBC, Marmaduke Hussey, recounted from the stage his gratitude to the Red Cross for repatriating him as a wounded prisoner of war after he had been wounded in the 1944 battle at Anzio, in which he lost a leg. Every aspect of British Red Cross work was on display through a variety of vignettes performed by staff and volunteers and compèred by the irrepressible John Gray in a sparkling multi-coloured waistcoat – somehow it felt as if we were 'on our way'.

Dominating everything in my own UK Operations Division, the subject of endless worry and debate, were the branches. Everything we wanted to do in terms of transforming the Red Cross in the UK began and ended with these fifty-three county-based 'business units' in England and Wales and their counterparts in Scotland and Northern Ireland (which were organized somewhat differently).

But the Red Cross wasn't a commercial business, and the branches weren't units in that sense at all. With services largely delivered by volunteers based in small local centres, they were more like families than business units strictly so-called. There was a branch director (usually paid), who reported to the branch trustee committee, and only a handful of paid staff.

It was to the branch, and its committee, not to the national headquarters, that volunteers and staff owed their fealty, imbued as it was with the very character and soul of the county in which it was located. It was the branch which paid their salaries (if they were staff), and provided their much-prized service badges and uniforms if they were volunteers (or 'members' as they were often called). It was the branch that told them what to do and where to go, the branch that rewarded them for their loyalty and long service, the branch which explained the Red Cross to them, fired them with its spirit and made them proud of its history. Hanging in the entrance hall of almost every branch was a large 'school photograph' of dozens of volunteer wartime Red Cross nurses in their starched white uniforms, a large red cross emblazoned on their nurses' bibs – the pictures a silent evocation of the halcyon days to which the organization might yet aspire afresh.

Most branches had their headquarters in large, gloomy and outdated Victorian or Edwardian buildings, often in the leafy suburbs of the county town. There, the branch director, usually a man, had his office, and the branch committee met every few weeks and attempted to exercise their proper governance function with as much common sense as they could muster and such business or organizational experience as they might possess.

Many branches were well led by people (paid and unpaid) who galvanized their colleagues, mobilized resources seemingly from nowhere and delivered services that were second to none in the voluntary sector. But there were others, in the early 1990s at least, where the overriding impression from some of my first branch visits was one of complacency. We called one branch, I remember, 'Sleepy Hollow', but it was a name that could have been applied to several.

National Headquarters seemed a long way away when you were in a branch. When the new head of my 'branch support' team, Martin Farrell, spent his first week or so at the Red Cross in a branch in the West Country, he was astonished to realize that, when volunteers or staff referred to 'Headquarters' they meant the branch office in the county town, not the headquarters of the organization in London. This sense of distance was magnified in Scotland and Northern Ireland, which were both designated as 'Central Council Branches' run, as the name suggests, by their own Council or board of trustees and responsible themselves for the county branches in their part of the United Kingdom.

Scotland was the more distant of the two, in terms of jealously-guarded autonomy, with visits from London discouraged; any attempt to direct or even suggest change or improvement was often rejected out of hand or put to one side with the response, 'That'll never work here', usually accompanied by a weary shake of the head.

Northern Ireland was less distant, if only because it depended more on London for financial support, but in those last years of the Troubles, in such a fiercely-divided community, it was difficult for the branch to tread and be seen to tread a strictly neutral and impartial path, with the result that it was always being criticized by one side or the other – which made it an uncomfortable place to visit as a result. One person stood out, though, in Northern Ireland and remains for me the very model of what a Red Cross volunteer should be – a model, indeed, replicated in one form or another in so many individuals, both volunteers and staff, all over the UK, people who understood to the very core of their beings what it meant to live the fundamental Red Cross Principles of Humanity, Impartiality and Neutrality. Her name, and let her stand for all the others, was Aileen McCorkell.

Aileen, Lady McCorkell, was born in India in 1921, the daughter of an Anglo-Irish aristocrat then serving as a Lieutenant Colonel in the Indian Army. On returning to the UK she enjoyed a privileged education but did not hesitate to join the WAAF (Women's Auxiliary Air Service) in 1939. In 1950 she married Michael McCorkell, whose family owned a large shipping business based in Londonderry and who subsequently became Lord Lieutenant of the County.

Aileen founded what became the Derry Red Cross Branch in 1962 and, throughout the Troubles, provided welfare services across the city, in particular in areas of tragic deprivation and poverty such as the Catholic Bogside, and a first aid post in an urban district with recurrent fighting. When the Bogside and the Creggan became 'no go' areas, she became a fearless fighter for those in need, as prepared to take an army commander to task as she was to remonstrate with the IRA, helping to find accommodation for people bombed out of their homes, looking after girls who had been tarred and feathered for drinking in soldiers' pubs, and delivering meals on wheels on her bicycle across the 'peace line'.

She was in the Bogside on Bloody Sunday, supporting the families of the dead and injured, and described staying on duty long into the night in the dark and fearful streets of the Creggan. It was entirely appropriate that, when top secret peace talks were proposed between the Heath Government and the IRA in 1972, the venue chosen was the McCorkell family home near the Derry/Donegal border.

I met Aileen many times, most memorably on my first visit to Derry, when she wanted to take me to the local Red Cross shop. When we arrived we found the whole area cordoned off and full of soldiers. I assumed we would beat a hasty retreat – but not a bit of it. Aileen marched straight up to the officer in command and demanded to know what was happening.

'It's a bomb, Ma'am,' he replied, 'in that car over there. You can't go through.'

'Nonsense,' she retorted. 'I've got Mr Young here from London' – and through she went, with me nervously in tow.

It was her spirit of courage and determination to help those in need, whatever the odds and whatever side they were on, that helped me understand what the Red Cross was all about. There were many volunteers like her, perhaps not operating in quite such dramatic circumstances or with the benefits of her education or position in society, but there they were nonetheless – turning out to help people flooded out of their homes, providing first aid cover at some muddy village fair, driving an ambulance or lending out a wheelchair. They didn't need to do it: they could have stayed at home. But something drove them on – and it was that 'something' that we wanted to set free and build on, as we started out to implement the National Strategy Five Year Plan.

Work started immediately on reviewing the services offered by pretty much all branches, in an attempt to reduce the list of 'fifty-seven' varieties of services then on offer in some places some of the time to a set of 'key services' to be offered by every branch, to a specified standard.

The new focus that had evolved was actually pretty ground-breaking, with its unifying theme that 'the heartbeat of the Red Cross is emergencies and caring for people in crisis', and that this care should be delivered primarily by highly-skilled volunteers who have been trained or otherwise prepared to be able to respond quickly and effectively. Logically, this led to the conclusion that we should be working harder to develop our emergency response skills (particularly around emotional and practical support, including first aid) in association with the emergency services; but also ensuring that the other services we provided should themselves have an 'emergency focus', and/or deploy skills that could be useful in an emergency.

This was ground-breaking in the sense, first and foremost, that it meant really developing and marketing our emergency response capacity to sceptical providers like the Fire Service. Secondly, it gave us a consistent logical focus to apply to all our services, including those that we wanted branches to drop – if the service wasn't clearly 'within the Focus', we shouldn't be doing it.

We intended to monitor Branch performance, pump-prime worthwhile development and provide training where needed. Opportunities for generating additional funds by securing contracts for services from local authorities and health services, and the possibility of partnerships with other organizations, were to be explored, and we started trying to persuade Branches to sell off outdated and under-used properties and replace them with something more fit for purpose. We determined to work closely with new colleagues in the fundraising and communications departments and, as a personal goal, I decided to try and help the organization feel a bit 'bouncier' and more optimistic about itself – 'bounce' became my watchword.

The first service we reviewed was 'emergency response', based on the concept that the Red Cross had a responsibility as a voluntary aid society (and therefore as an 'auxiliary to Government') to assist the statutory services in time of national or local crisis (severe flooding or a major train crash, for example). The British Red Cross had done little to resource or train its branches for this role, despite the fact that many of them were members of county emergency committees (which included all the major emergency services) and engaged in local exercises organized by them. However, some branches had no county emergency committee and little contact with the emergency services, and could be waved away by whoever was in command of the emergency response on the ground. Our goal here was to ensure that every branch could deploy a range of skills and resources that could be useful in any emergency, and that the police, fire and ambulance services were both aware of this and ready to use them.

Next came a collection of five other 'key services' that both met a current local need and developed in our volunteers skills and experience that were also applicable in an emergency response. These activities were: the provision of nursing and other support to carers in the community; the capacity to trace and exchange messages between people separated by conflict or other crises; training in first aid and the provision of first aid cover at local community events; the provision of 'transport and escort services' to patients who needed help getting from one part of the country to another; and the lending of wheelchairs and other basic care equipment to those who had need of them.

It will be readily appreciated that each and every one of these activities, if fully developed, had the capacity to become a very substantial nationwide charitable business in its own right, employing thousands of staff and volunteers and requiring millions to finance, but the challenge implied by that potential seemed a long way off at that time, and would have meant some very hard choices for the organization.

For now, Emma Tait (a hard-working former social worker) and her service development team contented themselves with devising new standards and a development plan for each of the chosen services; Alan Taylor and then Roger Smith (a former head teacher) worked on our first aid training offer; Helen Watson (one of a marvellous group of Red Cross 'old hands') started reviewing the way the Society engaged young people in its work; and we set up within UK Ops a National Strategy Steering Group, led by ever-energetic and enthusiastic Martin Farrell (another experienced social and charity worker), which embarked upon a review of the overall activity in each Branch and a programme of intensive assistance to local teams to help them devise a five-year development plan of their own, in the light of local needs, and with access to a limited pot of NHQ funding to provide some strategic investment. Five regional directors worked hard to advise and encourage branches on the ground.

On top of all that, we were looking, through the branch reviews, at what new services might conceivably be developed on a national scale, and at which services might conceivably be handed over to other organizations, or (a very difficult concept for committed Red Cross volunteers) discontinued altogether, particularly where they were absorbing time and resources that could be better spent elsewhere.

Looking back, it was in many ways an impossibly ambitious and intensive programme. Persuading over 2,000 (mostly part-time) staff, and (a probably over-estimated) 90,000 volunteers working actively in ninety largely autonomous branches to work in a new, much more centrally-directed way was a big challenge. But it infused the organization as a whole, at both local and national level, with a sense of optimism and purpose, and for many at local level a genuine spirit of enquiry about how we could best meet current needs, whilst remaining true to the principles, values and core mission of the Red Cross.

The branch reviews threw up an astonishing diversity of activity at the local level. There were branches lending pictures to brighten up the homes of sick people, providing welfare services for retired gardeners, cutting the toenails of the elderly, organizing holidays for the disabled, running canteens and book trolleys in hospitals, and dozens of other activities – all of them meeting a need of some kind and all delivered by some wonderfully passionate and committed volunteers, but few of them to scale, few of them really monitored or supervised or being delivered to a set standard, and some of them not in any real sense 'Red Cross' at all.

On the other hand, we identified some inspiring examples of innovation and good practice, like the 'Home from Hospital Service' in Lincolnshire and elsewhere, in which people coming out of hospital received a few weeks' ongoing care in their homes from Red Cross volunteers; the top quality provision of first aid cover at big public events like Burghley Horse Trials or the Isle of Man TT Races; professional first aid training delivered to companies and other organizations to help them satisfy the legal requirement to employ a minimum number of trained first aiders; work with the homeless in Glasgow; interesting services or bundles of community services being delivered under contract to local authority or NHS providers – and many more.

Our research and planning team, under thoughtful former lawyer and strategist Douglas Bennett, looked at and sometimes adopted ideas from other National Societies, like the American Red Cross 'Fire Victim Support Service', the Belgian Red Cross Blood Transfusion Service, Germany's Ambulance Service, Denmark's independent youth action teams or the Norwegians' work with refugees and asylum seekers, to see if they could be adapted to fit conditions and needs in the UK. John Gray started work on a Disaster Appeal Scheme, intended to act as an off-the-shelf model for a local fundraising appeal after a local disaster.

We thought hard about requests from left field, for example that we should take over the Air Ambulance Service, or all the residential homes in Warwickshire. We did weird stuff, too, like working with the film company Aardvark to devise an engaging film for seafarers about the dangers of HIV, featuring characters modelled in plasticine, including a ship's captain who turned into a penis, for the purposes of making the point, as it were. It was all grist to the creative mill.

We embarked on a series of roadshows nationwide to sell the national strategy to Branch volunteers and staff, introduced by Mike and with an enthusiastic arm-waving presentation from me, and were rewarded, after what seemed like weeks on the road, with almost unanimous acceptance.

I can vividly remember the moment when success seemed assured: it was at a roadshow in Devon, when an elderly and typically forthright volunteer stood up portentously at the end of another ding-dong Q and A session one Saturday morning. She looked fierce and disapproving, and I feared the worst.

'Mr Young,' she said, 'what you have described is nothing like the Red Cross I joined thirty years ago.'

She paused and glared about her, and then back at me.

'But I rather like it. Good luck!'

From the very start I had been sure that we needed to tackle the cumbersome local structure of the organization; so much so that, in my first appraisal, Mike rightly rebuked me for my importunate demands that we should get on with a structural review immediately. He was right – it was much too early.

We had at that point no real idea what the structure should be delivering, or how, and to our thousands of volunteers on the ground, and some at times embittered 'old hands' at National Headquarters, we were still 'the new kids on the block'. Had we tried to change the structure too soon, it would have taken us not the three years or so we hoped for but the ten (or more) that Lady Limerick had warned me about on my first day.

With its virtually independent county branches, each separately registered as a charity in its own right, with its own trustees and to all intents and purposes its own very strong sense of local family ownership, the Society was clearly burdened with an excess of structure, and sometimes with rebellious or indifferent local autonomy. But local ownership was a great strength in terms of energy, loyalty, and responsiveness to local need – albeit costly, terminally inefficient and ineffective for what purported to be a modern, dynamic, needs-led charity dependent on supporters' generosity and receiving little or no government funding.

We knew that the whole process of reviewing the structure would be complicated legally and fraught with practical and emotional difficulties and challenges. However, my legal training came to the rescue when I realized that, legally speaking, the local branches were 'unincorporated associations', and that our hundreds of local trustees were, each and every one of them, personally and individually responsible and liable for any debts of their branch. I devised a relatively matter of fact letter 'reminding' them of this fact, and sat back to await events.

In truth, this wasn't a 'reminder' at all – most if not all of them were completely unaware of the legal minefield they were in and had assumed that they were somehow protected by the same limitation on personal liability enjoyed by the members of our Council under the Society's Royal Charter. The news that this was not the case came as a sobering shock to many, and after a few days of stunned silence the phones in Grosvenor Crescent started ringing.

Within a few months there was general acceptance that a review of the structure was both necessary and desirable, and after lengthy debate about the form it should take and how it was to be accomplished, businessman Sir Christopher Benson was appointed to lead the task as an independent, objective non-Red Crosser. Working with a management consultant, and reporting to an internal Steering Group chaired by Mike Whitlam, Benson toured the country seeking the views of the membership at all levels, and held discussions at National Headquarters about what would be a more effective structure and yet still be acceptable to the branches.

The main goal from my perspective was to remove the separate charitable status of branches, creating a more unified national society, whilst establishing clear operational line management from the Director-General, through the Director of UK Operations, to the branch directors. Standing in the way of this were the ninety branch trustee committees, to whom the branch directors currently reported. Representatives of the Chairs of those branch committees comprised the overwhelming majority on the Council, the body that would have to agree the new structure. Many of them cherished their independence, and persuading them to give it up and replace it with a greater degree of control from the 'ivory tower' would not be easy.

The exhaustive and exhausting consultation process rolled on well into 1995. The complicated politics of the Red Cross, still dominated at that time by a frequently troubled relationship between volunteers on the one hand, who felt they 'owned' the Red Cross, and on the other hand an increasingly professionalized staff team, who believed they had been appointed to run the show and had the management skills to do so. Eventually, a somewhat uneasy compromise was reached and agreed by our Council. Charitable status for the branches would go – and with it the personal liability of the branch trustees – but the branch volunteer committees would remain in an 'advisory capacity'. There were some other changes – minor adjustments of branch boundaries, amalgamations of some smaller branches, and so on – but the main goal, of a more unified National Society, was achieved, and the focus switched to the Privy Council which, under our Royal Charter, had to approve the changes – and did so in 1997.

Deeply involved as we all were as a senior management team, and very busy, with what seemed at the time to be the Herculean effort of modernizing a much-loved institution, we were of course also having to continue with the day job of delivering a multitude of services all over the UK, as well as playing a very full part in the international work of the British Red Cross and of the Red Cross Red Crescent Movement as a whole.

The British Red Cross was a well-respected and significant actor in the Movement, and an elected member of the Governing Board of the League of Red Cross Red Crescent Societies (later to become the 'International Federation'). Lady Limerick, as the Society's nominated representative on the Board, attended its regular meetings with Mike Whitlam and reported back on what sometimes seemed (to us on the UK side at least) to be the rather theoretical debates of the League and its occasional wrangling in Geneva with the 'senior' part of the Movement, the International Committee of the Red Cross (ICRC).

Very loosely, the ICRC dealt with governments, victims of armed conflict and international humanitarian law, whilst the Federation looked after all the National Red Cross or Red Crescent Societies and focussed on victims of natural disasters and other emergencies. But the work of the two international bodies often overlapped, as war led to food insecurity and other issues, and vice versa, and the relationship between them was not always an easy one. It seemed obvious that the two should be working closely together – but sometimes that was easier said than done.

The same could be said about the relationship between the National Societies and 'their' Federation. They were all autonomous and independent and jealously guarded their right of action in their own country. But some, particularly in the south, were less well-equipped to deal with a major natural disaster, for example, than those based in wealthier countries. In those circumstances, the Federation and the wealthier national societies would provide both financial and practical help and support, and whilst this was always welcomed it wasn't always easy to lead and coordinate.

But I will never forget the extraordinary thrill of emotion when I first visited the ICRC Central Tracing Agency (which seeks to trace and renew contact between family members torn apart by conflict), and the director, Mme Scheinberger, rushed up to me just as I was leaving, clutching a small brown piece of card.

'We've found him, Mr Young!' she cried, handing me the card.

She had managed to locate my father's Red Cross Registration Card from the time of his capture in Tunisia in 1943. Issued in the Tunisian desert in April 1943, it bore my father's unmistakeable scrawl of a signature and acknowledged his capture by the Germans and his registration by the Red Cross as a prisoner of war. It had a serrated edge – the missing half of the card had been sent to his home in Epsom to notify his parents that he was alive, a prisoner – and known to the Red Cross.

I thought of the comfort that signing that card must have brought to him and to his family back home, one of millions of index cards held by the Red Cross, each representing a vulnerable individual captured during a conflict and separated from his family. I whispered a silent thank you for the luck that had brought me to work for the Red Cross.

There was always room for improvement, but the international work of the British Red Cross, and the Movement as a whole, seemed hugely impressive to me, and it was impossible not to feel an enormous sense of pride at being part of an organization that was operational in virtually every country on the planet on a daily basis, and during every crisis, bringing relief and support to individuals and communities at what was often the worst moment in their lives. Lady Limerick held a dinner at Brooks's one evening for Cornelio Sommaruga, the charismatic President of the ICRC at the time, and I will always remember how he talked across the shimmering silverware about the world as he saw it, his large and expressive hands seeming to encompass a wealth of understanding, compassion and comprehension that was somehow uniquely 'Red Cross'.

I think I saw the universality of the Red Cross, and the power of its emblem, most clearly during the terrible fighting between the states that had formed the federation of Yugoslavia, starting with the Croatian War of Independence and the Bosnian War which began in 1992, and the 'ethnic cleansing' which followed. These events dominated the national news but, as ever in the Red Cross, we were privy to the horror and granular detail of events on the ground, and the impact upon individuals, that went well beyond what was shown in TV news bulletins. We had staff *in situ*, some of them UK colleagues, and the stories they brought back from the field chilled and inspired us in equal measure.

When Muslim refugees from Bosnia started arriving at Stansted in December 1992 under a UNHCR programme, to be housed in centres hurriedly set up in Cambridge and elsewhere by my team, in a project brilliantly led at very short notice by Martin Farrell, the sense of involvement in a humanitarian endeavour that transcended boundaries of every kind became real for all of us. None of us will forget the moment at Stansted when the first group of refugees came down the steps of the plane clutching a few pitiful belongings, ignored the waiting police and civil servants and made straight for anyone wearing a Red Cross badge – the 'certain sign of hope in a crisis' that was our 'strapline' at the time.

There was an interesting sequel to these events, when one of our Branches in Northern Ireland took it upon themselves, without telling anyone in London (or even Belfast, and breaking BRCS regulations), to start delivering donated supplies to communities in Bosnia, using old second-hand Red Cross and NHS ambulances, which they then left behind for the locals to use. When a contact in MI6 phoned to warn me that there was evidence to suggest that these ambulances were subsequently being used by the military to transport guns and ammunition undercover, we had to take urgent action to cool the well-meaning volunteers' enthusiasm for direct humanitarian action overseas.

In the following year we had a chance in the UK to see the Movement itself in all its glory. The British Red Cross had agreed to host (in Birmingham's magnificent new conference centre) the biennial General Assembly of the Federation, and the Federation's formal meeting with the ICRC (Council of Delegates) which always followed it. As he had shown with the *Simple Truth* Appeal two years earlier, Mike had a good nose for an opportunity to make a public relations splash, a massive ambition for the organization to take centre stage and live up to its name, and an inexhaustible capacity for hard work – and the hosting of the 'statutory meetings' in 1993 was another example.

The Queen opened the proceedings and received an ovation from over 600 delegates representing the 161 National Societies in attendance. We also hosted some of the British Red Cross Overseas Branches, tiny Red Cross bodies from remnants of Empire like Antigua, Turks and Caicos, the British Virgin Islands, the Falklands and Gibraltar – and started discussions with them about the extent to which the National Strategy might be applicable in their contexts.

The evening before the General Assembly began, John Gray organized entertainment for the international guests with a light-hearted virtual 'tour of the UK' in film and song; it required Lady Limerick (who was elected a Vice-President of the Federation later in the proceedings) to take the role of hostess, parading in a vintage automobile driven by John Gray capering about in full chauffeur's uniform. We shrank deep into our seats in embarrassment, but our guests, many of them in their national costumes, loved it, and the days of formal meetings, debates and resolutions that followed showed both the British Red Cross and the Movement at their best.

The year 1995 marked the one hundred and twenty-fifth anniversary of the founding of the British Red Cross, and presented another big opportunity to promote the organization. John Gray was asked to lead the preparations and he soon had a list of more than 600 fundraising events and projects.

The year kicked off, literally, with Red Cross events at fifty-two first tier football matches around the country, and had its climax during Red Cross Week in May, which happily coincided with the celebrations to mark the 50th anniversary of VE Day. There was a massive Red Cross Street Party for children in Oxford Street, and a huge Red Cross refugee camp in Hyde Park displaying our work in conflict and overseas. We also mounted an intensive effort nationwide to mobilize wheelchairs for use generally in the Park, and used this opportunity to promote our community services.

The day finished with a glittering gala concert at the Royal Albert Hall at which Luciano Pavarotti sang and which was televised by the BBC. I managed to cover myself with glory in the eyes of the fundraisers by blagging my way backstage at the interval and persuading the Maestro and the entire orchestra to wear our new Red Cross fundraising lapel pin for the second half.

There was much more: the Queen attended a reception preceding a dinner for 500 guests at the Guildhall; the creation of a '125 Society' for high-net-worth individuals; parties in Red Cross Centres all over the country; the lighting of beacons; a concert at Westminster Abbey. It was what I think we all saw as a chance to celebrate our own five years of hard work, as well as a significant anniversary for the Society.

For me personally, though, it was also a time of some sadness. With the new structure virtually agreed, and our UK Emergency Focus firmly established as the way forward, I knew that I either had to commit myself to the Red Cross for several more years to implement all the changes – or move on to something new.

I had already been offered a new job in Geneva, working to create a better climate of cooperation between the two senior components of the Movement, the ICRC and the Federation, but I wanted to try my hand at being a chief executive myself and was offered the job of Chief Executive at Macmillan Cancer Relief (or Cancer Relief Macmillan Fund as it was called at the time). This was one of the 'plum' jobs in the sector, and I felt very lucky indeed even to have been considered for it.

Leaving the Red Cross was hard, though, like cutting off an arm. I had adored working for this revered institution and had made many good friends at all levels in the organization and within the Movement. Mike had been an inspiration as CEO and had taught me something about the toughness and singularity of purpose that you need to run a big organization.

I was fortunate indeed to get the job at Macmillan for my first experience as a chief executive. The organization had been phenomenally successful under two previous leaders, both of them with commercial experience, who had transformed a sleepy little support group for cancer patients into a fundraising phenomenon with their invention of the 'Macmillan Nurse', cancer-care specialists employed largely within the NHS but funded for three years by the charity – on the promise that the NHS would continue the funding thereafter, retaining the Macmillan name for the posts in perpetuity. This had been a stroke of marketing genius for, as the number of Macmillan Nurses grew in response to NHS demand, so the name Macmillan became ever-more familiar to grateful patients and their families.

By the time I arrived in 1995 the organization was ready for the next stage in its development. It so happened that Ken Calman and Deirdre Hine, respectively the Chief Medical Officers of England and Scotland, had that year published a draft plan for improving the 'postcode lottery' of cancer services throughout the UK, and we were using this plan as our organizational blueprint for the development of Macmillan-funded cancer services.

In the run-up to the 1997 general election we decided to try and persuade 'New Labour' under Tony Blair to adopt the plan if they came to power; and one afternoon, we corralled the Shadow Labour health team, Chris Smith and Harriet Harman, in a room with a dozen of the country's top cancer clinicians to talk about the Calman-Hine proposals, with a particular focus on breast cancer. About half way through the session, Harman turned to her boss and said, 'Chris, why don't we just adopt this as our manifesto pledge?' It was a wonderful moment, Macmillan being well placed to play a leading role in facilitating the implementation of the plan, with its extremely powerful local fundraising machine and popular fundraising events such as the Macmillan Coffee Morning – not to mention the Macmillan Nurses themselves.

The charity was an immensely happy one, for all the seriousness of the work, with a cheery bunch of top-quality staff at its national office (then in Chelsea) and around the country, hundreds of passionate and committed local fundraising committees and a delightfully relaxed and supportive chairman in investment banker Ric Hambro. Our message, with superb creative support from J. Walter Thompson and former BSkyB chief executive and trustee Anthony Simonds-Gooding, was a relentlessly positive and optimistic one about 'living with cancer' (at a time when many of our fundraising competitors were focussed on cancer as a cause of death), and the public responded accordingly.

My six years at the helm, blessed with continued fundraising and service development success and growth, and good relations with a responsive Department of Health under the energetic Alan Milburn, passed in a flash. To my astonishment, I was nominated for a knighthood in the Millennium New Year's Honours List, something which embarrassed me at the time because I felt that my chairman Ric Hambro (who had worked for the charity as a volunteer for twenty years or more, and whose nomination I had been pushing with the Department of Health at the time) had the greater claim; but I was persuaded to accept it as a tribute to the charity as a whole, and the staff gave me a resounding welcome when I returned from the Palace with the award.

Gazing across the Thames at the Palace of Westminster from our new offices on the Embankment, I was looking forward to the next few years at Macmillan, for there was plenty more to do to improve cancer services … but it was not to be.

Passionate though I was about the work at Macmillan, not least because my mother died of bowel cancer while I was there, I still dreamt one day of returning to the Red Cross. The red cross emblem and all that it stands for exerts a powerful hold on staff, volunteers and supporters alike, and when I heard that Mike Whitlam's successor as chief executive was leaving suddenly, after only a few months in post, I couldn't help wondering if my chance had come. I felt torn in two directions, unsure whether to apply or not … and then they called me, and my mind was made up. I started preparing for the interview process.

Chapter 2

Starting Back at the Red Cross, 2001

Archer and the Simple Truth – Dealing with the deficit –9/11

'They want you on *News at Ten*. You'll need a briefing.'

It was early in July, my first day back at the offices of the British Red Cross as chief executive, and I was about to address the whole staff team at an off-site meeting about the challenges the organization was facing. I had been away for six years at Macmillan and, in the meantime, the Red Cross had got into a mess. The 'Director-General' Sam Younger, Mike Whitlam's successor, had left suddenly after only eighteen months in the job (to become Chair of the Electoral Commission), and the organization was facing a crisis of cash and confidence.

The cash problem was due to a dramatic drop in income from legacies in one year, purely the result of happenstance, which coincided with a decision to invest very significant sums of money in the new and re-focussed services that I had been working on six years previously. Unfortunately, at around the same time, a whizzy new computer system, installed to cope with the centralization of all local branch income and expenditure following the restructuring of the Society (finally signed off by the Privy Council in 1998), had crashed. The result was disastrous – thousands of invoices and expense claims from all over the country piled up in Grosvenor Crescent unable to be paid – and the deficit caused by the drop in legacies grew inexorably, but invisibly because the accounts team had no means of making sure what was happening financially.

Meanwhile, those diehards who had said that the restructuring would never work shook their heads and rubbed their hands, whilst morale collapsed and the organization headed for the rocks. When Professor John McClure (who had just become Chair) rang to offer me the job of chief executive in January 2001, the deficit stood at a relatively modest couple of million pounds, but by the time I took up my post in the late summer, it had grown to over £14m, and I knew I had a full-blown crisis on my hands.

I had spent my first couple of days at the Lincolnshire Branch to gauge the mood on the 'front line' – it was dire, as Director Joy Clift-Hill and her team confirmed – and I was now preparing to talk to the staff at 'headquarters', to see what they thought of the situation and to hear their views on what needed to be done to resolve it.

But *News at Ten*, on my first day. What was all that about?

'It's Jeffrey Archer,' I was told. 'He's been accused of stealing from the Red Cross.'

It was hard to grasp. Exactly ten years previously, during my first stint in the Red Cross, we had run the global fundraising *Simple Truth* Appeal for Kurdish refugees fleeing from Saddam Hussein's regime in Iraq. Archer, the prime mover in getting the Appeal up and running, had been its volunteer chair and had played a big part in raising a record £57m for the cause. Now, though, Archer was in prison, jailed for perjury in the 1987 legal action for libel that he had brought against the *Daily Star*. On his very first night in the maximum security Belmarsh Prison, a fellow Tory 'grandee', Baroness Emma Nicholson, had popped up to raise questions about where all the appeal money had gone – the implication being that some of it had ended up in Archer's own pocket.

This would have been a difficult issue to deal with at any time. Archer was uniformly hated by the media because he had been accused and convicted of lying in a case against a newspaper in which he had won substantial damages – it was inevitable that, coming so soon after the drama of his perjury trial, they would have a field day with these new allegations from a seemingly unimpeachable source. On my first day in a tough new job, about to address a disillusioned staff team with the organization already in crisis, it was the last thing I needed.

I turned to the task at hand, talking to the staff. I felt that the main challenge was low morale rather than the deficit, so I opened my speech with what I hoped was a rousing call to arms:

We simply cannot afford to be anything but confident and proud. We are part of the biggest and greatest voluntary organization on the planet. From one side of the globe to the other, the Red Cross is regarded with awe and respect, as an organization that gets things done, that makes a difference. Throughout this country, mention the Red Cross and people will say, 'Fantastic – how lucky you are to work for the Red Cross. What an interesting job.'

There is a great team of people here in the British Red Cross, at every level in the organization, volunteers and staff, and we must have confidence in our ability to resolve the difficulties and move forward as one organization, working together ... We must baulk at no obstacle, shirk no difficult decision, falter at no hurdle. We just have to be successful, for what is at stake is not just a great organization: it is the lives and wellbeing of people who depend on us. Who look to us, in the Red Cross, to stand by them in their hour of need.

I highlighted four key challenges – meeting need, raising money, getting our message across and putting our house in order.

The first, a long-standing issue for the Red Cross, was the need to focus both on real crisis need (the *raison d'être* of the Red Cross) and on a manageable range of services both in the UK and overseas, in the face of almost unlimited demand.

The second was fundraising, then running at about £40m per year and nowhere near its full potential. Red Cross shops, first aid training fees and government grants added another £40m – but we needed much more. The culture at that time was that 'fundraising was for fundraisers', not for the volunteers or service staff. I wanted to turn that on its head with the message that 'we are all fundraisers in the British Red Cross'.

Thirdly, I expressed concern that the British Red Cross was still 'best known, least understood' (a phrase first used by our PR consultants in 1990) – and maybe not even 'best known' any more. On the basis that people give to organizations that they know and understand, I argued that we had to tell people loud and clear what we do and what we stand for, and that we had to 'speak up and speak out' more on issues that, as a humanitarian, independent organization, we felt strongly about, without necessarily always seeing ourselves as restricted by two other key Red Cross 'Fundamental Principles', i.e. neutrality and impartiality.

Finally, and turning to the issues most on everyone's mind, I said that I had placed 'putting our house in order' last simply because I took it as a given – 'Our house should be in order now'. I said that the £14m deficit had to be dealt with immediately and urgently and acknowledged that this would cause some pain. Trying to apportion blame, or just 'wishing it was different', was a waste of time. I paid tribute to Roger Smith, Mike Adamson and others who had held the organization together after my predecessor's departure; mentioned specifically the certainty that there would have to be some reorganization and staff cuts; and then finished with a heartfelt plea, on behalf of both myself and the Chairman: 'We cannot do it alone – nor do we want to. We need your support. I beg for your support.'

Thankfully, and in spite of the pain, I got it.

But first I had to try and deal with the Archer issue and my appearance on *News at Ten*. In the Red Cross at least, we all knew that it was inconceivable that Archer could have stolen money from the Appeal – quite apart from anything else, not one penny of money given to the Red Cross could ever have physically passed through his hands. But there were two difficulties about proving this.

The first was the logistical challenge of identifying exactly how the money had been raised ten years previously, and exactly how it had been spent. Eager to show what the Red Cross could do – at a time when the organization was again in the doldrums – the then Director-General, Mike Whitlam, and his sparky new fundraiser John Gray had included in the £57m total not only sums raised (and spent) by Red Cross national societies all over the world on the back of the international publicity which the Appeal generated, but also monies which Archer himself claimed to have persuaded governments to spend on support for the Kurds – which amounted to over £30m and which had not come through the Red Cross at all. It was obvious early on that it was going to be difficult to track down and account for all the government funds to the satisfaction of a sceptical media (let alone Emma Nicholson).

The second challenge was more subtle – how to defend the reputation of the Red Cross whilst not, at the same time, seeming to associate the organization inextricably in the mind of the general public with the disgraced Archer.

All these thoughts, and a jumble of numbers hastily pulled together by the press team, were racing through my head on the way to the *News at Ten* studio that night, and again the next morning as I set out for the first of several grillings from John Humphrys on the BBC *Today* programme.

At this relatively early stage in the saga the interviews passed off well enough, but it was the end of July, a quiet period for news, and the media were intent upon digging up more dirt to fling at Archer in his prison cell. The stories kept coming and, with each day that passed and with Archer himself out of reach for the media, the story focussed more and more on the Red Cross and its *Simple Truth* Appeal. When the Metropolitan Police announced that they intended to launch a Fraud Squad investigation into the allegations, as they were legally obliged to do, Archer being already a convicted offender, the clamour for 'answers' rose to a crescendo and I was once again summoned to the BBC *Today* studios.

This time, the questions were more probing, and it became obvious that the story was set to 'run and run'. I made the decision that I would deal with the Archer issue myself, rather than risk distracting other members of the management team at a time when there was so much else to do. But I was very nervous about it.

Rescue was at hand. In the taxi back to the office, I got a call from Patsy Baker, a partner in the PR firm Bell Pottinger.

'You've got a problem,' she said. 'Maybe we can help?'

Within an hour she was round at our offices with two of her senior colleagues, Stephen Sherbourne and David McDonough, and a strategy for establishing and defending the numbers began to emerge.

Crucially, the first piece of advice they offered was that the Red Cross had to take control of the investigation itself – the sight of detectives entering Red Cross offices and removing files and computers would have been catnip to the media. Instead, they suggested that we appoint one of the top firms of accountants to conduct a 'forensic audit' of the money raised and spent, to answer the concerns and questions raised in connection with the Appeal.

The next day, I met with Alex Plavsic of accountants KPMG, and he agreed to conduct the audit. A few days after that, we were able to persuade the Fraud Squad to accept KPMG's findings for the purposes of their own investigation, thereby obviating the need for a separate and intrusive police enquiry. As Bell Pottinger had expected, the announcement of this arrangement effectively dampened media speculation, for the time being at least, leaving me some time to get on with the day job.

There was no shortage of urgent matters to attend to. I had agreed with the chairman John McClure, a level-headed professor of pathology from

Northern Ireland and a keen Red Crosser, that although governance and management functions were normally kept separate, the situation that we faced was sufficiently serious to warrant setting up a joint working group of trustees and directors to tackle the £14m deficit, under his chairmanship and called, somewhat euphemistically, the Cost and Effectiveness Steering Group (CESG). This proved to be a successful and effective mechanism which facilitated speedy decision-making and a real sense of partnership between trustees and senior staff, as well as a great chance for me to get to know John personally and work closely with him.

It was obvious that what was required was a fairly drastic slimming down of the organization structurally, and in terms of the 1,500 paid full-time or part-time staff at National Headquarters and at Branch level. But we were also determined to enhance capability and effectiveness wherever we could, and this became a strong theme in our deliberations.

We started to look hard at some of our services, boosting the focus for example on responding to emergencies in the UK and providing 'home from hospital' care and 'community equipment' (lending out wheelchairs, commodes and the like), whilst cutting back (controversially as far as some of our dedicated volunteers were concerned) on non-emergency work such as running holidays for people with disabilities, and youth groups. We identified work with the growing numbers of refugees and asylum-seekers coming to the UK and the increasing incidence of HIV/AIDS as areas for further attention.

The CESG (aided by some incredibly generous pro bono support from top management consultants McKinsey, who had helped us at Macmillan) generated studies and working papers galore, and a great deal of anxiety around the organization, though most people realized that the work was essential and that the interim recruitment freeze and subsequent five hundred redundancies were unavoidable, though painful. Inevitably, this generated anxieties amongst the wider trustee body, too, most of whom were elected locally, and there were concerns about being 'steamrollered' into decisions that would inevitably have a major impact on local volunteers. The Chairman and I had regular debates about these issues, as did the CESG, and we did what we could to assuage these entirely understandable concerns, but there were inevitable bumps along the way, because we had to make decisions quickly.

We appointed external property experts to conduct a major review of the Society's hundreds of (mostly small) freehold properties, with a view to selling off as many as could reasonably be spared, often against considerable and understandable local opposition from the volunteers, who liked having somewhere to meet and felt quite possessive about them. We also started seriously to explore the possibility of exchanging our obsolete but valuable leasehold headquarters building in fashionable Grosvenor Crescent for something cheaper to run and more suitable as offices for a modern organization.

Fundraising was either regionalized or centralized, and the Society's 430 charity shops were brought under central control. The vital comms function was separated from fundraising and, despite the recruitment freeze, we started looking for a comms director to lead efforts to promote the work of the organization better, strengthen internal and social media comms and help us 'speak up and speak out' more.

We decided to invest substantially in trying to persuade people to give money to us regularly by direct debit, and had some early and successful experiments with the newly-invented 'face-to-face' method of signing up 'regular givers' on the street – or 'chugging' as it came to be known. By the end of the year some 80,000 people had signed up to make regular donations to the Red Cross – a good start, but some way off Oxfam's total of 500,000.

But, as I was to find so often in the Red Cross, the opportunity to do organizational 'housekeeping', however necessary or urgent, was quickly overtaken by events in the real world. I was sitting in the rather grand CEO's office one afternoon in September working on some papers, with half an eye on the BBC News Channel, when the extraordinary image of an airliner colliding with one of the towers of the World Trade Centre in New York filled the screen. I assumed at first that it was an extract from a disaster movie, but the 'breaking news' flash and urgent reporting quickly dispelled the notion.

As coverage continued, the initial assumption that there had been a ghastly accident began to give way to the nightmare possibility that this was a terrorist attack of some kind, a notion soon confirmed when the second Tower was struck by another plane, and reports came in of a similar incident at the Pentagon. In the building and outside everything seemed to go quiet, and I watched in dumbstruck horror as the coverage continued.

What struck me that afternoon, as chief executive of the British Red Cross, was that not one member of staff – no one from our International team, not a single fundraiser or representative of the press team – contacted me to ask, 'Have you seen what's happening?' or, better still, 'Should we be doing something?'

This was a sign to me that, in some senses at least, the organization was asleep on its feet, or so taken up with its own affairs as to be virtually oblivious to this trauma affecting our brothers and sisters on the other side of the Atlantic. I put this the next day to a gathering of those from all disciplines who I considered to be 'emergency responders' and immediately initiated an urgent exercise to sharpen up our reflexes and inspire the whole organization with a vision of what it really means to be in the business of emergency response. Modelled on the Government's COBRA emergency committee, we instituted a cross-divisional response system for emergencies in the UK and overseas, conducted regular exercises and set up a 'Disaster Fund', to which supporters could donate and which would give us the wherewithal to respond immediately to an emergency wherever and whenever it arose, without the need to raise money first.

This period also saw my first engagements overseas as CEO, with international Red Cross meetings of various kinds in Iceland and Italy, and a visit to the Indian Red Cross, one of our 'partner' national societies, to see what we were doing to support their work generally, and in particular in Gujarat, rebuilding fifty small nursery schools (or *anganwadis*) after the earthquake in January of that year. This was my first visit to the site of a major natural disaster, and I noted in my mission report the challenge posed by a devastating earthquake, in terms not only of the immediate response but also of the task of rehabilitation:

In Anjar particularly, where an extensive area of densely-packed shops and homes had been reduced to a vast wasteland of dust and rubble, it was hard not to despair: here at least the aid agencies seem to be barely scratching the surface. The Government has backed out of its promise to remove the rubble; compensation is paltry, and certainly won't cover the full cost of rebuilding to the newly-imposed earthquake proof standards; the legal task of sorting out who owned what will take years; and, in the meantime, apart from a few tiny shoots of recovery (the local sari shop has reopened in the middle of the rubble), local people pick about in the mess, mourning the loss of lives and livelihoods.

I was also taken to Mumbai to see the work of the Indian Red Cross in that teeming city and was shown round by veteran and well-respected politician Murli Deora, a former Mayor and later to become Minister of Petroleum. He insisted that we visit a slum area, where we were greeted by an enormous banner strung across the road, emblazoned with our names and a great cheering crowd.

'Give us a wave,' cried someone in the accompanying press pack, and the camera bulbs flashed.

'That's great,' said a minder, as I raised my hand. 'You'll be on the front page tomorrow: you've just given the Congress Party sign!'

Murli had inveigled me into supporting his re-election campaign.

During the visit to India I was also able to engage for the first time at field level with both the ICRC, in India mainly to fulfil its conflict-related mandate in the disputed territory of Kashmir, and the International Federation of Red Cross and Red Crescent Societies (the Federation) in its role supporting the local national society. The ICRC in particular came across as focussed, informed, strategic and highly polished.

Later that year, I joined the beady President of the ICRC, Jakob Kellenberger, at a meeting with Clare Short (Secretary of State for the Department for International Development) as part of DFID's review of its 'partnership' with the ICRC. Clare Short was forceful and direct, Kellenberger precise, very Swiss and almost pedantic, but they got along famously, and I began to see how the ICRC's very carefully nuanced language played well in dealings with governments and enabled even difficult and controversial messages to be delivered successfully in a non-confrontational way.

In November, at the Federation's biennial General Assembly, I joined over a thousand delegates from national societies all over the world meeting together to discuss common issues of concern and was invited to make a keynote speech about the importance of valuing volunteers. There were also elections for half the seats on the Governing Board of the Federation and, despite the fact that both John McClure and I were new in our jobs and virtually unknown to the national society electorate, we decided that the British Red Cross should put its name forward – and it was duly elected.

We took our seats for the first meeting of the fresh Board immediately after the General Assembly, and we were all surprised to realize that the new President, Juan Manuel del Toro Rivero from Spain, who had mounted an unlikely challenge against the effective if somewhat bossy incumbent from Norway, not only spoke no English but had no language in common with his French 'Secretary-General', former banker Didier Cherpitel. This was to cause problems for both of them.

I found it incredibly inspiring to be in company with the representatives of (at that time) 190 national societies, united by common humanitarian principles, values and work. As in many international institutions, the outcome of meetings was often couched in wordy resolutions full of sub-clauses and conditions, but sometimes that is what is needed for consensus to be achieved.

As I said in a speech to the Government's Immigration and Nationality Directorate on the evening of my return from the Geneva meetings:

> It was an extraordinary gathering of Societies – but more importantly people – from around the world, trying, not always successfully, but always passionately, to rise above political differences to address a common theme: the theme of humanity, the cornerstone of the Red Cross/Red Crescent Movement. This is the essence of what makes us a unique movement in the world today, binding more than 100m members and volunteers together in a common attempt to provide the glue in a world that seems sometimes determined to break apart.

I went on to talk about the resolution passed in Geneva for the Movement to take a more common global approach to the needs of refugees and asylum-seekers, reflecting upon the fact that, at virtually every stage of a refugee's journey, he or she is likely to come into contact with and receive help from the Red Cross Red Crescent Movement – an extraordinary measure of the Movement's reach, presence and reputation for true impartiality and neutrality.

After the heady days in Geneva thinking about global issues, the *Simple Truth* reared its head again. In reality it never went away as, day after day that autumn, I had to deal with further 'revelations' planted in the media by Archer's enemies; queries and questions raised by KPMG's exhaustive enquiries and searches for documentary evidence; requests for media interviews; a lunchtime encounter with an implacable Emma Nicholson; meetings with Bell Pottinger and the Charity Commission; and briefings for staff and trustees.

Mary Archer, desperate because her husband could not be released from maximum security prison Belmarsh until the investigation was complete, took to phoning me regularly for an update and urging me to speed KPMG along. I did my best, but was dismayed when KPMG returned from a visit to the man himself to report that he had been 'unable to remember' what individual governments had pledged to the Kurdish cause.

Eventually, in late November, KPMG presented me with their final report, and I prepared to face the media once again with the findings – hoping against hope that this would enable us to draw a line under the whole sorry tale. Their conclusions were pretty stark, and made uncomfortable reading:

> KPMG have concluded that statements issued by the British Red Cross when announcing the results of the appeal lacked clarity; not all the overseas figures had been or could be properly verified both in terms of amount and connection to the Simple Truth Appeal or concert ... KPMG consider that the unclear presentation resulted from a combination of factors. The ambitious timescale for announcing the appeal total within five weeks of the concert ... [reliance upon] information provided by other Red Cross Societies and Archer ... without sufficient challenge ... tried and tested procedures were not in place.

As to the £31.5m said to have been pledged by governments, the figure was not fully supported by documentation, and the British Red Cross 'substantially relied upon Archer to provide the figure'. Nevertheless, KPMG reported that Archer had 'no role to play in the collection of funds ... nor in deciding the distribution', and 'found no evidence of misappropriation and consider it highly unlikely'.

The KPMG report was released to the media, as we had promised. I gave a press conference and answered questions as fully as I could, pointing out that even though the final figure might have been exaggerated, the Appeal had nevertheless been a successful one and had resulted in a great deal of help going to the Kurds. I apologized for the mistakes made by the organization ten years previously and ended by wishing that the truth, in relation to the *Simple Truth* appeal 'could have been simpler and less opaque'.

I took some comfort from headlines the following day, which concentrated entirely on the Archer side of the story:

The Guardian:	'Archer rebuked over cash for charity'
The Independent:	'Audit concludes Archer made up charity total'
The Times:	'Archer cleared of defrauding charity'
Daily Express:	'Disgraced peer cleared of robbing Kurds' £57m fund'

I appeared once more on *Today* to 'discuss' the issue with Humphrys but was relieved to discover that he was saving himself for another encounter with Mary Archer later in the programme and therefore treated me quite gently. I met her, and son William, in the green room after my interview. William was profuse in his thanks for 'what you did for Dad' and urged his mother to agree that Jeffrey would 'feel honour-bound to do another big fundraiser for the Red Cross as soon as he comes out of prison'. Mary must have seen the pained expression on my face and hustled him into the studio before I could respond.

It had been a tumultuous first few months for me as chief executive, and I had sometimes wondered why I had ever left happy, successful Macmillan; but with the Archer affair resolved more or less satisfactorily, I allowed myself to breathe a small sigh of relief.

Chapter 3

The Recovery Begins, 2002

Reorganization – Sangatte Refugee Camp – Israel and Palestine –
South Africa and AIDS – Red Cross bans Christmas

After a punishing first six months in the job, it was good to turn the page on a new year. The annual deficit had already been reduced from £14m at the end of 2000 to a more manageable £4.5m as we went into 2002, and I was hopeful that the organization might soon be able to settle down and recover its confidence.

The first part of the year was taken up with the changes consequent upon our decision to reduce the number of branches in the UK to twenty-one, to be called 'Areas'. Each Area would have an 'Operations' Director, who would report to four new 'Territory' Directors – Scotland/ Northern Ireland, Wales and the West, the North, and the South-East. The Territory Directors reported to me and became full members of the Senior Management Team. It was estimated that these changes alone would save over £3m per year.

The Areas were to become the key operating unit, responsible for the development of services, all of which were to be prioritized around emergency response, first aid, tracing and messages to individuals caught up in conflicts, support for refugees and asylum-seekers, and 'emotional and practical support' for individuals with short-term health and social crisis needs. The changes were fraught with risk though. Forcing previously independent Red Cross counties to amalgamate and work together brought the benefits of scale and a more united, strategic and consolidated approach, but our volunteers did tend to identify strongly with their county or city, and I was concerned that an all-important sense of local ownership might be lost.

It was all a big upheaval, which would ultimately entail hundreds of redundancies, the sad and painful loss of many old and faithful Red Cross friends and a great deal of uncertainty and disruption for the remaining staff and the volunteers. I was very conscious that, having been welcomed back into the organization as a friendly and familiar face, I was now in danger of looking like the wolf in sheep's clothing.

We appointed reliable and steady Norman McKinley from Northern Ireland as the Project Manager, and it was his job to make sure that we communicated regularly and in detail with all those concerned at every stage, and answered every single one of the hundreds of questions and comments (and complaints) that we received. We recognized that we had to consult, and be seen to consult, openly and fairly, and we went out of our way, under human resources director Roger Smith's overall wise and steady leadership, to make the whole process as transparent as it possibly could be.

We knew that internal communications with the staff and volunteers in our local branches had been weak, and we installed a new information and communication system, whilst preparing for the introduction of a society-wide intranet to aid and improve communication generally around what had been an organization divided between 'Headquarters' (from now on to be called UK Office) on the one hand, and the volunteers and staff at local level on the other. Weekly organization-wide bulletins were instituted, and we agreed as a management team that we would all make every effort to visit the Areas on a regular basis and engage actively with local volunteers and staff.

Determined 'not to waste a good crisis', we moved fast to make decisions about closing residential care homes, selling off local centres that were no longer fit for purpose and dropping services that no longer met a need or were unaffordable – decisions that might have sparked serious objections from volunteers in years gone by but which soon came to seem almost routine. Our strategy director, the intellectually tough-minded Mike Adamson, led on proposals for reforming our structures for volunteer representation, abolishing county branch committees and replacing them by elected Area Councils with a purely advisory function and an annual Area Forum, which was intended as an opportunity to inform and inspire local volunteers and supporters about the overall work of the Area and the organization as a whole.

The Board of Trustees was also reformed, with the addition of some co-opted trustees with relevant skills and experience and a process for the election of Board members by the chairs of the Area Councils in each Territory. Led by John, the Board was enormously supportive of our efforts, and increasingly we felt able to move forward and make tough decisions with a degree of confidence. The Territory Directors were reporting positive local reactions, and new faces on the senior management team brought fresh impetus and enthusiasm.

In any event, we were not the only charity sharpening up its act, in an atmosphere of increasing scrutiny by Government and the media of charity performance and accountability. Several of the other large charities which had structures involving autonomous local branches looked at our new, more streamlined and unified organization with envy, as did several of the larger Red Cross national societies, and I was frequently asked to give talks on the subject and explain how we had overcome the natural objections and sensitivities of local volunteers and staff.

The Labour Government, keen to outsource as much as it could to charities and the commercial sector, had set up a Treasury review to look at how to improve the contribution of the voluntary sector in public service delivery, and this gave added impetus to our efforts; a Performance and Innovation Unit report on performance assessment was in progress; and the National Council of Voluntary Organizations was looking at accountability. Both Mike Adamson and I played an active part in these enquiries, and I joined the Board of Guidestar (which was looking to create a league table of charity effectiveness) and became an adviser on the creation of a £125m government investment fund in charities and social enterprise called *futurebuilders* – suddenly, what had looked like a purely internal crisis became part of a much wider initiative to improve the voluntary sector and make it more effective. Curiously, for an organization that, only ten years previously had been stuck in the past, we appeared now to be ahead of the game.

Discussing and agreeing these changes ate up my time but, as always in the Red Cross, events overseas proved distracting. No sooner had a threat by Mary Archer to sue Emma Nicholson for libel – which would have meant my being drawn again into the whole sorry *Simple Truth* saga – passed, than we found ourselves implicated in a series of articles in the *Daily Mail* criticizing the work of the French Red Cross at Sangatte in northern France, which (since 1999) had been running a camp for the thousands of would-be asylum seekers, mostly from the Balkans, Iraq and Afghanistan, who were hoping to enter Britain through the Channel

Tunnel. Prior to the opening of the camp, the refugees had been living rough on the streets of Calais.

In February, under the headline 'Riot of Sangatte', the *Mail* described what it called 'terrifying pitched battles' between 'migrant mafia gangs' at the camp and associated abuse, violence and intimidation in the area. On the same page, under the headline 'The Shaming of the Red Cross', there was a comment piece suggesting that the Red Cross had shown 'consistent failure to take responsibility for the political consequences of its action', and demanding that 'Sir Nicholas Young should ... condemn the role played by his French counterparts at Sangatte'.

I drafted an immediate response explaining the humanitarian reasons for the setting up of the camp and sent it off to the *Mail*, but they declined to print it and followed up with a second article in March ('Red Cross fears Sangatte row is hitting donations') alleging that, on a forthcoming visit to Sangatte in April, 'Red Cross chiefs are to stage a crisis meeting with French counterparts', at which, claimed the *Mail*, I would be complaining to the French about 'the scale of the public opinion backlash against the location and operation of the hostel'.

After a series of radio and TV interviews about the issue, I did in fact go to Sangatte, but in order to understand the situation for myself, not to complain to the French about it. And of course, the situation was complex, involving as it did the troubles in the Middle East post 9/11; EU migration policies and practice; the politics of the forthcoming French general election; the activities of unscrupulous people-traffickers; the allocation of responsibility for security in the Tunnel itself; arguments in the UK about benefits for asylum-seekers; and the suspicion in Britain that the French Government was simply trying to offload its own asylum problem on to us.

On 17 May the *Daily Mail* published a leader headed 'A Cause Unworthy of Your Support' which, after describing the 'immense problems caused by the camp', stated 'with a heavy heart [that] the time has come for *Daily Mail* readers to stop donations to the Red Cross and give their money to other charities.' The British Red Cross, it went on, 'must share culpability for what is happening', since it fully supports its 'French colleagues in their discreditable refusal to close the camp down'.

The camp at Sangatte was eventually shut down, as part of measures agreed between the two governments to deal with what was perceived as the refugee crisis. I was concerned that the *Mail*'s coverage had been unfairly critical of the Red Cross and related my concerns to the Press Complaints Commission. The Commission felt that any formal complaint might only serve to prompt further adverse coverage – which we got anyway, later that year.

In the meantime, since our election to its governing board, I had been getting involved in the workings of the International Federation of Red Cross and Red Crescent Societies. Most Federation initiatives were started from the 200-strong secretariat which was based in Geneva, but occasionally national societies themselves took the lead. One such initiative was the 'G24' – a group of two dozen of the Federation's wealthier national societies which met every year or so to discuss matters of concern to them all as 'participating' national societies (PNS) – i.e. societies which contributed most to the Federation's annual running costs and invested in the work of the 'poorer' or 'operating' national societies (ONS), often sending teams of delegates to work on the ground in those countries.

When the Chairman and I had attended a G24 meeting in Iceland in 2001 we had been both been concerned to discover that the meeting, with its overtones of privilege and colonialism, gave the impression of being an opportunity mainly to 'agree a line' on key issues at the Federation's General Assembly the following month. We voiced our concerns during the final session. Luckily, several other 'PNS' supported us, and we offered to lead a working group to see if we could re-purpose the G24 and make it less exclusive and anti-democratic.

Our working group met in April, on the fringes of a meeting of European national societies in Berlin, and we agreed to form the 'Donor Forum', not as a vehicle for influencing decision-making, but as an annual opportunity to discuss how the PNS could best co-ordinate their activities in the field, and how in particular they could work together to help the ONS with the development challenges they faced. It was agreed that the ONS would always be represented at our meetings.

These two issues had bedevilled the Federation for a long time – the less Federation-minded PNS sometimes tried to operate overseas without consulting the Federation Secretariat or other national societies, and failed to invest in the capacity of the host national society itself. This form of humanitarian colonialism was resented by the hosts, and it was a missed opportunity in terms of building a stronger Federation and therefore a stronger Red Cross.

The British Red Cross hosted the first meeting of the Donor Forum in Windsor later that year and attracted appreciative comments from our fellow 'donor' national societies, as well as from the ONS representatives. It was particularly exciting that representatives of some of the national Red Crescent societies from the Middle East joined us, as they had never been invited to the old G24 meetings. When I asked them to join me for breakfast on the second morning, they had a sorry tale to tell, of how they felt that their work (and the challenges they faced in their own countries) was not understood or appreciated in what seemed to them like a very Euro/North American-focussed Movement. I persuaded them to repeat some of their comments in a plenary session and, upon hearing them, the Forum agreed there and then to hold its next meeting in the United Arab Emirates. I felt encouraged that the Donor Forum had got off to a positive start, and would be a force for good in terms of improving cooperation within the Federation.

In June, the Red Cross participated in the Queen's Golden Jubilee Parade in London, with dozens of volunteers dressed either in the Red Cross uniforms of the 1950s or in modern day 'workwear'. The remainder of the year was taken up with visits to national societies that we regarded as our partners and in whose capacity we had chosen to invest, usually either because of the particular challenges they faced, or because there were historical links between our two countries.

In Nigeria I made headlines in the national press with a £100,000 donation to an HIV/AIDS Project. AIDS was a huge issue here, as elsewhere, with victims of the disease savagely stigmatized, and the whole country was in denial about the causes and the best way to prevent its spread. We saw the result of this confusion later in the trip in a moving visit 'up country' to a 'motherless baby home', where the children were all 'AIDS orphans'. The local Red Cross youth group gave us a demonstration of their peer education skills, which reflected all too well the societal, tribal and religious ambivalence about 'safe sex' messages. Their conclusion that 'abstinence is best' seemed hopeful but not particularly realistic.

The trip, my first to an African country, was a heady mix of public speaking and press conferences, exuberant and acrobatic displays of Red Cross dancing and singing, formal meetings with staff and local dignitaries, and emotional visits to Red Cross members working in their local groups. We saw some innovative fundraising schemes involving chickens and peanut oil extraction which brought in a few extra pennies for local groups; and I wowed the Otukpo Mothers Club, who had been sitting under a tree for hours in the bright spangled colours of their traditional costumes awaiting my arrival, when I joined in their lengthy chant of welcome.

We had made a substantial investment in the capacity of the Nigerian Red Cross, partly funded by the Department for International Development (DFID), and its leaders were keen to hear about our own restructuring, since they had themselves recently created a regional tier and forced all thirty-seven of their Branch secretaries to re-apply for their own jobs, which henceforth would report direct to 'HQ'. I was to find as time went on, in visits to national societies all over the world, that most of them had structures based on 'independent' local branches, and there was always significant interest (and sometimes amazement) that we had managed to move away from this model.

Much of the time was spent crammed in a Land Cruiser in the endless traffic jams of Lagos, watching the colourful street scenes outside or the anarchic antics of fellow drivers, who often seemed to be engaged in a jostling game of slow-motion dodgems. Outside the city, on our way to the capital Abuja, we came upon the aftermath of a hit-and-run accident, an elderly man lying in a ditch, his leg at a bizarre angle, watched in what looked like his final agony by a small crowd of interested but entirely passive onlookers. While I directed traffic and spectators, our popular delegate Paul Jenkins launched effortlessly into Red Cross first aid mode and soon had the man efficiently bandaged and bundled into a conveniently passing police car for transport to the local hospital – a relief for us, as it would otherwise have meant a lengthy detour and a likely bill from the hospital before they would treat him.

Later in the summer, I visited Israel and 'the Occupied Territories' (aka Palestine) with the Chairman, and we had some early discussions on a topic that was very current in the Federation at that time, namely the question of whether the Magen David Adom (or the Red Shield of David, the Israeli equivalent of the Red Cross) should be admitted to the Movement as a full member – a topic given added urgency by the previous year's startling unilateral announcement by the American Red Cross that it would not be paying its *barème* (or annual assessed contribution to the Federation, of several million Swiss francs in their case) until 'MDA' was allowed in.

This was a very controversial issue. Admission to membership of the Movement depended upon fulfilment of ten conditions for recognition, which included a requirement to use the name and emblem of the 'red cross' or the 'red crescent', in accordance with the Geneva Conventions – which MDA was not prepared to do. Given the enmity that existed between the state of Israel and most of its Arab neighbours at that time, it was unlikely that a vote to allow it to become a member notwithstanding would pass. The hope was that some kind of deal could be negotiated which would allow Israel to join, possibly by admitting the Palestine Red Crescent (PRCS) at the same time. (The reason why this had not happened before was that Palestine had not been recognized as an independent state.)

This 'deal' already existed as a draft 'Third Protocol' to the 1949 Geneva Conventions, which would allow the recognition of a third Emblem, plus a Memorandum of Understanding between the Israeli and Palestinian national societies as to future operations in their respective countries. Persuading both sides to agree to its terms (which would require MDA in particular to change its working practices by respecting the territoriality of PRCS), let alone the Government of Israel, let alone other governments, seemed a monumental task given the complex political sensitivities.

The tense and seemingly intractable discussions on this very difficult political and legal problem (in which our own Michael Meyer, as one of the Movement's leading experts on international humanitarian law, was playing a key role) were happening, most unpromisingly, during the second Palestinian *intifada* (uprising) against Israeli occupation, and it was against that backdrop, and the tensions that it caused on both sides, that our visit took place. Rockets were being fired daily into Israel from Gaza, whilst the Israel Defence Force had enforced a 24-hour curfew in the West Bank.

Our visit took in the work of MDA in Jerusalem, in Tel Aviv and in the north on the border with Lebanon (where, shockingly to our eyes, MDA volunteers carried arms for self-defence), also the work of the Palestine Red Crescent in east Jerusalem and in Ramallah and Hebron. In Israel MDA is the main ambulance service provider, and whilst we were trying out one of their new ambulances (one of many funded by supporters of MDA in the UK), there was a 'shout' and we shot off under 'blues and twos' to attend at the scene of a rather nasty road traffic accident.

In the light of the obvious tension, we had cautious and inconclusive but friendly talks with the MDA leadership on the subject of their admission to the Movement. They were, of course, closely aligned with the Government and its policy with regard to Palestine, and we were not expecting a breakthrough. Understandably, they expressed a degree of indignation that they were not full members of the Movement already but affected a level of cool disinterest on the question of whether they might be admitted now (as a result of the American initiative), particularly if it meant any restriction on their provision of services to Jewish settlements in Palestine or in the Golan. This sense of disinterest was no doubt also fuelled at least in part by the long-held view of many Jewish people that they had been let down by the Red Cross over the Holocaust and the Movement's failure to speak out against the horrors of the concentration camps, and that the Red Cross was therefore in some sense institutionally anti-Jewish.

In Palestine, or the 'Occupied Territories', we saw the full effect of the Middle East stand-off, with large bustling Arab towns like Ramallah and Jericho under curfew – no people, no traffic, no noise, just the sound of the breeze and an occasional darting cat, even at midday. Jerusalem was also completely deserted, with not a tourist in sight – the Via Dolorosa and the Church of the Holy Sepulchre, normally crammed with visitors, were silent and full of foreboding; and the beginnings of a 'security fence' (in reality a massive wall), dividing the two communities could be seen in parts of the Holy City.

Everywhere there were roadblocks and checkpoints manned by heavily-armed and unsmiling Israeli troops. Our local delegate's attempt at a friendly joke at one of these places resulted in us being told at gunpoint to leave the vehicle, whilst a full search was carried out – no doubt a response to a recent rumour, probably apocryphal, that a PRCS ambulance had been used to transport weapons for the Palestine Liberation Organization.

The shock of turning into a street in Ramallah and finding ourselves literally under the barrel of an Israeli tank was a sobering one. In Hebron particularly, Israeli settlers had moved deep into Palestinian areas. In the backstreets it wasn't unusual to see Israeli flags and loudspeakers festooning a first floor apartment, and we heard reports of refuse being occasionally showered on the heads of those below. When we approached one of the better-established settlements in our clearly-marked Red Cross vehicle, two groups of settlers sallied forth and threw stones at us.

We received a warm welcome from PRCS and its popular leader Younis al Khatib, who showed us round his threadbare headquarters and the ambulances parked outside, several of them holed, allegedly by bullets. We visited local centres of volunteer activity and an impressive but overstretched hospital, and came away both speechless with admiration at their bravery and determination and heartbroken at the agony and the pity of it all. Younis responded to comments about our 'talks about talks' with the Israelis and our hopes for a settlement of the 'Emblem' issue with a resigned shrug.

'*Inshallah*,' he said, but his tired eyes belied the optimism of the word.

We returned to London and reported back to the ICRC and the Federation in Geneva, making some tentative suggestions about the way forward, before flying to Washington two weeks later for meetings with our counterparts in the American Red Cross, who had precipitated the latest round of urgent efforts to solve the 'Emblem issue' by withholding their *barème*, an action destined to drive the Federation into a severe cash crisis.

The Americans accepted the draft Third Protocol as the only comprehensive solution and were keen to support efforts to bring governments together with the Movement as a whole in a special 'Diplomatic Conference' in November 2003, at which, it was hoped, the Third Protocol would be agreed and the Israeli and Palestinian national societies would be admitted to the Movement. The political situation in the Middle East at that time rendered this an optimistic timetable to say the least.

There was a grim reminder, soon after we got back, that the Movement's problem with the Emblem and the American *barème* was but a reflection of the challenges in the Middle East as a whole – the memorial service at St Paul's for the victims of the 9/11 bombing of the World Trade Centre. I attended with Sophie Brandt, one of our own welfare workers who had done so much for the families of the sixty-seven

British victims, and watched spellbound as 2,977 white rose petals, one for each victim, tumbled gently from the Dome, the sound of each single petal as it landed on the white marble of the altar clearly audible in the deep silence of remembrance and reflection.

Turkmenistan, a huge, sparsely-populated and arid country bordering Iran and Afghanistan, was another of our partner national societies. The country, though rich in gas and oil, was at that time at least unable to exploit its reserves because it could not sell to anyone but Russia until a pipeline was built to the south. As a result, its economy was rural and poor, apart from the capital Ashgabat, which had become a veritable Disneyland of white marble palaces, fountains, grand plazas and golden domes under the country's eccentric President Niyazov, who had renamed the days of the week after members of his family and erected a golden statue of himself which revolved with the sun in the main square.

The Turkmenistan Red Crescent was run, or rather ruled, by the delightful but steely Madame Zukhra, who had been appointed by the President, chaired his Emergencies Committee, drove around in one of his Mercedes and was constantly fearful that one day she too would fall victim to one of his capricious whims and be removed. The objects of my visit were to sign a Memorandum of Understanding regarding our three-year £500,000 organizational development partnership, and to try to get an audience with the President to secure a formal Status Agreement allowing the Federation itself to open an office in the country.

I failed in the latter aim, despite the best efforts of Madame Zukhra and the British Ambassador, but the MOU was signed with a flourish in Madame Z's office, celebrated with a game of darts on her personal dartboard and accompanied by my rendition of the theme music to The Archers (in the context of a description of British village life); then there was a long evening's drive north singing Beatles songs with her and our extremely able and personable Desk Officer, Alexander Matheou. She was a character.

During the week-long trip we visited several disaster preparedness projects, some of them way up in the mountains along remote tracks and across rushing streams; saw schools, feeding centres, lunch clubs, workshops staffed by people with disabilities, clubs for the elderly – indeed a cornucopia of Red Crescent projects, all demonstrating the incredible strength of the Movement at local level all over the world and in the remotest places. Everywhere I received the warmest of welcomes: from a regional volleyball team whom I was called upon to address across a vast windswept stadium, accompanied by a barrage of loud pop music and four cheerleaders dressed as Cossacks; and from an elderly man who tottered up a mountain track to present me with the bag of teacups he had just bought in the village below and his huge black woolly hat (which sadly I had to jettison when I got home as it was popping with fleas).

Finally came South Africa. I gained the impression of a country sleepwalking to disaster in the face of what was at that time an HIV/AIDS epidemic largely ignored by the Government, but affecting by some estimates 35 per cent of the adult population of the townships. I visited a number of township 'home-based care projects' which we were funding, where volunteers provided very basic practical and emotional support to affected individuals, many of whom had been abandoned by their families due to the stigma attached to the condition. It was heartrendingly basic stuff, as I reported at the time:

> Picture the scene: a dark unlit garage crammed between shacks. Twelve eager volunteers crouch on rickety wooden seats. In a corner, two elderly ladies knit bathmats and bead necklaces to sell. Half a dozen people living with HIV sit quietly as the volunteers talk about their 150 clients, all of whom they try to see every day … a young woman stands and declares for the first time that she is HIV positive. The young men shift uneasily and avoid all attempts to draw them into the conversation. We find no answers, only questions.
>
> We are taken to meet two people dying of AIDS. A 40-year-old woman, living with her son, daughter and granddaughter in a tiny shack in a vast shambling township, and a younger man of thirty living with his infected wife in an even smaller shack. I cannot begin to describe the sense of hopelessness and helplessness of these two and their families. They survive on a small Government benefit, which has to support the whole family – not many jobs around here, especially if your family is affected by AIDS. They sit and watch and wait, the older woman on a sofa turned away from the open door, the

young man huddled under the blankets in the dark, fetid bedroom. I felt very intrusive and uncomfortable, and was relieved when we left.

Later, in a township, we came upon an orphaned 13-year-old girl who was looking after her two much younger siblings and attempting to raise enough money to live on by collecting scraps of meat and vegetables from local vendors, turning them into a mess of stew and then selling the result in nearby bars.

At this point, back home, the year seemed to be coasting to an encouraging conclusion. Indeed, in my December report to the Board I talked about the green shoots of recovery that seemed to be springing up. The deficit was down to just over £2m; income was up; the necessary structural changes had been largely completed and seemed to be working well; we were establishing an exciting new process for engaging and consulting with our volunteers at the local level; the sense of 'them and us' between volunteers and staff, and between UK Office and the Branches, was beginning to dissipate; our UK emergency response capacity had been reviewed and strengthened (learning particularly from the US 9/11 experience); work with refugees and asylum-seekers was expanding; steps were in hand to reinforce the importance of first aid as a core Red Cross activity; and plans for the sale of the Grosvenor Crescent offices were well in hand, with the prospect of an eventual move to somewhere modern and brighter.

I was starting to relax when, on the Saturday before Christmas, one of our Press officers called, early in the morning.

'I think you had better go and find a copy of the *Mail*,' she said. 'It's not good.'

When I got to the newsagents, I nearly cried.

'THE RED CROSS BANS CHRISTMAS' yelled the six-inch-high front-page headline. The article went on:

Christmas has been banned by the Red Cross from its 430 fund-raising shops. Staff have been ordered to take down decorations and to remove any other signs of the Christian festival because they could offend Moslems. The charity's politically-correct move triggered an avalanche of criticism and mockery last night – from Christians and Moslems. The furore is a fresh blow to the image of what was once one of Britain's most-respected charities. The British Red Cross lost friends this year over its support for the French illegal immigrant camp at Sangatte and its insistence on concentrating large efforts on helping asylum-seekers. 'The Red Cross is a neutral organization and we don't want to be aligned with any political party or particular philosophy,' a spokesman said.

The impact, at least in the short term, was disastrous. Within hours the story was being covered on every radio and TV channel in the country. All the newspapers took it up, in one form or another, within the next few days. Our switchboard was jammed with callers ringing to complain, to mock, to scold and, most worryingly, to cancel their regular subscriptions. Throughout Christmas and into the New Year I was being called constantly to give interviews to explain the policy and to answer questions about 'why I had introduced this ridiculous ruling'.

'Political correctness gone mad' was the most frequent comment. 'Bending over backwards to be nice to Muslims' was another.

Initially, we were all mystified. The Red Cross had always been a neutral and impartial organization, politically, culturally and of course from a religious standpoint. We had for years avoided overt linkage with faith-based organizations, and although we did (wrongly, said some) sell greetings cards at Christmas to raise money, our offices and shops were always devoid of religious imagery. It was simply something we did, and neither I nor anyone else had issued any recent edicts to reinforce this: there was simply no need. Everyone in the Red Cross understood.

After a few days the truth emerged. In a small shop in Kent a recently-recruited volunteer had been asked by the manager to refresh the shop window display. When the manager returned to inspect the result he was concerned to see that the volunteer had installed a nativity scene and other seasonal decorations. The manager, recognizing that the celebration of any religious festival was contrary to Red Cross policy, removed the tree, thereby sparking ill-feeling amongst the volunteers. This was reported in the local newspaper and featured on local radio. Somehow the *Daily Mail* got hold of the story and put it on the front page as another example of 'political correctness'.

Our careful, earnest explanations about why Red Cross neutrality and impartiality was so vital in terms of bringing aid to all sides, particularly in conflict situations, seemed to gain no traction and win us no friends (at least in the media). In interview after interview, the examples we gave to show how important that stance was were listened to (usually politely), but were then met with a sceptical 'But surely …?'

Shoals of extravagantly 'holy' Christmas cards began to arrive in Grosvenor Crescent, addressed mostly to me and filled with fervent blessings and Christian messages. They kept coming for years. It all sounds hilarious in hindsight, but it wasn't at the time. On a conservative valuation, the thousands of letters and phone messages, and no doubt the outraged feelings of many, many more who didn't bother to contact us at all, cost the Red Cross £4m in lost donations, direct debits and legacy pledges.

So much for Christmas.

Chapter 4

Turning the Corner, 2003

Invasion of Iraq – The Balkans and Siberia – Nelson Mandela

T he 'Banning Christmas' story put a blight on the first month of 2003, but after that, with the new emphasis on building emergency response capacity and activity and on establishing much stronger links with local statutory emergency response providers, the mood seemed to lighten, and we all began to see light at the end of the tunnel.

We started a push to demystify first aid skills and to encourage the public at large to learn the basics of how to save a life, whilst at the same time restating our commitment to the practice and teaching of first aid skills as a fundamental part of our core purpose – this emphasis delighted thousands of our volunteers, for whom 'saving a life' was what it was all about. We even researched at length the possibility of launching a 'Big Campaign', with a strapline of 'Don't be a Bystander', aimed at recruiting 'a first aider on every street', and only dropped the idea, sadly, a few months later, for fear that it would be too costly. First aider Joe Mulligan, with his relaxed style and friendly manner, was the perfect front man for our efforts to make the skill more accessible, and he was regularly called on by the media to charm readers, listeners and viewers with his topical and non-technical first aid tips.

This somewhat traditional 'emergencies and first aid' emphasis for the Red Cross contrasted with the development of a more edgy workstream, supporting the increasing numbers of refugees and asylum-seekers heading for the UK, mostly from the Middle East. They faced dispersal to local authorities around the UK, and even destitution, as a result of recent changes in benefits legislation which made it illegal for local authorities to provide support to an individual if the Home Office was not satisfied that he or she had sought asylum at the earliest possible opportunity (i.e. usually within three days of arriving in the UK). I had been concerned that the Red Cross had been doing little in this area of work, partly due to its political sensitivity and partly because organizations like the Refugee Council seemed to have it covered, but as the need increased, we set up a small unit at UK Office to encourage our Areas to offer help such as small cash grants, simple emotional and practical support and signposting.

Fundraising also appeared to be doing well, with a record £2m coming in from direct mail in December, shop sales up and one or two big donations from trusts and foundations in response to our appeals for Africa. Building on the theme that we were 'all fundraisers in the British Red Cross', we started gearing up for a big push to make our long-established Red Cross Week in May a successful and high-profile money-spinner, encouraging everyone to get out on the streets to rattle a tin. We also launched a very successful series of ads called 'I owe my Life', featuring individuals whose lives had been saved by the Red Cross; these included Maddie Sparrow, the daughter of close family friends, whose life had been saved at the age of three by a first aider volunteer, who had pulled her out of a pond at a village fete and resuscitated her.

All this good news was tempered, necessarily, by the ongoing restructuring programme which, whilst saving over £2m in employment costs, meant nevertheless that, tragically, over 400 colleagues lost their jobs, with many more enduring a lengthy period of uncertainty and change. Roger Smith and his team did a brilliant job trying to minimize the pain, but we all hated having to do it, and for me it remains one of the saddest periods of my professional career. We raised a further £4m from the sale of unsuitable or redundant properties and used the money to provide better buildings locally and to establish our organization-wide IT network.

All of these developments featured in our new-style National Assembly in March, the annual gathering of 2,000 or so volunteers from around the country, this year held at the National Convention Centre in Birmingham. The Assemblies I had attended before had been miserable affairs, mainly used as an opportunity for local volunteers (and some staff) to beat up senior management. I was determined to change the tone this year and put on a real 'show', to reflect the fact that we had turned a corner and were regaining our confidence. We had uplifting speeches, exciting audio-visual presentations, some music and dancing and, in what was to become a tradition in future years, the CEO dressing up – this year as a gross game show host, complete with frizzy wig and gold lame jacket. It was a great success – tragically marred for me that very night by a ghastly road traffic accident in which my son Tom was run over on a pedestrian crossing and ended up in hospital with a smashed pelvis, necessitating painful rehabilitation for him and weeks of worry for us.

But all the while, the possibility of another armed conflict with Iraq loomed, over the possibility that Iraq possessed 'weapons of mass destruction' and that it accordingly posed a threat to the US and its allies. The Movement began to gear up its response, with the ICRC leading on preparing for high numbers of casualties, the maintenance of key humanitarian supplies in Iraq and relief for those displaced by fighting. The Federation focussed on helping neighbouring countries prepare for an expected influx of refugees, buying and pre-positioning emergency stocks of tents, food and blankets, and working with the wealthier 'donor' national societies to coordinate their financial and other contributions.

Our own specialist logistics emergency response unit (ERU), led by our much-admired 'old hand' Mike Goodhand, was put on standby; we seconded an emergency response officer to Geneva; released £10,000 from our newly-formed Disaster Fund; and lobbied DFID for a £1m contribution towards the work of the ICRC. Our International Humanitarian Law (IHL) display at the Bovington Tank Museum was attracting such numbers that we were invited to keep it open for a further six months, and we maintained the spotlight on IHL with a gathering at Lancaster House of Red Cross and Red Crescent societies and their governments (hosted by Princess Alexandra) to discuss what might be done globally to promote better understanding and acceptance of these 'rules of war'.

In the Gulf, Red Crescent societies from across the region gathered in the United Arab Emirates (UAE) to discuss how they could best respond to the challenge of war on their doorsteps. At the same time, I was in the UAE preparing for the second meeting of the Donor Forum, to be held (somewhat incongruously for the Red Cross) in a vast, brand-new military academy on the outskirts of Abu Dhabi. The need for the Movement to build up the capacity of all national societies had never seemed more urgent.

The issue of national society development was discussed again at a regional Red Cross conference in Chile that month, and when I visited Colombia on the way home, my counterpart Walter Cotte expressed his frustration that the few 'PNS' (or donor national societies) operating in his country often tried to impose their own programmes and ways of working on the national society, whilst doing very little to build its own capacity to cope with the ongoing consequences of the 40-year struggle between the central government and the FARC guerrilla movement: 2m internally-displaced people; regular killings, kidnappings and beatings; and the domination of virtually every aspect of daily life by armed groups and the drugs trade. Two of his branch directors had been shot by guerrillas recently, he told me, and suddenly my own challenges at home seemed very small.

The war in Iraq, for all the political and humanitarian mayhem it has caused since, was over very quickly, ending with the fall of Baghdad in April 2003. We launched an Appeal early and got a good response, as did both the ICRC and the Federation. DFID contributed an unprecedented £30m to the Movement as a whole, predicated on the widely held but unrealized expectation of a large-scale exodus of Iraqis into neighbouring countries. We had to work even harder than usual, in the event, to ensure that the money was used carefully to meet emergency needs, and to build sustainable humanitarian response capacity in the country, given the extremely difficult and constrained working environment in Iraq – the narrow 'humanitarian space' caused by the power vacuum left by the collapse of Saddam's regime, and the consequent breakdown in law and order.

I visited Baghdad in May, part of a 'high level' Federation mission to determine priorities on the ground for spending the large sums raised by the Appeal. Our tiny plane spiralled downwards from high above the airport in the Coalition 'green/security zone', hoping thereby to avoid the very real danger of a rocket attack from dissident forces, and we soon got our first glimpse of the devastated city – bombed-out buildings, largely deserted streets and dust everywhere. US troops were out in force, usually in armoured vehicles, wearing full body armour, guns to the fore and finding it difficult to make personal contact with the locals. Looting was rife, shops were closed and shuttered and nobody was working. As my mission report noted:

The visits we made to hospitals, water-pumping stations and power stations were deeply depressing. The impact of the looting is quite astonishing to behold – in one water-pumping station, for example, on the banks of the Tigris and just opposite one of Saddam's vast palaces, huge generators and pumps had been removed by crane, light fittings and doors had been ripped out, virtually everything useable or saleable had been taken – and everything else had been trashed, even the panes of reinforced glass high up in a wall above the staircase. The Americans have not responded to repeated requests to protect these key installations from successive waves of looting and destruction.

As ever, the ICRC came over as professional, efficient, dedicated and focussed, painstaking in their attention to security – this was a delegation which had seen one of their number, the Armenian Vatche Arslanian, caught in crossfire between Coalition and Iraqi forces and killed whilst taking an Iraqi colleague home at the end of the day. We passed his burnt-out Landcruiser later that day, riddled with bullets, its Red Cross emblem scorched and its engine gone.

As we drove around, it was clear that, for the Iraqis at least, the emblem, normally the only protection we relied on, meant nothing – if anything, we were seen as part of the problem. Visiting an ICRC water station and seeing that the large plastic storage bladders were empty, we got out of our vehicle to take a look and were instantly surrounded by a large angry crowd shouting and waving their fists. We beat a hasty retreat as hands banged on the roof and windows – I had never before seen such anger directed at an humanitarian organization, and it was an uncomfortable demonstration that, even in the Red Cross, we could not always rely upon being seen as 'the good guys'.

The situation on the ground in Baghdad was grim, and the mood uneasy. One of the nurses at the Al Rashad Psychiatric Hospital described how looters came and took away all the female patients. A young Swedish doctor, who had been working there for years, stirred the patient records which littered the floor and shook his head. There was a photograph on the wall of his team, two of whom had died in a bombing attack. Later, as we were visiting another water-pumping station, there was a huge explosion just across the muddy waters of the Tigris, then another.

Our ears popped as we looked wildly round and at each other, and a pall of smoke rose into the sky.

'Oh yeah,' said the engineer, 'they're a bit late today. They're still clearing the Iraqi ammunition dumps. There's over eight hundred of them.'

We nodded nervously.

Perhaps most shocking of all, though, in some ways, was a reception organized by the Office for Reconstruction and Humanitarian Assistance (ORHA) and attended by several senior American officials and military leaders. They openly acknowledged their difficulties in restoring law and order or protecting key buildings and appeared to have no coherent plans for the future of the country.

'Say,' said a US officer, as he sidled up to me with another beer, 'if you guys have any ideas ...'

To me it seemed obvious that the main task for the Federation was to build the capacity of the Iraqi Red Crescent itself, recruiting local volunteers to help rebuild civil society and provide care for the thousands of people injured or displaced in the fighting. Some of my donor country counterparts, however, were keen to provide aid and assistance themselves, and I was concerned that this would lead to a short-term approach and a security risk for their teams.

My mission report continued:

Shortly afterwards, calling in at an hotel for directions, having lost our way in the unlit streets, dodging through road blocks, a French photo-journalist, his face swollen and sweating, grabbed me. For taking photos at night at the airport (not a sensible activity it has to be said) he had received a night-time visit from four soldiers and a man in civilian clothes. He was beaten and hauled off to what he described as a 'Guantanamo detention centre', where he was shown handcuffed, kneeling Iraqis being interrogated in the burning sun. 'You're next,' they said. 'Now beat it.' He was on his way out by road that night.

It's a scary place and a scary situation, in every way. Early the next morning, waiting outside our small hotel for the ride out to the airport, I chatted to three young Iraqi boys on their way to school – about Manchester United and their algebra homework. It was the only normal conversation I had in three days.

Returning home, on one of the strangest journeys I took during my time in the Red Cross, I flew straight from Baghdad (via Frankfurt, Gatwick and Inverness) to Kirkwall in Orkney for an annual volunteers meeting, followed by three days observing our work in the Highlands. Coming in to land on that small island in the afternoon sunshine, across a sparkling blue sea, was like waking from a nightmare after the grim atmosphere of Baghdad.

The situation in Iraq continued to deteriorate and, as a national society, we played a strong role in supporting the ICRC, which lost another delegate, executed on the main road just south of Baghdad, and had their offices tragically destroyed in October by a car bomb, with the loss of twelve lives. The sense of being under attack was a rare and deeply unsettling experience for the ICRC, and there was concern that this was due in part to the organization mistakenly being seen in some sense as part of the Coalition effort. The Prime Minister, Tony Blair, was particularly vociferous in his condemnation of the attacks and, whilst he meant well, his remarks were seen as possibly reinforcing this perception. I had been invited to a Downing Street reception the next week and decided to speak to him if I got the chance. I approached his minder and asked for a word. Somewhat nervously, I broached the topic, and Blair's laser-like stare hardened; the message had got through but had clearly not gone down well.

So pleased was the ICRC with our overall support that we were offered the opportunity of a formal agreement for a five-year working partnership (the first ever offered to a national society) and a commitment to use our people and resources in future ICRC operations. We jumped at the chance to form a closer bond with the ICRC and to have the opportunity to influence thinking to some extent, particularly at a time when the Federation had internal difficulties of its own with the recent departure of the French Secretary-General, Didier Cherpitel.

It would have been easy, at that time, to become completely taken up with internal Movement politics and politicking. We had already become recognized as a strong member of the Federation's Governing Board: John got on well with del Toro and other Board members, who appreciated his dry wit and ability to think laterally, whilst I had formed strong bonds with my counterparts in other national societies. The Donor Forum (whose coordinating group I chaired) was already proving useful in securing greater cooperation between the wealthier national societies, and our participation in other cooperative Movement ventures was often sought. We were busy with our own group of 'partner' national societies, too – Bangladesh, Bulgaria, Cambodia, Ethiopia, Mozambique, Nigeria, Russia, Sierra Leone, Turkmenistan and Uganda – actively discussing the way we worked together and what we could do to support their development.

But I still felt like rather a 'new boy' on the international stage, so when the time came to recruit a new Federation Secretary-General, I was surprised to be lobbied to 'put my hat in the ring'. I had been asked to act as an adviser to the interim replacement, Markku Niskala from Finland, so I nervously agreed to apply for the permanent appointment, very much aware that it was too soon for me to leave the British Red Cross and too early to have gained sufficient experience of the Movement. I was disappointed but not surprised when President del Toro and his vice presidents chose Niskala, who had been involved with the Red Cross for years. I was also pleased to be able to carry on in the British Red Cross, where we had just appointed an interesting new Fundraising Director called Mark Astarita, who was destined to transform the financial health of the organization in the coming years, plus a strong-willed and dynamic secondee from the NHS, Virginia Beardshaw, to head up the service side.

There was more than enough to do, as I had just been appointed by the Blair Government to chair the committee charged with producing a much-needed 'Concordat' between the Government and the voluntary sector, and was at the same time campaigning for the role of the sector in responding to emergencies to be recognized in the upcoming Civil Contingencies Bill.

We had also just secured the Prince of Wales' agreement to become our President, in succession to his late grandmother, so I was able to build on the relationship I had formed with him at Macmillan, where he was our Royal Patron. I felt that he would value the opportunity to be involved, through the Red Cross, in the most pressing humanitarian issues of the day, and so it proved. His office was in touch after pretty much every major disaster or conflict thereafter, offering a personal donation and other support and asking for a detailed briefing, or even to discuss the possibility of a visit to the area. His support in subsequent years was invaluable.

We held some spectacular fundraising events in London and elsewhere, including a 'Havana Nights' ball run by amazing fundraiser Maria Shammas, a Remembrance Sunday concert at the Royal Albert Hall and a 'Jewels for Life' auction at Christies. Most memorably of all, we hosted an evening with Nelson Mandela at the QE Conference Centre, at which we reunited him on stage with Jacques Moreillon, who had been the Red Cross representative on Robben Island and who had had to negotiate with the authorities on behalf of the prisoners for 'luxuries' like soap and clean underclothes. Listening to the two of them swapping yarns about the difficulties they had faced was completely enthralling, and the looks on the faces of the invited audience as we walked together back up the central aisle confirmed that they had all been as moved as I was. Talking to him quietly on my own in the Green Room before we went on stage was an experience I will never forget – overcome by unwonted shyness at his extraordinary aura of calm patience and wisdom, not to mention terror at the thought of having to follow him as a speaker onstage. But he put me at my ease completely with a few questions about my family and about the British Red Cross, and then we chatted quietly about Robben Island, which I had visited the previous year. His power, as the inspirational leader of the brutal fight against apartheid, seemed to lie in the very simplicity of his humility and humanity.

Returning to my programme of visits to 'partner' national societies, I headed for Serbia, where the British Red Cross had been supporting the Federation's efforts to re-establish the work (and reputation) of the Red Cross in the wake of the terrible conflicts in the Balkans eight years earlier. It was clear that Belgrade remained heavily scarred both emotionally and physically by the Milosevic years and by the devastating NATO bombing campaign. The national society, having been effectively controlled by the previous regime, was struggling to maintain a wide range of services for an impoverished population (50 per cent unemployed), with little local funding available. It was heavily dependent on the Federation, the ICRC and national societies like ours, and worried that, were the external funding to dry up, the national society would be blamed for the closure of services. I met a health minister and, somewhat bizarrely, the Crown Prince and Princess, who were living in some luxury in a castle overlooking a large park and were busy clearing up after his birthday party the day before (400 guests at a candlelit dinner). I praised the work of the national society and urged the minister to support its campaign for a law enshrining its independence – he didn't look very convinced.

Montenegro was still, at this time, part of a federation with Serbia, so technically its national society was part of the Serbian Red Cross. Its Secretary-General, 'Slobo' as he was more or less affectionately known by his team of bright young assistants, twenty-eight years in the job, was impatient for independence. The main programme of the society was the provision of food relief for about 40,000 people from Kosovo displaced by the fighting there years earlier (when there had been more than 150,000 internally displaced people, nearly a quarter of the population of Montenegro).

From Podgorica we drove through lyrically beautiful plains and valleys to Kosovo, where the Kosovo Albanians had formed an army (the KLA) in the late 1990s to fight against Yugoslav/Serbian persecution. Serbian forces then began a campaign of retribution against KLA sympathizers, and NATO eventually intervened to stop the fighting. An interim administration under the aegis of the UN was established, and peace of a kind prevailed. The country remained divided, though, between the Serbs in the north and the Kosovo Albanians in the south, and there were as a result two Red Crosses to visit, one serving each community. The Kosovo Serbian organization was a tragic shadow of its former self, its elderly volunteers largely busy distributing food parcels from Belgrade   both the President and his Secretary General had had their houses in the south occupied by Albanian families, one of whom caused huge offence while we were there by ringing up to complain about the property's deterioration.

Further south, in Pristina, the Kosovo Albanian organization was more dynamic but hampered by lack of money and bitter memories of Serbian domination and atrocities. Their office was next to what had allegedly been a Serbian 'rape factory'. For reasons which I found hard to understand, the Federation was trying to persuade these two organizations to merge – this might have been appropriate if Kosovo was recognized as a country (which it was not) and if it had not so recently been ravaged by bitter ethnic conflict, the flames of which still flickered in numerous different ways. UN armoured vehicles and Red Cross Landcruisers roamed the streets, giving way at night to prowling gangs of disaffected youths and pitifully young-looking prostitutes lining the streets outside the few shabby hotels: I was chased by one of them into the lobby of the hotel and had to dodge into a lift to escape her. It all seemed a terrible mess.

Pausing only for a Red Cross General Assembly in Geneva, where John was appointed to lead a reflection upon 'The Federation of the Future' and I was asked to lead a team of secretary-generals to conduct a mid-term review of the Federation's *Strategy 2010*, I then travelled to Russia, another of our partner national societies, where we had been supporting work on TB and HIV, both of which were rife in Siberia. Tatiana, the President of the Russian Red Cross, was a fellow Federation Board member and she wanted me to give her some advice about managing her impossibly unruly local branches, so the five-day visit involved long drives and flights in rickety, ancient aeroplanes between and around St Petersburg, Novosibirsk in western Siberia, and Moscow.

We met Tatiana in St Petersburg Branch, having first visited some of their activities, including a centre for educating and feeding the children of single parents, alcohol- and drug-abusers and people with disabilities, a legal advice centre and a health clinic for refugees (mostly from Afghanistan), and a small club for Afghan women. Tatiana chattered away fairly inconsequentially, but one of her colleagues, a large black-bearded bear of a man who clearly disapproved of her rather laid-back approach, took me on one side and talked movingly of the thousands of street children who had flooded into the city from surrounding areas seeking a better life and who scrabbled a living in and around the warmth of the metro stations.

The flight to Novosibirsk in Siberia was grim and packed with hard-faced manual workers returning home from a weekend in the city. It was 2.00am and freezing cold when we arrived, nearly 4.00am by the time we got to bed and 9.00am when we had our first formal meeting with the Chairlady of the local Branch. Almost immediately, we set off for the three-hour drive to Kemorova in -40° temperatures, through snowy wastes and birch woods, past frozen lakes punctuated by lonely men dangling fish hooks through the ice, villages of ramshackle huts and farmers driving horse-drawn sleds to market.

On arrival, we were led straight into a vast welcome meal of cold meats and salmon steaks, washed down with vodka, a bottle beside each place for ease of refilling after the ritual toasting. After a press conference and a visit to the local hospice, we returned to the Branch to resume the meal, before eventually being escorted to our boarding house, which was presided over by an enormous tattooed and grinning skinhead.

The following day, after a dog-meat kebab for breakfast on the road, we drove another three hours south to the mining and smelting centre of Novokuznetsk, a place seriously challenged by endemic tuberculosis (TB) and rapidly rising rates of HIV infection amongst the young. We visited the treatment centre and met the local Mayor, who blamed drug-takers for the HIV problem – 'They hang them in Thailand', he remarked, wistfully. We gave another press conference, ate another large and vodka-fuelled meal and drove back to Novokuznetsk in the dark, arriving in time for another huge 'snack' at the Branch to set us up for our flight to Moscow and the headquarters of the Russian Red Cross, next morning.

I arrived home a day later, and the next morning, the head of our press team phoned to warn me of another *Daily Mail* headline: 'Red Cross Bans Jesus from its Christmas Cards'.

I even got my picture in the paper this time and in a subsequent article earned the title 'Commissar of Political Correctness'. The *Sun* featured the story, too, complete with a picture of Jesus looking in the direction, presumably by design, of the paper's adjoining 'page three girl', Krystle. The Tory MP Nigel Evans called it all 'beyond the pale' and 'political correctness gone mad' and suggested that the Red Cross, instead of banning the three wise men, should 'employ a new one, at the top'.

The story was then covered in a further thirty national and local papers, was featured on twenty-five radio stations and generated 1,200 telephone, email and postal enquiries, as well as another shoal of holy Christmas cards for me. It went on longer, in fact, than in 2002. As before, we had done nothing to prompt these stories and gave dozens of interviews trying to scotch them: as before, we failed to persuade anyone to listen, despite the hard work of our excellent and creative communications team who, as usual, pulled out all the stops.

Another happy Red Cross Christmas.

Chapter 5

Across the World and Around the Corner, 2004

Earthquake in Iran and the Prince – The Civil Contingencies Bill and the Contract Culture – North Korea – Ethiopia

There was to be no respite. On Boxing Day, a massive earthquake struck the ancient city of Bam in south-eastern Iran, killing an estimated 25,000 people and injuring many more. Its 2,000-year-old Citadel, which was constructed entirely from mud bricks, as were many of Bam's houses, disintegrated almost completely into a huge heap of dust.

We launched an immediate Appeal, and our newly-formed Emergency Response Unit with its expert logistics capability was immediately despatched to Bam to help manage the supply of relief goods via the nearby small airport, which had itself been badly damaged in the earthquake. As part of what became a standard routine, I contacted the Prince of Wales' Office, to update them on the disaster and what the Red Cross was doing, and told them that I was intending to go to Bam myself in January on my way back from a planned visit to Bangladesh, one of our partner national societies. The Prince agreed to host a reception at St James' Palace in support of the Appeal, and his office then raised the possibility that he might be prepared to go to Bam himself, as President of the British Red Cross, whilst visiting British troops stationed in Basra, Iraq. Would I be prepared to meet up with the British Embassy in Tehran and do a recce? This was all moving very fast.

First, I had the pre-arranged visit to Bangladesh, initially in Dhaka to the headquarters of the Bangladesh Red Crescent, then travelling north to inspect the flood response activities of Branches situated in the flood plain of the Brahmaputra River and its tributaries.

Rural poverty was the big issue, with three quarters of the country's 146m people living in remote villages and subjected to the constant risk of lost livelihoods and savings due to flooding and cyclones. 'Like a jigsaw puzzle floating in a bathtub' (as one Minister described it to me), large tracts of the country are underwater for months of the year, as great swirling, shifting sheets of water flow towards the Bay of Bengal from the Himalayas, eroding vast acreages in one place or creating huge new islands in another. I spoke to a farm labourer on a first aid course who told me:

> Every year, my house is under five feet of water. My family has to sleep on a small tower of piled up beds. We cook on a stove balanced on a bamboo raft. There is no work. Wages drop as the number of unemployed people in the area rises. Everyone turns to the moneylender and his extortionate interest rates, or sells what they can at a giveaway price.

Local resilience, or 'Community-based Disaster Preparedness', is vital, and we had been working with local Branches in Bangladesh to help them build cyclone shelters (huge circular towers big enough to house local villagers and their animals until the floods subside); delivering training in early warning systems, first aid and health maintenance; and funding regular cyclone response exercises such as the one I saw south of Chittagong in a village several hours drive out in the countryside.

After a long drive through a kaleidoscope of rice paddies, overloaded rickshaws, roads filled every inch of the way with animals and children, and brightly-painted lorries loaded with produce, I sat as the guest of honour in a small grandstand, with thousands of villagers perched in trees and atop buildings, to watch the show. As we raced back to the airport to catch the flight to Dhaka, a four-hour drive in the evening light, watching workers returning from the paddy fields and cooking fires being lit in the roadside villages, I marvelled at the resilience and resourcefulness of the Bangladeshis and at their cheery acceptance of the hardships of life.

The next day, I was on my way to Bam via Dubai, arriving in Tehran in the late morning and being whisked straight off the tarmac by the Iranian Red Crescent for a lunch with some of the society's leaders. The following morning, we were up early for the flight to Kerman, followed by a terrifying drive along the main truck route to Bam, hugging the tails of huge lorries before squeaking past to overtake amidst a blaring of horns.

Bam was a terrible mess. Three miles from the centre you could see collapsed mud-brick houses and shops: closer in, everything had been flattened – not a single building remained unscathed. The Iranian Red Crescent (a large and extremely capable national society enjoying massive government support) had done an impressive job by way of response, both in terms of organizing their own relief activities and in coordinating those of PNS like our own who had flown in teams and materials. There were tented casualty and orthopaedic units, a huge 240-bed field hospital, neat rows of tents for survivor families, plastic tent 'Rubb Hall' warehouses, a water-treatment plant – and everywhere tired but determined Red Cross relief workers from across the world working together to get on top and stay on top of a desperate humanitarian crisis. Our own work was centred on the logistics function, but it was also in Bam that we first started to use cash vouchers to enable people to buy what they wanted in the local markets, rather than rely on the supplies that we chose to give them – a system that we were to develop into a speciality over the coming years.

After a couple of TV and radio interviews, we drove around the town, saddened to see people still poking about in the rubble of their lives to salvage whatever they could; tiny temporary plastic shelters and tents perched amongst the ruins; burka-clad women queuing at standpipes to fill their cooking pots. The extraordinary Citadel was a pile of dust.

I was due to meet the British Ambassador, Sir Richard Dalton, for a briefing session and discussion about the Prince's visit the next day, so we raced back to Kerman (narrowly escaping death at the hands of sleepy lorry drivers along the way) for the late flight back to Tehran. The morning was filled with meetings with the Red Crescent, followed by lunch with the British Ambassador and someone from the security services, then more meetings at the Embassy and dinner with the Ambassador, before a ride out to the airport (armoured Range Rover, a flag and armed guards) for a midnight UN flight back to Bam with the Ambassador and two of his staff.

The next day was a full-scale recce for the Royal visit, with a tour of the town, another visit to the Red Cross Red Crescent relief compound, meetings with the local Governor, sitting cross-legged on the floor in his tent, and a representative of the Ministry of Agriculture. From his perspective, the key issue was dates. The dates from Bam are amongst the best in the world, but the orchards had been devastated, most of the palms uprooted and the complex structure of ancient underground water supply channels or *qanats* very badly damaged. It was pollination time, but many of the farmers had been killed. Indeed, the Ministry's offices had been destroyed and twenty-seven of their staff had died, too, while the rest were living and working in tents.

We met Akbari, the owner of a guest house popular with foreign visitors, who had rushed to save his guests before his family and proudly showed us a visitors' book that had survived the quake, filled with messages and drawings from his grateful customers. Then it was another UN Beechcraft flight back to Tehran and on to London for a planning meeting the next day with the Prince's team at St James's Palace.

The next week was a whirl of planning and briefings and preparation for our Bam Appeal event at St James's the following Friday – interspersed with an address to the Finance Directors of all the main government ministries about the voluntary sector; a meeting of the Strategic Partnership Forum of Department of Health and voluntary leaders (which I chaired); and one of our own managers' conferences in Kenilworth. A couple of days later, after a very successful Appeal event, I was back in the Tehran Embassy waiting for the Prince to return from his morale-raising visit to Basra.

He arrived late and tired. After a quick supper, the final briefing began, and then we headed upstairs for a couple of hours' sleep. Early the next morning, we set off through the chaotic Tehran rush hour traffic in a long motorcade, sirens wailing, for a courtesy visit to the President, Dr Khatami. A loudspeaker on one of the police cars blared out instructions, and anyone not shifting out of the way was moved off the road.

Dr Khatami seemed quite jolly and gave us all a friendly welcome before we set off again for the airport, passing on the way a desperate-looking Nick Witchell, BBC Royal Correspondent, surrounded by the Palace Guard. If he could not come to Bam with us, the trip would receive much-reduced publicity back home. Frantic phone calls from the car ensued, but by then we were at the airport, and there was the Royal jet gleaming white with a red tail fin, flag flying and the red carpet already laid out on the runway.

With the Prince impatient at the delay, take-off was stalled long enough (just) for Witchell and his cameraman to be seen panting across the runway as we taxied. Lunch was served on board, and I caused much amusement amongst the Prince's staff by mistakenly using the royal loo, instead of the staff one for'ard.

Then we landed in Bam, and a hectic day ensued, the Prince charming and engaged with everyone he met, the rest of us following in a pack behind chatting to anyone he had missed and struggling to keep both the Press and the crowds of onlookers from flattening him in the crush. Early on, we visited the historic Citadel, and the cameramen duly got their shots for the next day's front pages of HRH in his cream summer suit and accompanied by his security detail, all similarly-clad, picking about in the dusty ruins.

Then it was on to a date palm orchard, where a wizened elderly farmer pushed his way through the crowd and presented the Prince (to the consternation of the security men) with a large box of dates.

'Nick,' said HRH, calling me forwards, 'why don't we ask for more boxes, then you can send them to everyone who has supported the Appeal? It would be a nice thank you.'

Before I could say a word, his harassed-looking Private Secretary, thinking no doubt of the tangled logistical, security and customs challenges ahead, had been instructed; negotiations ensued with the farmer, and the local Governor beamed.

The day finished with a lengthy tour of the Red Cross Red Crescent compound and all the relief teams, then a reception for all the other British and Commonwealth NGOs working in Bam. Throughout, the Prince was interested, delightful, warm and solicitous, completely on top of his brief and apparently tireless and unfazed by the crush, the heat and the appalling dust. As he boarded the plane once more, I did a quick interview with Witchell for *News at Ten*, and we were off once more. The Prince immediately picked up his pile of files and started working.

But the day wasn't over yet, at least not for me.

The agreement was that I would hitch a ride in the Royal jet to Riyadh – the next leg of the visit – and make my own way back to London from there. The two-hour flight was quickly over, fully occupied with a debrief on the Bam visit, and soon we were drawing up at the enormous marble dome of the special Royal terminal at Riyadh. The Prince and his entourage said their goodbyes and then stood at the top of the steps to observe the glories of a right royal Saudi welcome, complete with a large military band and escort, numerous politicians and functionaries in spotless white robes and a fleet of Rolls-Royces, spotlit in the darkness on the tarmac and ready to whisk the visitors away.

I waited a while for the dust to settle, then thanked the RAF crew for the lift and made my own way down the aircraft steps, managing not to wave regally at my own reception committee – an elderly guy with a broom. I looked about me. I was on my own – not a flight attendant, driver or consular official in sight. I looked at the guy with the broom. He carried on sweeping. A dustcart arrived, bringing momentary hope of a lift to the main airport, whose lights I could see gleaming brightly across several acres of bleak empty concrete, but it swept on past me. I approached the gleaming terminal and banged on the locked door to attract the attention of the solitary security guard inside. He opened the door a crack, and with a few exasperated gestures I managed to convey my predicament. He went away to make some calls, leaving me outside. Twenty minutes later, a battered minivan arrived, and with a brusque 'You get in!' I was on my way at last.

At Riyadh's enormous airport, I checked in with a sigh of relief and then headed for the necessary passport inspection before going through to the departure lounge.

The official looked at my passport.

'When you arrive?' he demanded.

'Oh,' I said, 'just an hour or so ago.'

'Why no entry stamp?'

'Ah, well, I came in with the Prince of Wales.'

His eyes narrowed. I could see this wasn't going to be easy.

'Where you come from?'

My heart sank.

'Er, Iran,' I said, very quietly, conscious that the two countries were mortal enemies.

His eyebrows shot up, and he rubbed his chin.

'Why no exit stamp?'

I tried the Prince of Wales line again, but he simply shook his head.

'No understand. Wait there.'

Urgent-looking phone calls followed. As the people behind me in the queue stared at me curiously and shuffled their feet, I searched my pockets for some documentary evidence to support my story, but all I found was an elderly date from our tour of the orchard that morning.

Then the soldiers arrived, three of them, with very real-looking guns. I was marched away to a small cell just off the guardroom and left to contemplate my fate. Eventually, an officer in plain clothes arrived, and I went through my story again. He, too, shook his head, and withdrew to fetch a more senior colleague, who seemed similarly unimpressed. The time for my flight came and went.

Suddenly the door was flung open, and the head of the Prince's security detail was pushed in.

'Gosh, am I glad to see you!' I said.

'Don't get too excited,' he said, 'I've just been arrested, too. They didn't seem to buy my story about the Prince of Wales!'

When the senior security guy returned, we had another go at explaining our undocumented presence in his airport. The fact that he now had two people on his hands with the same unlikely story seemed to impress him just a little, and when the Prince's man gave him a phone number which he said was the number for the British Ambassador in Riyadh, his head-shake seemed ever so slightly more impressed.

Twenty minutes later, he returned, all smiles, and handed us back our passports, pointing vigorously to the new entry stamps which had just appeared.

'You go home now,' he said firmly.

When I got back to the office, there were several large crates full of dates waiting in reception.

'These are for you apparently,' said the receptionist. 'From St James's Palace?'

Delivering the dates, box by box, to supporters took up a lot of time for our fundraisers, but they were rewarded when we received an extraordinarily generous anonymous donation of £640,000 for our Bam Appeal from a well-known children's author. Our high profile in the region also attracted the attention of the People's Mujahideen of Iran, a proscribed terrorist organization, some of whose members were stuck in a camp in Iraq. Their families and friends now began a series of noisy and disruptive pickets outside our offices which went on for some weeks.

Meanwhile, on the home front, there were green shoots of recovery everywhere – or light at the end of the tunnel, as they called it at our centre at Croxley Green, where they presented me with a large torch when I went to give a talk at their annual meeting. It was an exciting time, perhaps best symbolized by the news that, thanks to a series of successful deals by our finance director David Causer, we were to move from our dark and dusty offices in swanky Grosvenor Crescent (our home for over seventy years) to a more modern open-plan block near the Barbican.

We were able to capitalize on the mood of recovery and optimism with a new overarching strategy, much of it the work of Mike Adamson's successor as strategy director, Richard Blewitt. We called it *Across the World and Around the Corner*, to capture the unique reach and spread of the Red Cross. The strategy opened with a bold statement:

> We are a dynamic organization which prepares people for, deals with and helps them recover from crisis. It could be a catastrophic event or personal crisis – across the world or around the corner.
>
> The people of the Red Cross come from many different backgrounds and have different skills. But what distinguishes us is our passion to help actively, supporting the most vulnerable. We help whenever and wherever we're needed.
>
> The British Red Cross is an open and welcoming organization. Always caring, always professional, always there.

We recognized the challenges posed by the growing complexity of natural, man-made and conflict-related emergencies; population movement; more older people; uncertainty about access to water, security, health and food; and HIV/AIDS and other health challenges; and we set a course for the organization based on building emergency response skills and preparedness, enhancing resilience, engaging with the most vulnerable and providing ever more opportunities for people to volunteer and give money and active support.

The strategy document was wonderfully full of smiling faces and dramatic images that captured the sense of a modern, dynamic and responsive organization, brimming with confidence and at the top of its game. We had commissioned Rita Clifton at Interbrand, who generously undertook a virtually pro bono review of our branding and positioning, and this led to a fresh new look for the organization's buildings and printed materials.

I even attempted to get the *Daily Mail* back on side. Paul Dacre, the editor, had always declined to respond to any of my attempts to speak or get into correspondence with him, but I had lunch with a deputy, who seemed reasonable enough. I was allowed to make all my points, and the result was a period of relative peace from the paper – marked the next Christmas only by an amusing extravagantly holy card, with a Nativity scene and 'blessings from the Managing Editor'. I can laugh now, but the negative coverage cost us millions.

Our finances were back in the black, and our investment in local emergency response capacity under the strapline 'Skill Up, Scale Up and Sustain' was paying off. Our local teams were being increasingly called out by local authorities to take part in practice drills and to help with local emergency 'shouts' (including, around this time, the tragic drowning of twenty-one Chinese 'slave labour' cockle-pickers in Morecambe Bay, a major fire in Glasgow and flooding in Boscastle) and were being seen as an important adjunct to the statutory services. After decades of being frequently ignored as 'mere volunteers', this was a major development. The statutory services were recognizing that, particularly in a big emergency, their resources were overstretched, and that the Red Cross in particular had plenty of trained and equipped people who could play a key supporting role. Our contribution to the rescue effort in Boscastle included an Appeal that raised over £150,000 and the wonderful sight of a fleet of German Red Cross vehicles arriving with donated dehumidifiers – a dramatic demonstration of both our growing fundraising confidence and capacity and our ability to call on resources from the rest of the Movement.

Unfortunately, the Cabinet Office Minister Douglas Alexander was resisting our campaign for the contribution made by charities in an emergency to be recognized in the draft Civil Contingencies Bill, which was designed to encourage local authorities to plan and prepare effectively for local disasters. It took another few months, detailed evidence at the Committee Stage and a revolt by supporters of the Red Cross in the House of Lords to persuade him to change his mind, and I can well remember the sense of satisfaction on getting a call from his office asking me to drop everything and meet to discuss amendments to the Bill, which duly received the Royal Assent in November.

At the same time, as part of a cautiously enthusiastic attempt to take advantage of the then prevailing 'contract culture', whereby charities were encouraged to bid for contracts to deliver local services rather than apply for grants, we had just won a flagship contract to deliver medical aid equipment all over Leicestershire. Some Areas embraced the new culture willingly, and we set up a small unit at UKO to support them, but as time went on, our caution (though criticized by some within the organization) proved justified as it became clear that many local authorities hoped to use the contracts to cut costs and to persuade unwitting charities to assume responsibility for subsidizing services that didn't pay – or face the unpopular alternative of closing them down.

This issue dominated the next few years. I chaired the Government Working Group tasked with drafting the constitution for a Strategic Partnership Forum between the Department of Health and the voluntary sector, and many of the Forum's early meetings were taken up with the vexed question of how to ensure that charities were not asked to carry an unduly heavy burden of financial risk in taking on these contracts. Government ministers went out of their way to give appropriate reassurance; but at local level it was a different story, and several charities, both big and small, came severely unstuck financially, forced to maintain loss-making services and accept short-term contracts that made it impossible to plan effectively or develop the service. These were risks that we largely managed to avoid.

Internationally, this was a time of considerable tension. The fallout from the Iraq conflict continued, as the Coalition under American leadership struggled to impose order and stability in the country; and the situation in Afghanistan with a newly-elected government was also unstable. This resulted in increased numbers seeking asylum and refuge in the West.

In Sudan, a terrifying campaign of ethnic cleansing had been launched against the non-Arab population in the Darfur region of west of the country, resulting in the death eventually of hundreds of thousands of people and the displacement and forced migration of millions more.

Through our new partnership with the ICRC, which now had a permanent representative based in our offices, we became actively involved in these conflicts, providing our own funding, access to DFID funding and personnel in support of the ICRC. The unauthorized publication of a highly confidential ICRC report on the alleged ill-treatment of detainees in Iraq caused a flurry of media interest – and was another opportunity to explain why impartiality and neutrality were such vital Red Cross principles.

Massive flooding in Asia and Haiti and a devastating hurricane (Ivan) in the Caribbean meant that our fundraisers were kept busy launching a new emergency appeal almost every month – thereby, of course, fortuitously raising our profile and generating new names for our expanding database of supporters and regular givers.

In June I was asked to join another 'high-level' Federation visit, this time to North Korea (DPRK). The main purposes of the mission were the delicate political tasks of encouraging the DPRK to feel fully part of the Red Cross Red Crescent Movement and link up more strongly with its sister organization in South Korea, particularly for the purposes of the forthcoming tenth annual reunion of 100 families separated by the war between the two countries – a war that was still theoretically ongoing. The Federation had been investing in the development of the DPRK Red Cross for some time, and it was fascinating to see the fruits of this work in a national society apparently thriving in the midst of unpromising circumstances.

Arriving from Beijing, after two days of meetings with the Chinese Red Cross leadership, we spent a day in the eerily traffic-free modern capital city of Pyonyang, each road junction policed, entirely unnecessarily, by smart baton-waving and rather robotic young women, who shrieked menacingly at any motorist or pedestrian who seemed inclined to disobey their imperious gestures.

Our first field visit was by ancient helicopter, across a damp green/brown rural landscape still scarred by bomb craters, to Ryongchon, where thousands of volunteer labourers were rebuilding the centre of the small town after it had been rocked by a massive explosion on a train carrying, it was alleged, fertilizer. There was speculation that the explosion had actually been an attempt on the life of the 'Dear Leader' Kim Jong-Il, whose train was passing through Ryongchon at the time – but this was impossible to confirm.

Red Cross volunteers, led by their tiny, shy Vice-Chairwoman (herself a victim of the blast), had rescued 2,000 individuals and their families whose houses had been destroyed by the huge blast – which had flattened the entire central area and most of the key buildings. An extraordinary rebuilding effort was now in full swing, manned by large squads of 'volunteers' all beavering away like ants amongst the dust and rubble, encouraged by improving songs blaring raucously from loudspeakers all around the explosion crater.

In the afternoon we drove to nearby Sunchon City along country roads crowded with bicycles, ox carts and ancient army trucks, the fields full of maize, and gangs from the collective farms and nearby army bases all working apparently harmoniously together. The hospital, a dank, rundown concrete building, staffed by doctors and nurses in filthy white coats and odd conical hats, was horribly basic, its wards and operating theatre devoid of the most basic equipment. The Federation was supplying something like 60 per cent of the medicines in this hospital and most of the medical equipment. We questioned whether it was appropriate for the Federation to take on this basic responsibility – but then what do you do if the Government can't or won't?

Further visits followed, to a community first aid post/clinic, a small Red Cross water-pumping station and a community-based disaster preparedness project in a small flood-prone village – or CBDP as it was known in the acronym-strewn landscape of the Red Cross in those days.

After dinner with the Swedish Ambassador, and a night in a large, sparsely-furnished hotel in Pyongyang, we spent the next day in formal meetings with senior colleagues from the DPRK Red Cross and an audience with the President of the Praesidium (effectively the Head of State) in his gaudily be-flagged Palace, its walls decorated with the patriotic and highly-coloured landscape paintings of which the North Koreans seem to be so fond. Then there was a night at the circus, hugely popular in North Korea and a riot of gaudy costumes and extraordinarily acrobatic performers.

The next day, it was back to Beijing, more meetings, a press conference about our visit to North Korea and then packing for the journey home – or, in my case, for the flight to Tokyo to plan for the next Donor Forum meeting in October, which was to be in a conference centre in the foothills of Mount Fuji.

The remainder of the summer, apart from a short visit to Cambodia (with its 82-year-old Secretary-General, still haunted by memories of Pol Pot) to sign a five-year partnership agreement with the local Red Cross, was spent in consultations about our new strategy and the changes in style and positioning consequent upon our work with Interbrand. We were the subject of a successful Blue Peter appeal which raised nearly £600,000, and installed a new IT system, recognizing for the first time that the successful integration and use of information technology was a fundamentally important part of everybody's work – not just something to help the Finance team crunch numbers. Charities were coming under media, public and government scrutiny like never before, and accountability and 'impact reporting' were the new buzz words – even if nobody really knew how to interpret them in terms of the softer side of charity work, where there is often no hard-edged bottom line by which progress can be judged.

We were preparing for our big move, too, and in the autumn held our last Board meeting in Grosvenor Crescent, in one of the dark, dusty, grandiose reception rooms. We had all the staff on balconies and leaning out of their windows for a farewell photo, and the general mood was one of excitement at the prospect. Many, myself included, felt a tinge of sadness, however, to be leaving the offices from where the Red Cross had run its extraordinary efforts during the Second World War, leased to us at a peppercorn rent by the Duke of Westminster's Grosvenor Estate. As it happened, we were also in the process of selling another relic of the war at that time, the Society's gracious Edwardian training centre at Barnett Hill in Surrey, given to us as a convalescent home in 1940 by the Thomas Cook family. The place was loved by thousands of staff and volunteers who had attended training courses or conferences there, many of them with fond memories of the early morning tea trolley, but we had concluded in our review of the Society's freehold and leasehold properties that it had to go.

Before the move, I had two more trips, the first being back to Japan for the third meeting of the Donor Forum, and the second to Ethiopia to sign another five-year partnership agreement with a sister national society. The Forum was another successful step along the way of persuading our fellow 'donor' national societies to work together better in supporting our less well-resourced brethren. There was lots of hard work, compensated by the glory of breakfast each morning looking up towards the snow-capped peak of Mount Fuji and the sheer exuberance of our final dinner, where we enjoyed a whole range of Japanese cultural experiences, from the tea ceremony to flower arranging, and from mass drumming to a

Haiku competition. An amazing evening finished with some local children performing the 'Last Ride of the Samurai' on horseback in the rain, and the elderly and very formal and much-respected President of the Japanese Red Cross, Tadateru Konoe, performing Nat King Cole's 'Mona Lisa' for a few of us in the bar afterwards, absolutely beautifully, in an impromptu karaoke session.

The trip to Ethiopia was extremely moving. The country had moved on, of course, from the terrible famine of the 1980s, but life in rural areas was still incredibly basic and precarious and this, thanks to a £4m grant from DFID, was where we had been working for the previous four years, supporting the prodigious efforts of the national society. Two paragraphs from my mission report help to paint the picture:

> One of many memorable moments on this trip came after a long drive literally across the fields to a tiny hamlet called Dimji where, amidst the thatched round straw huts, ambling cattle and scrubby coffee bushes and avocado plants of the villagers, we met the Red Cross Water Supply Unit and its Water Committee. Men and children gathered around to look at the *farangi* (foreigners) and to tell us about their new clean water supply and how it used to be in the bad old days when they had to fight over the untapped spring water in a muddy, worm-infested bog in a small ravine.
>
> 'But where are the women?' I asked, and eventually a shy group of the water-carriers, cooks, cleaners, child carers, cheap labourers and household slaves (aka 'women') were allowed a break from their labours to tell us about the difference the new arrangements had made.
>
> 'We don't have to queue any more.'
> 'I had to fetch water three times a day – it took an hour to and fro.'
> 'The worms have gone.'
> 'The children don't get diarrhoea.'
> 'The animals drink somewhere else.'
> 'We can get the clothes clean.'
> 'The water tastes nice.'

On and on they went – about a simple installation that had cost less than £1,000.

They gave a series of wild, ear-splitting ululations as we left – which we echoed back to them, to their amusement and applause. It was a happy moment.

HIV/AIDS was a huge issue in Ethiopia at this time, with an estimated 2.9m adults and 250,000 children living with the disease, and numbers rising. As in South Africa, those with the disease were stigmatized and shunned, the Health Ministry was a chaotic mess and even the country's President seemed glum at the prospect of dealing with it. What was inspiring, however, was the determination shown by young people in tackling the disease, in spite of the lack of leadership and health care facilities:

> In Gore, a wonderful young teacher put his youth group through their paces on peer education, and a charming young girl demonstrated how to put a condom on a model penis – then invited me to have a go, with a shy smile. In Jimma, a devout young Muslim Red Cross branch secretary showed us his home-made teaching aids – drawings of an STD-infected vagina and a list of 101 ways for a girl to say no to sex. The local director of social services said, 'I don't know how they do it – where would we be without the Red Cross?', whilst outside in the road a sad little group trudged past, carrying their sick relative on a stretcher the fifteen miles to the nearest clinic.

On my return, preparations were in hand for the move to open-plan offices in a 1970s block in the City. I was the last to leave the building on the day of the move, and I had a final walk round, hoping to catch a glimpse of our ghost, the elusive grey lady who was said to prowl the corridors at night. I felt she deserved a proper farewell. David Causer, the Finance Director, and Roger Smith on the HR side had done a brilliant job organizing the legal and practical issues around the move, and over the weekend of 10–12 December it was accomplished without a hitch. When we arrived on the Monday, all we had to do was unpack our personal boxes at our allocated desks and start work. I could feel the organization lift three feet off the ground immediately, freed from the shackles of an ancient pile where nobody could see each other and every formal or informal meeting required you to negotiate yards of labyrinthine corridors and endless fire doors.

We were all able to look forward to Christmas with a fresh start ahead of us – apart from a quick last-minute trip visit to Grenada and our Overseas Branch in the Caymans, to assess the damage wrought by Hurricane Ivan and work out what we could do to help, and to nearby Miami to talk to the American Red Cross about what they could to help our half dozen branches in the Caribbean. Finally, I was in New York talking to the various UN institutions about how they perceived the Red Cross, as part of the Federation's mid-term review of 'Strategy 2010', which I was leading. I met directors from UNOCHA, UNICEF, WFP, the World Bank and WHO, and they all spoke of their appreciation of the work of the Red Cross, whilst regretting that it seemed to hold itself aloof, on grounds of impartiality and neutrality, from the debate and discussion about global issues that they were all engaged with. I also attended a session of the UN General Assembly and sat in on a meeting of the Security Council.

I was pleasantly surprised to find that several of the individuals I met had read a recent interview in *The Guardian*, in which I had expressed concerns at worrying signs in Iraq of the Red Cross emblem, our only protection on the battlefield, being increasingly seen as less than neutral and impartial, both by Coalition forces (who saw us as being 'on their side'), and rebel forces (who tended to agree). I referred to attacks on Red Cross personnel and buildings in both Iraq and Afghanistan; of the Red Cross being denied access to prisoners and victims; and of Coalition troops describing themselves as humanitarian workers, thereby further muddying the water. I said:

Caught in the crossfire, there may eventually be conflict situations around the world where it is simply too dangerous for even the Red Cross to operate, and who then will be in a position to remind governments and non-government forces alike of their responsibilities under the Geneva conventions to protect the victims?

The humanitarian space we operate in has been narrowed, on one side by the sense that the white guys in the Land Rovers must be part of the Coalition because we seem to be doing the same kind of job as them, and on the other by the fear that non-state groups don't understand international humanitarian law and don't understand the strictly neutral and impartial role of the Red Cross.

I arrived back in London on Christmas Eve, just in time to host my traditional lunchtime mulled wine party, and headed home for what I hoped would be, for once, a peaceful Christmas ...

Chapter 6

The Tsunami Strikes, 2005

Boxing Day 2004 – India, Sri Lanka, Indonesia and the Maldives –
UK flooding – Strategy 2010 – The London Bombings – Darfur –
The Kashmir earthquake

I had Christmas Day off, but the next day the phone rang at about 8.30 in the morning. It was David Alexander, our international director.

'You'd better switch on the TV. There's something dreadful happening in Thailand.'

When I did I could hardly believe what I was seeing – it was like a scene from a disaster movie. What seemed like a tidal wave was engulfing seaside towns and islands off the coast, and we saw horrific live footage of people, cars, furniture being swept aside as the waters poured inland. The initial reports were vague as to the cause of this extraordinary phenomenon: it wasn't until a little later that the connection was made with a massive earthquake off the north-western coast of Sumatra, Indonesia, and the word *tsunami* began to be used.

As the morning wore on, and reports began to come in of tidal waves, loss of life and severe damage on the east coast of India, in Sri Lanka and eventually from a dozen other countries, it became clear that the world was facing a catastrophe of immense proportions. I set off for the office, attention glued to the radio, arrived in the early afternoon and found the place practically full already – the international team, of course, were there in force, but also a nearly full complement of communicators, fundraisers, the IT team and many others just there to offer help and support. This was one of the things I so loved about my time at the Red Cross – the impulse to respond to crisis immediately, with passion and complete commitment.

The media were already clamouring for news, and the Federation comms unit in Geneva was quickly overwhelmed. Offers of money started pouring in, and once we had worked out how to do it in our new offices, incoming calls were re-routed from the switchboard to a special helpline team. Mark Astarita called from his holiday hotel in Colombo (on Sri Lanka's west coast) to say that he was up to his knees in water, and Stan Fitches, our northern territory director, rang to say that he and his partner had been rescuing people in their hotel in Thailand.

We launched an appeal almost immediately and had raised £4m within a few hours and £26m by the time we closed it down a few weeks later. Tesco, in particular, responded magnificently with a wonderful fundraising effort, including bucket collections in all their stores, which raised over £3m in a week; other corporate and individual supporters were equally keen to help. The Disasters Emergency Committee (DEC) – of which I was a trustee, in common with my fellow aid agency directors – launched a joint appeal on 29 December and went on to raise £392m (of which our share was over £60m). Within forty-eight hours the logistics team was despatched to Sri Lanka, in response to reports of disaster along the south coast, and we had sent off the first of many relief flights containing essential items such as tarpaulins, blankets and hygiene supplies, one of them packed by Princes William and Harry, who offered to help in the early days. Within a few days we had sent disaster, health, water and sanitation, logistics and family tracing experts to Indonesia, India, the Maldives and Thailand.

British survivors started arriving back from Thailand in their thousands, and we set up teams of volunteers at Gatwick, Heathrow and other airports to help receive them and deal with the injured. After listening to the British Ambassador in Thailand, David Fall (later to become a trustee), describing the work he and his consular team were doing to support British victims in Thailand, I suggested putting in a call to the Foreign and Commonwealth Office to see if they could use some of our trained welfare volunteers to help with the task. The offer was snapped up, and our overseas Psychological Support Team (PST) was born. We launched a Tsunami Support Line to help people affected by the disaster, particularly those who had loved ones in one of the affected countries, and its phones, manned by volunteers, were soon busy.

The public response was extraordinary. At UK Office alone 50,000 people gave online to our initial appeal, and we received another 100,000 postal donations and 15,000 donations by phone (this was in the relatively early days of online and telephone fundraising); this generous outpouring was repeated at most of our local offices as well. In the Channel Islands, where the tsunami coincided with the 60th anniversary of the arrival of the Red Cross ship the *Vega* with the first relief supplies after the ending of German occupation, £2m was raised.

Thousands of individuals rang in to offer voluntary help rebuilding houses in the affected countries, or to bring gifts in kind to our offices, and we had to put a special team in place to handle the calls and try to persuade people to send money instead. As ever, our shops were swamped with old blankets – which we couldn't use, simply because the logistical effort of collecting them all up and sending them out would have cost far more than simply buying new blankets in the countries concerned.

It was an extraordinarily intense period, and I can vividly recall taking a morning off to attend a service in our parish church in Suffolk and bursting into tears as I walked in to find the sun streaming through the stained-glass windows upon a scene that was so utterly normal and peaceful compared to the misery I had been dealing with all week, in so many different parts of the world. Later, as we walked beside a tranquil local river, David Alexander called to update me, and I was back with the tsunami once again.

By March, as the DEC Appeal wound down, we had £70m. It was a huge sum, more than we had ever had to spend on one disaster, but then there had never really been, in living memory at least, a natural disaster like the tsunami. Like many agencies, we felt daunted. We had spent nearly £14m on immediate short-term relief work, mostly in Indonesia and Sri Lanka, plus some in the Maldives, and had given another £2m to the Federation's own Appeal – but the need for this type of short-term aid was limited, and we started to turn our minds to the question of how best to spend the rest in rebuilding shattered lives and livelihoods in those countries most seriously affected by the disaster.

As a specialist emergency response agency, the Red Cross is not a development agency, so our experience of longer term work rebuilding lives and livelihoods was limited. We had no experience at all of rebuilding houses, and yet this was what was needed, tens of thousands of them. There was some thought that perhaps the Federation itself, funded by national societies, could take on this development role, but it rapidly became clear that it did not have the operational capacity or the experience, and neither, of course, did the national societies of the affected countries, all of them overwhelmed by the scale of what had happened.

The challenge was huge. The tsunami had killed an estimated 230,000 people and rendered nearly 2m homeless. At that stage, none of the governments in question had established systems for coping with such a huge rebuilding task, still less the task of coordinating substantial numbers of overseas relief agencies with large sums of money to spend. Even UNOCHA, the UN agency charged with strengthening the international response to complex emergencies and disasters, was overwhelmed, possessing neither the experience nor the authority at that time to take on the vital coordination role. The result was that, in the early stages at least, we all had to fend for ourselves, pick an area to work in and get on with the job.

At the end of February I had a chance to see for myself. The Federation's Secretary-General Markku Niskala had called a 'Tsunami Conference' in Hong Kong, and I attended with our new International Director Matthias Schmale. On the way, I stopped off in India, where the Government had set its face against overseas aid, and then in Sri Lanka, where I was to meet up with our President, Prince Charles, who was on his way back from a trip to Australia and wanted to see the tsunami damage for himself.

Compared to what I was to see later, both in Sri Lanka and Indonesia, the damage in India was relatively slight. The coast south of Chennai had borne the brunt, and there was work to do to help local fishermen repair or replace their boats and in repairing houses and hotels in the area, but not much else.

Sri Lanka was very different. I arrived just in time to meet up with HRH, and we flew together by helicopter to Batticaloa in the north-east of the country (parts of which were still controlled by the Tamil Tigers) to see the damage there. All of the coastal area had been devastated, with thousands of people still missing, homes destroyed and livelihoods (especially those of fishermen) ruined.

There were protests going on about a recent Government ruling that no rebuilding could be undertaken within 200 metres of the high water mark, which effectively meant that the fishermen would never be able to return – a matter which I took up with the country's President, Mrs Kumaratunga, when we met her in Colombo the next day. The Prince was supportive, and there was an amicable but 'full and frank' exchange, which continued after he left, when I was invited back to the Palace for a further private session with the President and two of her ministers (one of whom was assassinated a couple of months later). Up to that point, the President had not appreciated that the Red Cross Federation (with $400m to spend in Sri Lanka) was going to be one of the biggest players in her country's recovery, giving added power to my arguments – which along, no doubt, with those of many others, eventually prevailed, and the 200-metre rule was substantially rescinded.

Later, I set off south by car to Matara, a five-hour drive down a heart-rendingly shattered coastline – on one side sandy beaches, palm trees and the glittering ocean; on the other, a wasteland of wrecked shacks and houses, mud and rocks and meagre plastic tents awaiting inevitable destruction by the coming monsoon season. The emergency relief phase was nearing a close, and the Red Cross and many other agencies present (both large and small, international and local) were beginning to think about the recovery phase. Talking to groups of local fishermen while they recited what they needed – a new boat here, more nets, the replacement of or repairs to the house, the chance to learn a new skill – two things became very clear.

First, that the needs varied from individual to individual and were many and various; I could see that the old methods, of talking to the people we were trying to help, making a list of what each needed to assist with their recovery and then supplying it, would be impossibly cumbersome and slow. These people needed help now, fast. I became convinced that, for everything short of house-building, the method we had used in Bam, of giving them money or vouchers so that they could buy what they most needed for themselves, would be far quicker and more effective – and that it would help to maintain the local economy.

Secondly, I realized with a sinking feeling that, given the relatively simple lifestyles along the coastal strip, and seeing how many other NGOs (far more than usual, due to the scale of the public response) were already here and marking out 'their' territories, we would be very hard-pressed to spend the vast amount of money we had raised unless we were to become involved in actually rebuilding some of the tens of thousands of homes that had been destroyed – and that was something we had virtually no experience of at all on anything like the scale required.

Furthermore, the situation here in Sri Lanka had been complicated by the ruling about rebuilding close to the coast, because it meant that a fisherman who, for generations in some cases, had lived on the family plot of land beside the sea would have somehow to acquire both land to build a new house further back and potentially the skills to build a new career if he no longer had access to the sea and somewhere safe to store his boat. These complex issues would take months, even years, to resolve and threatened to keep us tied up in Sri Lanka far beyond our usual time commitment as an emergency response organization.

As I flew on to Hong Kong for the Federation conference to discuss the overall Movement response to the tsunami, it was very clear that we were in uncharted territory and that a massive and well-coordinated Movement effort would be required if we were to meet the needs of the millions of those in need, and be able to demonstrate to our donors that the funds raised (over £1bn for the Red Cross Movement as a whole) had been wisely spent and well.

The Conference was a reasonably successful attempt to reach an agreement between the Federation Secretariat, the fifteen or so PNS present and the national societies from the affected countries as to how and where we were all going to work, but it was fiendishly complicated and made more so by the fact that the Federation Secretariat itself had several hundred million Swiss francs to spend as well, and so would also be in operating mode on the ground as well as playing its normal coordinating role.

It is difficult to imagine how we coped with anything else at the same time. But of course, we did – in our case, flooding in the UK.

In January, Red Cross volunteers and staff from all over the country converged on Carlisle to help cope with the effects of terrible flooding, the first real test of our campaign to enhance our ability to respond to a major UK disaster and to encourage Areas to work together. I visited after the worst of the flooding subsided and was saddened to see pitiful heaps of soaked belongings piled in front gardens, identical to those I had seen only a few months previously in Grenada and the Caymans. We ran a rest centre for 3,000 evacuees, provided support to the ambulance service, four-wheel drive vehicles to access the worst-affected areas and, perhaps most important of all, emotional and practical support of all kinds to those who had lost their homes. It was exciting to see our new emergency response strategy paying dividends, with practically every Area having something to contribute.

Her Majesty the Queen, our Royal Patron, graciously paid us a visit to open the new offices, and in another example of the growing and generous recognition we were receiving from the Royal Family, I was also asked to advise St James's Palace about the setting up of a new charity for Prince Harry on the back of money we had helped him raise from a recent documentary about his work in Lesotho with the Crown Prince. Both men had lost their mothers early and so decided to call the charity 'Sentebale' (or 'forget-me-not' in the language of Lesotho) in their honour.

Meanwhile, I was spending my 'spare' time conducting consultations (in person, in group meetings and over the phone) with national societies all over the world, gathering evidence for the mid-term review of Strategy 2010. In April, after some intense hard work in Geneva with my 2010 Review Team of secretary-generals from Singapore, Finland and Rwanda, we pulled our final report together for the Governing Board. The Review ran to nearly fifty pages and included the findings of all our consultations, detailed commentary and recommendations, a suggested Performance Framework to aid implementation of the Strategy during its remaining five years and examples of good practice from around the world.

The Report identified a number of global trends and developments to worry the humanitarian community, including increasing political polarization both internationally and within communities (in the wake, particularly, of the fall of communism, the 'global war on terror' and the surge in separatist activity), all of which had played a part in creating a world that was becoming more divided and in which security and the space for humanitarian action was threatened.

We pointed to the glaring inequalities that still existed, between rich and poor, between those with access to the basic necessities of life and those without, between those living under stable and open regimes and those who were not, and to the importance of initiatives like the UN's Millennium Development Goals with which, at that time, the Federation had not yet fully engaged. We welcomed moves towards greater self-determination for countries in the south and the east and the slowly strengthening concept of 'civil society' and a more inclusive community-based approach, and we recognized the potential benefits for all of improved global communications.

We found that Strategy 2010 had had very significant influence and take-up, at least in name, throughout the Federation's national societies, a significant achievement in five years, especially given the diversity of the member societies. Nevertheless, there were large gaps in the implementation of its actual recommendations, including poor management of the global response to large-scale disasters and a failure to develop a clear response to world-wide health emergencies. Efforts to improve national society governance and development were found to be weak, and we called for improvements in the way national societies, the Federation's secretariat and the ICRC worked together.

We had received a strong message from major UN and international NGOs that the Red Cross punched below its weight intellectually in global policy debates, and our Report finished with a ringing plea for humanitarian leadership from the Red Cross Red Crescent Movement:

> In the early years of a new century, and during a troubled time in the history of our world, do we in the Red Cross Red Crescent Movement have the strength of purpose and the determination of spirit to ensure that the drumbeat of humanity, of dignity and equality, of trust and mutual respect is heard, if nowhere else, then at least here in this Movement of ours?

The Report was well received by Board Members and generally throughout the Movement, and John's 'Federation of the Future' working group undertook to incorporate its findings in their own recommendations, due later in the year. My personal concern, though, was that unless the Federation Board and Secretariat was strengthened, mandated and resourced to fulfil its leadership function effectively, the charge that we 'punched below our weight' internationally would remain a valid one.

But it was the tsunami that continued to dominate the year for the British Red Cross. In May, Kofi Annan's special representative on the tsunami, former President Clinton, came to the offices of the DEC for a meeting to discuss the response, a reminder if one was needed that the eyes of the world were on us. By June we had decided to prioritize the province of Aceh in western Sumatra as the main focus of our overall response: the scale of the damage there was immense, the Government of Indonesia was doing little, as Aceh had been a hotspot of insurgency and civil unrest for years, and there were relatively few international agencies able to operate there. I flew out in June to see for myself. My report noted:

> It is hard not to feel daunted by the scale of the task facing us in Indonesia. Flying over Banda Aceh by helicopter, the horizon is filled with a desolate wilderness of mud, flattened buildings and fallen trees, as far as the eye can see. A massive generator-ship has been driven by the surge of water into the centre of Banda Aceh. Almost the only buildings left standing near the coast are the mosques.
>
> Walking around the ruins of a small village called Seurapong on the 'paradise' island of Pulau Aceh, details become sharper – the mud was once rice paddies that gave food and income to the villagers, the rubble piles were once houses where families lived and loved, the trees brought shade and shelter and sweet coconut milk.
>
> Around this shattered landscape, thin tendrils of life appear. Plastic sheeting roofs a shack that survives, and a farmer pecks away at the mud to clear his land; fire clears a patch of forest where some villagers have decided to move their homes – just a little further away from the sea; barrack accommodation built by the Government waits empty for expectant families to come back to start rebuilding the work of generations.

By the time I arrived, six months after the tsunami had swept away 'life as they knew it' for all the inhabitants, the immediate relief operation was more or less over. Around 170,000 people had lost their lives in Aceh as a whole (the highest total of all the tsunami-affected countries) and an estimated 380,000 people had lost their homes in the earthquake and subsequent tidal wave.

We had decided to invest some of our £70m in re-establishing a fishing community of 300 families on Pulau Aceh, giving each of them cash to rebuild their homes and their lives. They had lost everything. The work involved helping them to replace identity papers (without which they could do nothing) and, for the first time, open bank accounts; trying to prove title to the land where their houses had been (in the absence of any kind of national land register); planning new houses with them and working out how to build them as a community; and, in the meantime, assisting them either to return to their former way of earning a living or to learn new skills. At every stage we had to negotiate with local government officials, themselves completely overwhelmed by the task and being pulled in a dozen different directions every minute of the day.

This was detailed, painstaking, intricate and sensitive work for our team of just ten people, with a community still in shock, living in tented accommodation in a huge camp on the mainland and impatient to get back to their island. Good communication with all those affected as a group, and as individuals, was vital but hugely time-consuming and dependent on a few overworked interpreters. Rumours in the camp spread quickly, and the overall atmosphere was tense and volatile.

And the problems were immense. Just in 'our' small community, which was replicated along the whole coast of Aceh, around half had perished in the tsunami: sometimes whole families, sometimes one or both parents. Bodies were still being pulled from the mud and wreckage, sometimes miles from where they had lived. Boundaries had been obliterated, identity papers washed away.

In addition to the need for houses, schools, health centres, water and sanitation units would all have to be repaired or rebuilt. All of this would require large quantities of wood, bricks, roofing materials, cement and other materials – for all of which there was now enormous demand, so local prices were rising daily, and we (and all the other agencies) were having to look further and further afield for supplies. Negotiations were tense. Supplies were short and delivery, whether by boat to the islands or by truck on the mainland, was problematic, as many roads had been washed away.

I had numerous meetings with the following people: Mar'ie Muhammad, chairman of the Indonesian Red Cross and as head of the country's national society (the PMI), nominally at least in charge of the whole international Red Cross relief effort; Kuntoro Mangkusubroto, recently-appointed chief executive of the government's reconstruction agency, who was charged with bureaucracy-busting and the enforced coordination of the entire rebuilding effort; Gareth Thomas, a DFID minister; the British Ambassador; the governor of the Aceh district; Pulau Aceh's headman; the country director of the World Food Programme and the local representatives of many of our fellow DEC members; various colleagues from the Federation and the ICRC; and dozens of PMI volunteers and staff. A local council leader chaired a coordination meeting of NGOs and burst into tears when I described how generously the British public had responded to the tsunami appeal.

I think it's fair to say that we were all completely flummoxed, frightened even, by the scale of the task in front of us. Certainly I was.

On the last day I met up with Ben Brown from the BBC and Brendan Gormley chief executive of the DEC. The BBC wanted to film a piece for the *Ten O'Clock News* on Pulau Aceh, and Ben asked if I thought someone from one of 'our' families would be prepared to come with us, to be filmed revisiting the island for the first time. I had serious misgivings about this but promised to ask in the camp and was surprised when a young woman called Romaini volunteered.

We set off by helicopter early the next day and flew out to what looked from a distance like a paradise island, across a brilliant blue sea. As we passed low over the remains of the village of Seurapong, where Romaini had lived, we all gasped. There was almost nothing there: a few bedraggled palms, some random piles of wood and mud, the remains of a small jetty. I looked at Romaini; she was rigid with shock.

The ask had sounded so simple: 'If Romaini could show us where she used to live, I will do a quick interview, through the interpreter, then talk to you and Brendan about the overall recovery effort. It's a short 3-minute piece.'

For nearly an hour we trailed about as Romaini attempted to find where her house had been. Every so often she would dart forward, only to stop and shake her head, then set off in a new direction. Her small son, aged six, tugged at her hand and kept asking her something.

'Is he OK? What does he want?' I asked the interpreter.

'Oh,' was the reply, 'he is asking, "Will we see daddy here?"'

She looked away, tears in her eyes.

I called off the search, Ben did an interview with just Brendan and me and had a quick kindly talk with Romaini on camera; then we packed up for the day, motoring back to the mainland in a high-prowed wooden fishing smack with a suitably piratical crew, drenched by the monsoon rain.

As I flew home, the penny dropped. It was going to take years for this ravaged community to rebuild their own homes. In the meantime, they would either be stuck in a tented camp on the mainland or struggling in temporary accommodation on the island, coping for themselves with minimal facilities. We were going to have to build the homes for them, and fast. We needed building contractors to do the job.

This was a shock for our team, who had invested huge amounts of time and energy in developing a wonderfully consultative and inclusive scheme, which would have resulted eventually in a marvellous co-operative community effort. But it just wasn't practical, and we all agreed that we had to find a new approach – going out to tender internationally to find a construction company to build many hundreds of new British Red Cross homes in Indonesia. For our international director Matthias, and finance director David Causer, it was a new and massive challenge.

On 7 July, following an unusual whole week in the office and then the annual Board/SMT 'awayday' in the new look Manchester Area headquarters, I set out for a day in Harrogate attending a conference of senior local authority leaders to discuss the new Civil Contingencies Act; I was due to speak about the role of the Red Cross in responding to emergencies in the UK.

I never got there. As the train approached Darlington, I got a message on my phone from Roger Smith.

'There's been a bomb on a tube in London.'

All around me, people were receiving similar messages.

Then Roger texted me again: 'Three bombs.'

I got off the train at the next station and tried to call the office, but couldn't get through as the mobile system seemed to be jammed. I called Ian Temple, the local area Red Cross director, who lived nearby, and he came to collect me and took me to his home. By this stage it was clear that there had been a further bomb on a bus, all apparently terrorist suicide attacks, but the number of casualties was unclear. The Red Cross had been asked to provide ambulances and crews in support of the London Ambulance Service. Drivers were being urged to stay away from London altogether, and the city was in effective lockdown.

For an anxious few hours, unable to contact UK Office as the phone lines seemed to be jammed, I sat stunned and silent with Ian and watched the TV coverage of the unfolding drama. In the early afternoon we managed to find a local taxi driver who was prepared to take me back and, after lengthy delays, I arrived in the capital at around 4.30. The eerily silent streets were filled with people trudging home, quiet, thoughtful, tense, some of them almost in a trance, completely overcome by the emotion of the day and the rising toll of dead and injured. It was the most chilling and extraordinary atmosphere.

At the office, anyone not involved in helping to deal with the response or answering the constantly-ringing phones had been sent home. I drove to King's Cross, where our ambulances and their crews had mustered, in a Red Cross Land Rover. I found them in the small car park, about twenty or thirty volunteers gathered around their ambulances, and got them talking about the things they had seen and done that day. They were quiet and reflective, in shock still, but proud that they had been able to play a part in the response. Listening to them was like being back in Baghdad.

A call came in from the London Mayor's office and, the next day, Mark Astarita and I shot round there for a meeting to discuss a national appeal. Within hours we had launched 'the London Bombings Charitable Relief Fund' for the victims, supported by the *Evening Standard*. It raised in the end over £12m, which was distributed by the Fund, a separate charity which we set up and staffed at short notice, to the families of the fifty-two people who had died and to the 300 or so who had been seriously injured. In the days after the bombings we also set up, in cooperation with other charities, a helpline, and an assistance centre for families affected by the bombings, and provided emotional support to staff and visitors at the temporary mortuary in Moorgate.

On the day of the bombings the Mayor, Ken Livingstone, made a memorable speech in Singapore (where he had just been told that London would be the venue for the 2012 Olympics), which I cannot resist quoting:

> I want to say one thing specifically to the world today. This was not a terrorist attack against the mighty and the powerful. It was not aimed at Presidents and Prime Ministers. It was aimed at ordinary working-class Londoners, black and white, Muslim and Christian, Hindu and Jew, young and old … Londoners will not be divided by this cowardly act. They will stand together in solidarity alongside those who have been injured and those who have been bereaved … and to those who came to London today to take life … [and] to destroy our free society, I can show you why you will fail.

In the days that follow, look at our airports, look at our seaports and our railway stations and, even after your cowardly attack, you will see that people from the rest of Britain, people from around the world, will arrive in London to become Londoners and to fulfil their dreams and their potential.

They choose to come to London, as so many have come before, because they come to be free, they come to live the life they choose, they come to be able to be themselves. They flee you because you tell them how they should live. They don't want that, and nothing you do, however many of us you kill, will stop that flight to our city where freedom is strong and where people can live in harmony with one another. Whatever you do, however many you kill, you will fail.

Of the fifty-two people who died in the attacks, twenty were from overseas.

A week later, back in London, Livingstone hosted an electrifyingly moving gathering in Trafalgar Square, attended defiantly by thousands in an act of commemoration and solidarity. It was a wonderfully bright clear warm evening, London at its best. Several people who had been involved in the bombings, whether as victims or responders, were invited to speak or read poems. I was asked to read John Donne's poem *No Man is an Island*. It had been an extraordinary week.

In Sudan, in the meantime, another desperate humanitarian crisis had been bubbling. The country was largely split along ethnic lines, with broadly Muslim Arabs in the north and controlling the government; non-Arab animists/Christians in the south; and non-Arab Muslims in the west (particularly the province of Darfur). These divisions had led to years of civil war and insurrection. In the south, just before I arrived on my first visit, a Comprehensive Peace Agreement was due to be signed between the Government and the rebels. It would lead, in time, to independence.

In the Darfur region, meanwhile, rebels had been fighting against government forces, alleging that there was a policy of apartheid against non-Arabs. At the same time, there were local conflicts between semi-nomadic livestock herders and sedentary farmers, and between those who had access to water and those who had none. These clashes had led to a campaign, allegedly government-sponsored, of what amounted to 'ethnic cleansing' led by an armed militia (called the Janjaweed), which backed the nomadic herders, and the mass migration of around 2m people, many of whom died from starvation and disease in the harsh, isolated desert regions of Darfur.

We had been working in Sudan as part of our operational partnership with the ICRC, helping them to access DFID funding, and raising money ourselves from a special appeal. We were using this money to fund the costs of seventeen British Red Cross delegates, to buy relief supplies and equipment and to help the Sudanese Red Crescent. We also had a joint project with the ICRC and the Australian Red Cross, providing supplementary feeding, water supply and health care programmes in a massive camp at Gereida in southern Darfur.

The purpose of my ten-day visit was to meet with senior ICRC/ Federation and Sudanese colleagues; to discuss the continuance of our work in the country; to look at how we could help Sudanese Red Crescent development; and to prepare for the relatively imminent prospect of independence for the south and the establishment of a new Red Cross society in country.

I started in Khartoum with the usual briefings, then flew in a tiny ICRC Beechcraft plane to Lokichokio in northern Kenya, to see the ICRC tented field hospital which was providing care for those wounded in fighting in the south, mostly between farmers and nomadic pastoralists, and to observe training for community health workers. Then it was on to Juba, capital of South Sudan, lolling in its humid tropical atmosphere on the green banks of the Nile. The whole of the south was depressingly underdeveloped, with one hospital and 12km of tarmac road in a country the size of France with a population of 10m.

The hospital was our first stop, its four or five chaotic wards crammed with patients drenched with sweat and fever, whilst volunteers folded bandages or dished out steaming plates of hot sorghum porridge. The nurse in 'intensive care' described how, a few weeks earlier, a secret ammunition dump in the town had exploded, firing bullets and shells around the town for hours and killing ... no one knew how many. I spent the afternoon with John Labor, head of the putative future South Sudan Red Cross, and his team, and had a wonderful tour of Juba itself in the gentle evening light – bustling street markets, barges on the mighty Nile, armed police and UN troops lounging in the heat, burnt-out tanks, little boys playing with a tortoise, cattle in a stockade awaiting buyers, the owners taking their ease in the dappled shade, and beautiful women in a kaleidoscope of yellow, turquoise and lime green dresses making a stately progress home with the day's shopping perched on their heads.

The next day, we visited a primary health centre run by the Netherlands Red Cross with local volunteers in a tiny mud-brick, tin-roofed oven of a building surrounded by the thatched *tukuls* of a village full of internally displaced people, many of them packed tight on the wooden benches of a shaded veranda awaiting treatment – or perhaps a pack of the free condoms prominently on display. Then it was back to the airstrip (where, straying inadvertently on to the dusty runway, I was nearly run over by an incoming cargo plane) and a hair-raising flight back to Khartoum, skirting gingerly around towering storm clouds – 'You would have been bouncing off the ceiling if we had tried to get through that lot', was the laconic comment from our grinning Sikh pilot, drenched in nervous sweat, as we taxied to a halt outside the hangar.

After more meetings the next morning with the new British Ambassador and the local heads of DFID and UNOCHA, we drove north to two dismal IDP camps established twenty years before at the start of the fighting in the south, filled with shambolic huts and battered compounds in a vast, flat desert landscape. Women huddled and shawled against the searing, dusty *haboub* wind and heat struggled with their chores, whilst neglected, stunted children peered from doorways or scuffled in the dirt, goats rootled about in the fly-blown rubbish, donkey carts tottered about and sickly young trees bent in the stiff breeze. Nearby, at a bleak road junction, two volunteers spent all day calling the attention of passers-by to large boards filled with the photos of children who had lost their parents, or parents who had lost their children – a ghastly living metaphor for the ruin and heartache caused by war.

It was Friday, the Muslim day of prayer, so no one was working, and I spent it with our desk officer Ros, walking along the White Nile at its confluence with its sister Blue Nile and visiting the remains of 'Kitchener's Gunboat' and old Palace, the scene of his death at the hands of the Mahdi after he had failed to hold Khartoum. There was a museum filled with mementos of that time, the spears of the Mahdi army and the brutal snouts of the British Maxim machine guns, where we were accompanied by the strains of tambour and triangle, and wafting incense from the square outside, and then we drifted outside into the labyrinth of alleyways and shady courtyards that is old Khartoum.

In the evening, as sunset approached, we were met by a devout Sufi friend of our Red Crescent guide who agreed to take us along to his regular Friday evening meeting at the Hamed-al Nil Tomb. In front of the Tomb a small crowd had gathered, all men, all robed in white or green; in the background, lightly-veiled women chatted together. Slowly a procession formed and moved towards us, the men chanting and clapping, a few out in front bobbing and weaving as they led the way into the Tomb itself. A small band appeared, and then the procession emerged from the Tomb and moved towards the centre of a small ring of worshippers and spectators.

The band started to play, plaintive wailing notes with surging wild beats on the drum, and as the rhythm took hold, small groups formed in the centre of the ring, the men shifting and twisting towards and away from each other, coming and going, testing and teasing, shoulders in, heads back, sticks raised, arm in arm or alone.

In the very middle of the ring a young man hurled himself about, hitting himself ferociously on the forehead with the palm of his hand, while another in a multi-coloured coat whisked around the circle, never hesitating in his madcap reel. Friends greeted each other, a touch on the shoulder, a hug here and there, ducking and bobbing, a kiss on the cheek, a nose rubbed on a forehead. The sense was of delightfully smiling old friends, veterans of a thousand Fridays, enjoying each other's company and dancing to the sun, to the crowd, to each other as sunset approached.

New dancers joined the white-robed group whirling and skirling around the ring; on and on they went, the tempo rising and falling, the whirling dervishes of Khartoum. The sun set, and still they went on, as darkness fell and smoking torches lit up the wild sweating faces of the dancers and the watching crowd. Cries of 'La ilaha illallah' (There is no God but Allah) heightened the excitement. They dance till ten or eleven sometimes, joined later by a group from another Tomb, until exhaustion and slaked passion signal the end of another week and another night of devotion to Allah.

More meetings and visits to projects in Khartoum followed the next day, including a trip to the ICRC Orthopaedic Workshop where they make the large numbers of prosthetic limbs required to meet the demand created in a country riven by conflict, and a meeting with the Head of Delegation for the ICRC in Sudan and his Scottish colleague charged with the task of vaccinating 50,000 camels threatened by a killer disease that would damage the country's economy. So typical of the ICRC this – they see a problem and deal with it.

We scrambled to get to the airport the next day in time for the chartered flight to Nyala in South Darfur, where we joined an absorbing but tense four-hour Landcruiser convoy south to Gereida, along rough tracks deeply rutted by ICRC trucks supplying a huge IDP camp housing, at its peak, 120,000 people displaced as a result of Janjaweed violence in the region. Our small four-vehicle convoy was led by a taciturn Belgian, who forced a stiff pace past fields and mudflats and deserted silent villages of empty thatched huts, and through *wadis* greasy with the glutinous, sucking mud of the rainy season. Occasionally we caught sight of a villager scurrying to plant a sketchy crop near his former home, hoping not to attract the attention of a Janjaweed patrol.

At the Camp, in the late afternoon, our backsides numb from the bumpy, jolting journey, we met up with our nine British delegates, living in extremely basic conditions themselves, and shared their standard meal of rice and spaghetti, before retiring for a sweaty, mosquito-plagued night. In the morning we toured the Camp briefly, its thousands of mud and thatch or plastic and stick shelters sprawling and huddling around three sides of Gereida, itself no more than a scattered criss-cross grid of small family compounds enclosed by a lattice of thin woven branches. But we saw warm beaming smiles of welcome and friendly curiosity wherever we went, despite the bleak physical squalor and meagre protection offered to people facing an uncertain future.

That day, we heard the grim news from South Sudan that the charismatic opposition leader John Garang had died in a helicopter crash, putting at risk the tenuous progress that was being made towards independence and making another period of suspicion and unrest a certainty.

In the supplementary feeding centre, patient lines of 'moderately malnourished' children and their mothers waited to be methodically weighed by a chirpy Geordie called Elizabeth clad in a large straw cloche hat, prior to receiving their allocation of extra food for the week. After a brief stop for refreshing *karkaddy* (hibiscus tea), we carried on to the Therapeutic Feeding Centre, where tiny, bony, wide-eyed bundles were clinging precariously to life, whilst nurses tenderly encouraged them to take their first teaspoons of milk or suck ruminatively upon morsels of Plumpy Nut peanut paste. We watched transfixed as two-months-premature Fatama, orphaned at birth, whimpered and writhed in her fever, before finally accepting a drop or two of milk from his aunt, who beamed with relief.

We sat in a tent with a group of sheikhs from a village called Otech, dignified and serious in their white robes and turbans. They described their village with its fields, *wadis* and cattle – all now deserted and destroyed. They talked about the village meeting at which they had decided to give all this up and come to the Camp, their frustration that no immediate help was available and that they have not got enough to eat. I struggled to find anything to say that would relieve their distress and sense of dignity lost, but spoke of my hope that there would soon be peace and a return to the life they lived before. Tears coursed down their cheeks as they murmured their '*inshallahs*', and I left reflecting that here was the aching human reality behind the jumbled statistics, slogans and acronyms of humanitarian relief.

Nearby, clustered under the sparse branches of a shading tree, twenty women clad in a riot of yellow and reds pored over a board filled with the pasted photographs of children whose parents were missing.

After another sweaty night it was time to return to Nyala, spurred by the news of rioting in Khartoum and cancelled BA flights, the fretful trek back leavened by the haunting landscape of Sudan. one passing image, of a rainy season pool in the tan sand under an azure sky, the thatched huts of a village and a line of women dressed like a tube of Opal fruits with water pots on their heads remains etched in my mind.

I was back in Africa again later in August, for a meeting of the 'New Partnership of African Red Cross Societies' (NEPARC), which had been established following a regional conference in Algeria the previous year. As I read the papers on the plane out to Algiers I had discovered to my horror that a group of PNS like ours had given certain undertakings at an earlier event in Burkina Faso, designed to put relationships between African national societies and the PNS on a more equal footing. Nothing had been done by the British Red Cross, and I called a meeting of fellow PNS as soon as I arrived to try and establish if they were in the same boat – as indeed they were. We therefore agreed to have a further meeting with our African brothers and sisters before the conference proper began, to admit these failings – which turned into a most encouraging dialogue, described by Abbas Gullet of Kenya later as the occasion when 'African national societies found their tongues, and the PNS found their ears.'

The dialogue led to the formation of NEPARC, with its ambitious aspiration to be a centre of excellence for African national societies, and the means whereby they would take charge of their own destinies by developing models of good governance, service delivery and advocacy themselves (assisted by the Fritz Institute), instead of being to some extent at least 'told what to do' by the wealthy PNS. I was privileged to be invited to attend and to co-chair, with the great Tom Buruku of Uganda Red Cross. It was a tremendously exciting development for the time, and one which we continued to support for a number of years, as the national societies in Africa began to create their own agenda for change and development.

In September, John presented his 'Federation of the Future' document to the Governing Board with his co-chair from Tunisia, setting out a 'Global Agenda' for the whole Federation aimed at reducing the impact of disasters and health emergencies, improving capacity to respond,and promoting respect for diversity and human dignity. A global planning process was proposed, with the decentralization of many secretariat functions, and a new system of 'operational alliances' between national societies. The Report was accepted with acclaim but, as I commented to our own Board at the time, 'The challenge of leading and implementing some fundamental changes in culture and working methods, and securing buy-in from some powerful PNS who prefer to act bilaterally, is a substantial one.'

The other major item on the agenda for that Board meeting (accepted for further research and discussion) was a proposal from UNOCHA that the Red Cross should take global responsibility for coordinating the provision of 'shelter' (tents, huts and houses) for the victims of major natural disasters worldwide, starting with the tsunami. This was part of a UNOCHA strategy to improve the international response to a disaster by forcing agencies in particular sectors to work together. This was both an opportunity and a risky challenge for a relatively inexperienced Federation secretariat that would have to cope with a politically sensitive and complex operational task in the full glare of world media attention.

I was to see these difficulties clearly later in the year, when I visited our own building efforts in the tsunami-hit Maldives.

On 8 October a terrible earthquake struck, centred on Kashmir, killing an estimated 65,000 people in northern Pakistan and India and rendering more than 3m homeless. Both the ICRC and the Federation launched emergency appeals, as did we, soon followed by the DEC. We immediately deployed our expert logistics team (only just returned from New Orleans) and, by the end of the month, we had contributed £9m to the Red Cross relief effort. The logistical challenges of providing relief high up in the mountains of Kashmir were enormous, and I was summoned to a meeting at 10 Downing Street with Tony Blair, Hilary Benn, the DFID Secretary of State, the RAF and others to discuss how the UK could best help – particularly with the deployment of urgently-needed Chinook helicopters. There seemed to be no end to the surprises the year had in store for us.

Then it was off to Seoul for another Federation General Assembly. Apart from the four-yearly round of elections to the Governing Board (we were re-elected for a second term), and the adoption of John's Federation of the Future proposals, there were only two contentious items, namely proper oversight of our overall tsunami response and the UNOCHA shelter proposal. On both issues the Federation's Secretariat won the day, despite the significant misgivings of a number of PNS, who feared that the Secretariat was being over-ambitious. After four long days in a hot conference centre with 800 other national society representatives, I took myself off to an extraordinary museum dedicated to the Korean national dish of *kimchi*, or pickled cabbage, to cheer myself up.

By this stage I was looking forward to a break over Christmas, though I was fearful that, as in previous years, I would be disappointed. But first I was due out in the Maldives, where we had just started work on a £17m reconstruction, livelihoods and disaster-preparedness programme on six tsunami-affected islands in one of twenty atolls comprising over 1,100 mostly unoccupied islands, scattered like the tail of a comet across the choppy blue ocean, just off the west coast of India.

The tsunami struck the islands three hours after the earthquake, with virtually no warning beyond a loud noise 'like a helicopter', five minutes or so before 'the horizon disappeared' and the sea simply rolled silently over the tiny low-lying islands, to a depth in places of over 10ft. Then it simply rolled eerily away again minutes later, leaving over eighty people dead, hundreds missing and much of the country a disaster area.

On the 'ordinary' islands, those not taken over by fancy hotels and tourist resorts, life was very simple:

Imagine yourself standing on a sandy path. Look to your left – you can see the sea clearly 200 yards away, through an avenue of palms. Look to your right – 200 yards away is the small harbour, the light blue of the coral lagoon, and then again the wide open sea. Behind you is your house (single storey, concrete block, tin roof), where you live with your family of five children, your wife and your parents, maybe an aunt or two. In the harbour is the fishing boat on which you crew each day – it's your livelihood. In your small garden are a few tomato plants, a mango tree, maybe some peppers. Around you live perhaps another couple of hundred people or so, sharing this simple, very basic existence … until the tsunami wipes it all away, in a quick surge of the sea.

We had realized a little late that the Maldives had been virtually ignored in the main tsunami response, and we were now racing to catch up – one of the very few NGOs working on the islands. We were to build 744 houses on six islands in the south of the chain, about four hours by fast speedboat from the capital island Malé, provide livelihood support for individuals and communities on the islands and prepare them for future disasters – plus promote some organizational development for the national society.

My first duty was to attend ground-breaking ceremonies on two of the islands – Fonadhoo and Maabaidhoo – so I flew down in a seaplane with no fewer than four government ministers, to dig a trench and shovel some cement for the first 111 houses. The families who were to live in these houses helped us with the shovelling, then stood back speechless, with tears in their eyes, as they realized that eleven months of waiting was drawing to a close, whilst a group of local women sang and danced and drummed their welcome, before beckoning us to an enormous celebration lunch in the school hall.

But on 'our' four other islands, we were nowhere near so far advanced, as I found the next day after a long bumpy speedboat ride to Kolhufushi.

Each island is run by a Chief. This one, maybe four hundred yards long, was riven by an ancient dispute between the families living in the north and those in the south. According to the Chief, who lived in the north, the two groups were barely on speaking terms. Since most of the houses on the island (especially those in the south) had been destroyed or badly damaged, the Chief's plan (opposed by at least half the islanders) was to rebuild all the houses in the middle. Impasse.

We spent the day on the island hearing sad tales of the day the tsunami struck. A man gripped my arm as he told me how his two small children were swept from his arms, never to be seen again, and an elderly lady poked about in the ruins of her small garden as she described how she and her husband had clung for their lives to a coconut palm. I met the Women's Committee, then the Men's Committee, hearing everyone's views on what they wanted and on the Chief's radical proposal. Then I told them all, as gently as I could, to stunned silence, that there was no way we could solve their problem – they had to agree amongst themselves what they wanted us to do.

The next island we visited was Vilufushi, smaller than Kolhufushi but with more than twice its population, most of whom had decamped to nearby Buruni. The government planned to raise their island three feet and build a large wall round it, leaving us then to build the 250 houses needed. My heart sank at the very thought of this unlikely plan, and it sank even lower when we visited Buruni, where we were set upon by an angry group of displaced islanders, who had apparently been told very little about the government's plans for their homeland. Somehow we survived the lengthy encounter, and were given some fish curry for our pains, before we set off again at dusk for another bumpy and painful speedboat ride to Thimarafushi, our supply base for the building project.

Here we received a very different greeting, from 'Dusty' Miller and his logistics team, all smartly at attention on the jetty in their Red Cross T-shirts like a guard of honour, with five huge 'Rubb Hall' storage tents behind them ready to receive building materials for the project. It was very nice to be amongst friends again. Dusty cooked a great supper of steak and tuna, and everyone laughed like a drain when I was assailed by a toothless elderly female passer-by in a gaudy pink veil who insisted on serenading me at length and, apparently, proposing marriage. I strongly suspect it was a set-up.

The following morning, we met the island Chief, who had been a generous host to our team, in return for which we had installed some lights for the harbour, undertaken to leave the Rubb Halls behind when we finished and trained some of the young men on the island to help with our work. On the long, buffeting speed boat ride back to Malé, under lowering skies, I couldn't help dwelling on the difficulties – coping with the politics on each island; how to establish ownership of each plot; what to do about absentee owners who had left their island; how to weed out the occasional cheat from those really in need; how to improve conditions for our team; where to buy materials and how to ship and store them on remote islands in time for the building work to begin; how to supervise the building work and make sure the new houses will withstand future disasters; how to communicate with understandably impatient local people.

I had plenty to think about over Christmas, as usual.

Chapter 7

The Emblem Debate, 2006

Hokey-cokey in the hills – The Third Emblem debate – Hurricane Katrina – Child soldiers in Sierra Leone – Syria before the war

The year, John's last as Chair, started well, with news that we had raised a total of £116m from voluntary sources, including £36m from Emergency Appeals and an additional £9m for the Mayor of London's Bombings Appeal – a truly remarkable year, nearly double our original budget and a great tribute to Mark Astarita and his dynamic team. Having been in the fundraising doldrums for several years, we were fast becoming one of the strongest performers in the sector.

We were also lucky enough to attract an offer of virtually unlimited pro bono management consultancy support from Booz Allen, a leading global consultancy. Our relationship with them, particularly the lead partner Jake Melville, blossomed over the years, and their insightful, encouraging and innovative approach to problem-solving proved a substantial boon.

In the UK, our increasingly crisis- and emergency-focussed offer had continued to attract interest from statutory providers looking for partnerships, and it was encouraging to see the new Areas develop radically improved relationships with the emergency services. This led to Red Cross volunteer teams being called out regularly to assist with fires, floods, road traffic accidents and other local incidents, and to provide 'winter pressures' support for an under-resourced ambulance service.

We were putting a great deal of effort at the time into winning contracts for our 'medical loan service', lending out wheelchairs, commodes and other basic equipment to patients in their own homes, building on the county-wide service we had been operating for the NHS in Leicestershire. Our 'home from hospital' scheme also attracted a great deal of interest from NHS commissioners, as hospitals looked to discharge patients ever earlier, sometimes to empty homes and meagre support at local level. It never ceased to amaze me, on my many visits to such schemes, how frequently hospital beds were emptied on a Friday afternoon, apparently with little or no thought as to what support might be available for the patients once they were back in their own home, and with little or no warning to the family.

I remember, on one visit to a scheme in Nottingham, being told of a very disabled person with severe hearing difficulties who was left in her home one Friday with a packet of biscuits and no heating. Her daughter, who lived some distance away, was not informed, and it wasn't until the Red Cross volunteer broke in, three days later, that the poor woman received any help at all.

'Where does that rank in terms of the seriousness of the cases you deal with?'

'Oh,' said the coordinator, 'that's about a six.'

Our volunteers, usually led by a paid full-time coordinator, did a superb job liaising with the wards, preparing houses for patients' return and then supporting them in their first few days or even weeks thereafter.

From refugees and asylum-seekers, too, facing an increasingly restrictive, even hostile immigration regime and considerable difficulties in terms of settlement and integration, there was growing demand for our orientation and support services. Entitlement to state benefits was drastically reduced around this time, and many became destitute whilst trying to overcome the administrative hurdles in the way of their applications for 'leave to remain'. Our teams (which were often able to recruit former asylum-seekers as volunteers) provided practical and legal advice, emotional support, limited financial assistance, interpretation – and just friendly and sympathetic company. It was inspiring stuff, entirely funded from donations rather than government grants or contracts, and it enabled us to add the strength of the Red Cross name and reputation to campaigns for improvements to the asylum system.

It was the first anniversary of the tsunami, and the media was mostly determined to concentrate on what hadn't been done for the victims. This was difficult to handle. The response to any major disaster is primarily the responsibility of the government of the country affected, supported by UN institutions like OCHA, WFP, etc. The international aid agencies, the Red Cross, Oxfam, Save the Children and so on, have a supporting role but certainly do not have the money, capacity or expertise to rebuild whole towns or large communities, such as those destroyed by the tsunami and the Kashmir or Bam earthquakes.

But we raise our money direct from often incredibly generous members of the public, in whose name the media, not unreasonably, seek to hold us to account. We are far more accessible than the officials of the government in question, or the UN, and so inevitably we are in the firing line and often faced with a hostile line of questioning based on partial information and unrealistic expectations of what could possibly be achieved in a few short months.

We felt we had done well to get hundreds of thousands of displaced people under some kind of shelter and in receipt of access to basic facilities and necessities. For some members of the media this was not enough, as I found in an embarrassing *Newsnight* interview with Martha Kearney in January. Briefed by our media team to expect a reasonably routine 'update' piece, I got into my seat in the studio opposite Kearney to find to my horror that the interview was to be preceded by some film, from an island off the Indonesian coast that I had never heard of, alleging that the Red Cross had failed the islanders completely, and that nothing had been done for them.

An excited and indignant Kearney then proceeded to interrupt my every attempt to explain or put in context the overwhelmingly negative impression conveyed by the film. We had been given no warning that the film was to be shown, no opportunity to establish the facts in relation to that particular island; and now, in front of a large live TV audience, I was given no opportunity to try and help people understand the huge and complex challenges that we faced. I'm sure I became increasingly rattled, and I tottered out of the studio to do another couple of interviews elsewhere feeling wretched, my humiliation completed by the discovery that the plastic cup of water I had been given by Kearney's assistant had leaked all over my trousers. I received a half-hearted apology from Kearney via our media team weeks later, but it was a miserable experience.

As ever in the Red Cross, however, there was no time to dwell on it, as I had a busy two weeks ahead of me, leading a pitch to Tesco for the opportunity to be their Charity of the Year (one of the biggest and most prestigious corporate partnerships around in those days); speaking in an Oxford Union debate about the recent Make Poverty History Campaign; attending a Royal reception at Buckingham Palace for charity leaders;

talking about 'Leadership' to a group of senior commercial managers for Windsor Leadership Trust; formally launching our new corporate plan *Across the World and Around the Corner*; accompanying Dr Hany El-Banna, the passionate and dynamic president of Islamic Relief, to a conference in Cairo of Egyptian voluntary sector leaders (part of an initiative that I had launched with Dr Hany and Jan Egeland – head of UNOCHA – aimed at helping to develop the humanitarian sector in Muslim countries), followed by a similar meeting in Amman, Jordan; and then going to Geneva with John for a Governing Board meeting.

A month later, I was on my way to Pakistan, where we had £12m to spend on the response to October's terrible earthquake in Pakistan-administered Kashmir. Nearly 90,000 people had been killed, another 70,000 had been injured and more than 2.8m had been displaced. In the worst-affected areas, more than 70 per cent of the houses had been destroyed, as had most of the hospitals and schools. About one third of the population had lost their livelihoods. My trip report read as follows:

At Balakot, we met a Norwegian Red Cross mountain rescue team, who turned up to collect us (me, three people from the Federation and an Associated Press camera team who were filming the visit) in a convoy of 'all-terrain-vehicles' (ATVs), comprising a mix of four-wheel motorbikes and chunky Volvo 'belt-wagons' on caterpillar tracks, accompanied by police outriders.

All around us were high hills and snow-covered mountains, patches of fir and dull grey shale slopes lowering above a rushing slatey river and the ruins of the town. Everywhere we looked there were tents, blue tarps and new corrugated metal sheeting. The whole place was one large camp, clustered thick in the centre of the valley, with tentacles stretching up into the hills.

With the ATVs in the lead, we ground our way up a narrow mountain track, our route carved out of the bleak hillside by the Pakistan Army only a few weeks earlier, to reach areas that would otherwise have been completely inaccessible. We clung to each curve and contour of the road, which was wet and muddy in places, collapsed and built up again in others. Along the way, more tents and rebuilt shacks, occasional splashes of colour from terraced rice paddies, tiny burial grounds with fresh graves decked in shimmering silver tape, like sodden, bedraggled and forgotten Christmas presents left out in the rain. Whole families sat beside some of the graves, and smiled wanly as we passed.

On and on we went, engines grinding, for nearly two hours, clawing our way upwards, past tiny clusters of dwellings as if sprinkled on the mountainsides around, until we came to Satbani, where Pakistan Red Crescent volunteers were supervising the distribution of blankets, tarps, corrugated metal sheeting and other materials to local people, so that they could build new 'houses' to replace those destroyed in the quake. We did some interviews with relieved local people, and then set off back down the hill in the encroaching dusk, standing up through the hatch of the ATV for a better view of the desolate scene.

At Federation 'base camp' at Mansehra, we joined the drivers for a whisky around the camp fire, before grabbing a quick scratch supper and settling into our tents and sleeping bags.

After an early start the next day, we drove up and over the mountains again to what had been the epicentre of the earthquake at Muzaffarabad, situated at the confluence of the Jhelum and Neelum rivers in the foothills of the western Himalayas. Deep in a valley, beneath beetling hills gashed with the scars of fresh avalanches, the town must have been beautiful once, with its ancient winding streets, crumbling storeyed houses and crowded alleyways. Now it's a shocking, sad shambles of fallen timbers, smashed bricks and piles of rubble.

We visited a Turkish Red Crescent bakery turning out delicious freshly-baked loaves, and an extraordinary treatment plant built by the Swedish Red Cross, sucking water up from the river and purifying it for use further up the valley. The enthusiastic designers showed us round with great pride, for it all looked kind of home-made and cobbled together, and somehow worked entirely by gravity. When I pointed to a small shed and asked, 'What's in there?', their faces beamed as they swept open the door to reveal a little sauna, complete with a fake window showing a view of a Swedish lake.

After several more interviews, both with the Associated Press team and Pakistan TV, we spent the night in the ICRC compound amongst the ruins, listening to the drenching rain outside and thinking about the thousands huddling still in their tents and temporary shelters on the hillsides around. But the next day, after a foggy start, the sun shone, and we were able to join an ICRC helicopter flight in an elderly Russian M18 up the Neelum valley to a community isolated 8,000 feet up, who were to receive that very day their first supplies of food and building materials.

By the time we landed, after an exhilarating but depressing flight above the devastation in the valley bottom and rocky hillsides gashed by landslips, the sun was hot. We stood transfixed in the silence of a sylvan scene. On all sides, hills rose sheer greeny-brown above us, dotted with pines and terraced maize fields. Three bright red flags fluttered in the breeze. We could see a small mosque across the valley and, sprinkled about every slope like scattered little piles of flotsam, small wood and mud dwellings, mostly collapsed, beside the blue plastic of Chinese tents. We realized we were standing on top of one surviving dwelling, a few large beams and a heavy roof of wood, grass and earth – great for protection from the snow and bitter cold, but a killer in an earthquake.

For a while we were on our own, so we trekked a short distance to the three terraced maize fields that had been cleared for the distribution of relief goods where a small crowd of men and bits of boys gathered, shyly observing our every move and muttering quietly together. Soon the helicopter re-appeared, with its first load of rice, ghee, sugar, tea and soup trailing in a bundle underneath, and the Pakistan Red Crescent volunteers started to organize themselves into a reception committee. With a roar and a clatter of blades, the load bumped gently on the lowest field, and the designated team of bearers hurried to release it from its sling and carry the precious cargo to the distribution point.

Meanwhile, we were getting to know the locals, and hearing patchily-translated stories of the earthquake: the stunning shock of the first tremors in the early morning; the collapsing homes; the screams of injured people and livestock; the rumble of landslides and renewed tremors echoed and magnified by the surrounding hills. These were grim tales, told by small groups of three or four, each person adding a memory, a number, a shake of the head. Aid had arrived slowly, two weeks or more before the military were able to blast a way through, and several more days before tents and food supplies appeared.

Most of the animals died, a disaster, this, as each family group owned at least one buffalo for ploughing the heavy soil and a cow for milk for the children and sale down the valley. The ICRC, we knew, was conducting a continent-wide search for tens of thousands of fresh cattle able to cope with the altitude and extremes of temperature in Kashmir.

But these were strong, proud, resourceful people, used to hardship, and obviously delighted to be receiving help now. Two weeks ago, they were wading through five feet of snow, today the sun was shining and there was the excitement of the helicopter and the foreigners.

'We will have all we need,' they said, 'apart from our animals.'

As the men bustled about with the distribution, we faced a growing audience of scraggy children, with a few women hovering in the background. We tried to get a conversation going, in pidgin and hand gestures, pointed at each other and exchanged names. Shafeez, Nadeem, Saheel, Nick, Stacey, Ted – the list grew

'What about school?'

Grins – 'No lessons, school broken.'

'What do you learn?'

Scratching of heads – science, arithmetic, English, Holy Koran.

'What do you want to do when you grow up?'

Blank looks, as if any future beyond the valley was simply impossible to imagine.

The questions, and the answers, faltered.

'Let's sing,' I said slightly desperately to my Red Cross colleagues, and we launched into a shaky version of 'Red Cross Spirit' ('I have the Red Cross spirit in my hands', etc.), complete with all the appropriate gestures. There were a few seconds of aghast amazement from men and boys alike, followed by hoots of laughter and appreciation.

'Now your turn,' I pointed.

They responded with a long and lovely chanting song, the refrain tossed to and fro between them, and then another, equally lively.

Then it was our turn again. We scratched our heads.

'How about the hokey-cokey?' I suggested.

Within minutes, we had them all lined up, hokeying and cokeying to their hearts' content, and I think they would have gone on all afternoon, if one of the ladies hadn't summoned us to lunch, an incredibly generous picnic of curry, rice and fruit laid out on the damp grass.

Soon it was back to work for the men, as further helicopter loads swung up from the valley below and the piles of goods to be distributed grew higher. I took myself off for a walk, and soon found myself chatting with a delightful young man clad in white and on his way to work. His wife was a health visitor, coping with a huge extra workload of injuries, pneumonia and childhood diarrhoea since the earthquake.

'And you,' I asked, 'what do you do?'

'Oh, I work over there', he said, pointing to the tiny corrugated iron mosque, distant across the valley.

'Ah,' I said, noting his youthful looks, 'so you must work with the Imam.'

'No,' he said, smiling, 'I am the Imam.'

'Are you the one who does the wonderful call to prayer?' I asked, and was astonished when he leapt to his feet.

'Yes,' he exclaimed. 'Would you like to hear it?'

So saying, he cupped his hands and began to chant, his voice rising and falling as the holy cadences of the haunting cry '*Allahu akbar allahu akbar*' drifted across the valley.

Down below, everyone looked up amazed, inspected their watches and shook their heads. It wasn't time for prayer. Clearly the world had gone mad since these foreigners arrived. It was a magical moment.

All too soon, the last supply run of the day grew from a small speck deep in the valley below to the gleaming white and red of the clattering ICRC helicopter, hovering above our heads sending grass and dust whirling into the air about us, before settling on the field, waiting to take us home. We gathered everyone together, reluctant to leave, as the villagers huddled in close tight circles around us. We all hugged each other, arms about shoulders, faces close.

'Auld Lang Syne,' I called, and the Red Crossers launched gamely into Burns' ancient, mournful song. Eyes glittering, smiling and crying, the locals urged us on, linked arms pumping up and down as our eyes misted over and the singing petered out. They had understood not a word, but our meaning was clear. There were hugs and handshakes. An old man seized my shoulders and looked hard into my eyes, then dropped his head and sighed. He put his hand on his heart, his gesture mirroring my own.

The helicopter's whirling blades grew faster, and we knew it was time to go. A sprint across the field, a turn, a wave, and we were gone.

Within a month I was off again, to join another of the Secretary-General's 'high-level visits', this time to discuss the overall Red Cross response to the tsunami. We split into three groups, one for Sri Lanka, one for the Maldives and the third (which I joined) for Aceh. By this time we had gone out to contract for the building work which we were funding, to a firm in the Philippines, and I was keen to see how the preparatory work was progressing and what other national societies made of our decision.

I was relieved to find that, overall, the recovery in Indonesia was well underway, with new roads and harbours being built to support the rebuilding, and houses beginning to go up – though not as fast as the Government wanted, with its newly-imposed target date of June 2007. Sourcing adequate quantities of raw materials (timber, sand, aggregate, reinforced steel bars and mesh, etc. of the right quality) was difficult, with prices already up 50 per cent from the previous year. Poor infrastructure made the running of large building operations in remote areas challenging, and it was clear that meeting the target date was going to be a stretch to say the least. Our own projects, though, were going well, and our team (now up to 120 delegates) was in good heart.

When the three teams of national society leaders met up in Bangkok a few days later to compare notes, we heard that progress in the Maldives was also being maintained (though as I had found on my own visit at the end of 2005, everyone was having difficulties agreeing exactly who needed help and where house-plot boundaries were). Our own team led by Jill Clements was singled out for particular praise.

In Sri Lanka the story was not so good, due partly to the ongoing confusion caused by the Government's 'buffer zone', which prevented building within 50 metres of the shoreline. This distance had been reduced by the President, but the principle remained and was causing significant difficulty.

The 'high-level' meeting broke up, having been encouraged by the progress so far, but recognizing major challenges ahead around high staff turnover due to poor conditions in the field, and high pressure to get on with the work – not least from increasingly (and understandably) impatient local people. We agreed that we needed to work ever closer together in updating our strategies, and I was asked to join a 'task force' looking at the finances for the entire operation, led by the New Zealand secretary-general, Andrew Weeks.

This turned rapidly into a real challenge. In an understandable hurry to meet needs and commit the large amounts of funding it had received (in common with all the other major aid agencies) to specific building projects, the Federation's secretariat team had failed to keep a fully accurate count of the commitments it had made to the governments of the affected countries. When we started to add them all together, we realized that the Federation had over-extended itself to the tune of 800m Swiss francs (about £350m) on a total budget of over 2bn Swiss francs. Finding ways of reducing the deficit (e.g. by negotiating our way out of specific commitments), or somehow chipping in ourselves as PNS from funds that we had, of course, mostly already promised elsewhere, was very testing.

As we all tussled with this scenario, and struggled with the operational worries on the ground, another enormous international Red Cross Red Crescent Movement issue was coming to a head. This was the forthcoming Extraordinary General Assembly of the Federation to discuss the admission to the Federation of the Israeli Magen David Adom organization, with its red shield of David emblem, alongside the Palestine Red Crescent (PRCS).

For the final vote to take place, the states party to the Geneva Convention had had first to agree to the adoption of the Third Protocol measures which would allow the creation of a third 'Emblem' for the Movement – the key to the admission of MDA as a full member. This meeting ('the Diplomatic Conference') had been successfully completed in 2005. Next, in June 2006, the whole Movement (i.e. the ICRC, the Federation and all the national societies) had to meet with all their governments ('the International Conference') to agree to adopt the third emblem itself (a red crystal shape), to be used by any national society (such as Israel) that was unable to use the existing Cross and Crescent Emblems when operating outside its own territory. This was the legal device, worked out over many months of delicate negotiation and legal argument, that would enable the admission of Israel to the list of countries whose national 'red cross' or 'red crescent' organization was a member of the Red Cross Red Crescent Movement.

To the outsider, this would no doubt seem an arcane debate. But the political significance was enormous, in the context of the tangled and bitter politics of the Middle East. For the vote to be passed 'by acclamation', as was the custom, it would be necessary for the Arab states and those countries with a predominantly Muslim population to support it; and in so doing, it could be argued, they would in effect be voting in favour of a tacit admission of the right of the Israeli state to exist. At the same time, as part of the 'agreement', Israel would have to accept the right of the occupied territories of 'Palestine' to their own national society.

This was all a very big deal indeed, in Red Cross terms, a deal with which we, as a 'senior' national society, were very much engaged, particularly through our Michael Meyer, one of the world's leading authorities on the specialist field of international humanitarian law and the constitutional statutes of the Movement.

The series of meetings began on 19 June, and it quickly became clear that the 'Organization of the Islamic Conference' (OIC), an inter-governmental grouping of Arab and predominantly Muslim states, was intending to try and have the International Conference adjourned or to disrupt the proceedings in some way. Various amendments to the resolutions were put forward but rejected. The Syrian Government then made several objections on process grounds which, over the course of several hours of backroom negotiation (in which Michael was heavily involved), were eventually discounted.

There followed various reports on progress in implementing the Memorandum of Understanding between MDA and PRCS (which required MDA to stop, for example, using ambulances badged MDA in Jewish settlements in the occupied Palestinian territories), to which the Syrian Government made further objections (on the ground, for example, that an ICRC delegate had once stayed in an hotel in a Jewish settlement), after which the formal resolution to admit MDA and PRCS was introduced.

Yet more backroom negotiations ensued, throughout the third day of the Conference, about the precise wording of the resolution. No sooner was text agreed than the OIC would propose further changes – and so it went on all day until, late at night, the suggestion was made that the text of the OIC amendments should be put to the vote, with two OIC speakers proposing and two (including ourselves) speaking against. The amendments were overwhelmingly rejected, and we were back on track.

The International Conference vote paved the way for the Federation's General Assembly to reconvene, which it duly did at 3.00am and agreed to admit MDA and PRCS by acclamation (i.e. without a formal vote). Applause rolled on and on throughout the conference hall, with many of us struggling to hold back tears at the thought that the Movement was now, in a sense, complete and that, in the field of humanitarian response at least, there was unity in the Middle East. The Federation breathed a sigh of relief that the American Red Cross might now resume paying its substantial *barème*. An historic moment.

Before these meetings, the Governing Board held the first of two special meetings about Africa, prompted by the national society representatives from African countries on the Board, all active members of NEPARC, whose plea was that concerted Federation action was needed to address the continent's multiple challenges and to make good 'decades of broken promises and disappointed expectations'. The founder of the Grameen Bank, Muhammad Yunus, came to talk about microcredit schemes, and Jeffrey Sachs, the inspirational American economist, gave a masterly overview of the problems facing African countries – which he summarized as failing agriculture, failing healthcare systems and lack of internet connectivity – and suggested that the Red Cross should focus on anti-malaria bed nets, the training of outreach health workers and the empowering of local community development schemes.

The Board agreed to produce a 'Red Cross Strategy for Africa' in response, and the African national societies expressed their satisfaction at being heard at last.

Soon after, I was on the way to New Orleans for a Donor Forum meeting to discuss the Federation approach to disaster management. The city, eleven months after Hurricane Katrina, was a shocking sight. The hurricane, and the subsequent flooding as the levees were breached, had overwhelmed the poorer, largely black, parts of the city, and thousands of homes, whole districts and streets, had been inundated and abandoned. The front door of house after house was barricaded against looting and marked with a cross to denote flood damage and a number to show if the inhabitants had been amongst the 1,200 people who had died. Tens of thousands had decamped to neighbouring cities and towns, many never to return, and the general air of decay and neglect was palpable.

We became quite indignant on hearing how little government aid had been forthcoming, and how reluctant the insurance companies had been to pay out, often to customers ill-equipped to argue or fight for their rights. Some of us, remembering how we had been hounded by sections of the media for not working quickly enough to rebuild after the tsunami, were especially irritated

Back at home, we were working hard to encourage and assist Areas to build up strong and effective emergency and community health services. The old county branch structures (and often antiquated buildings) were in many respects now defunct, but it was to the notion of the geographical county that many volunteers still owed allegiance, and the best Area directors were the ones who respected that and tried to work with it – not always an easy juggling act. The four Territory Directors, all full and active members of the senior management team, had a key role to play in bridging the gap between UK Office and the front line, and did it extremely well, constantly reminding those of us who worked in the London 'ivory tower' of the realities 'out there', whilst pushing the 'party line' back out the other way.

In a big break with tradition, the trustees advertised and interviewed for a new Chair from outside the organization to replace John McClure; they chose James Cochrane, a former director of Glaxo-Wellcome who had been involved in the distribution of cheap HIV drugs in Africa and so had both excellent commercial skills, as well as some understanding of the humanitarian challenges we faced.

We held a big conference for all our fundraisers (where, determined as ever to make a fool of myself, I launched into the Abba song *Money, Money, Money* as part of my opening remarks). Soberingly, I also attended a two-day security training event with members of the International Team, in the light of the increasing amount of work we were doing in conflict areas and the increased threat of kidnap and hostage-taking. This made us all more conscious that the risks were real and, for those of us who travelled regularly to dangerous areas, ever-present, and I immediately added a list of 'proof of life' questions to the 'final letters' that were kept in my PA's drawer.

It was also time for another visit to a partner national society, this time Sierra Leone, a humid, green, fertile little country on the west coast of Africa, just above the equator. Its 5m poverty-stricken people were slowly returning to normal after eleven years of civil war. We had invested £250,000 in the national society in the past year, one of the few PNS to show any interest, and Britain was popular there anyway thanks to a well-timed military intervention at the end of the civil war and ongoing DFID investment since.

The roads in the country were the worst I had ever come across and, as they wanted me to visit four branches some distance from the capital Freetown, we spent hours on long bone-grinding drives, which would end abruptly in a jungle clearing, where we would find hundreds of people from the villages and hamlets around, waiting patiently to greet us with dancing, evil-looking black-masked devils, pounding drums and maracas, singers in gorgeous costumes, a clown or two, and crowds of cheering clapping locals. Apart from joining the dancers, I was dressed up several times as a 'Paramount Chief'; became the proud owner of two chickens; joined twenty rocking, chanting schoolgirls as they cheered on their local football team; watched a magical play lit by hurricane lamps in a jungle clearing; drove over the bridge where the vicious rebel leader 'Rambo' was blown up; and attended a teaching session with traditional birth attendants.

In Sierra Leone the civil war and its bitter legacy still loomed large, and everywhere I saw the evidence, in still-shattered buildings, heavy security, the guarded look in people's eyes and the ghastly souvenirs of limbs hacked off as punishment by the rebels. The programmes of the Red Cross were orientated towards very necessary rehabilitation, and I spent a moving afternoon with a community 'animation and peace support' project, where we crammed into a tiny open-sided meeting hut, as the rains began again, to watch a spirited re-enactment of the health and sanitation problems they faced in the wake of the recent wholesale wartime destruction of local clinics and established traditions of community participation.

One of our biggest investments had been in the establishment of several intensive programmes for the re-education and rehabilitation of the thousands of young people and children who had been forced by the rebels to take an active part in the war – raped and abused, made to watch or even participate in the brutal killing of their parents and then recruited into the rebel army and forced to join its rampage around the country. I was privileged to be invited to attend a graduation ceremony at one of the 'schools', where the national society had acted as a quasi-family for these children, and had educated and trained them in a range of skills so that they could support themselves and re-integrate into their former home village (if it still existed) or somewhere new.

Two incidents still haunt me. On the night before the graduation ceremony, eight young female victims in raffia skirts danced around a much younger girl by torchlight. They sang and weaved and stamped their feet in the dust, seeking to recapture from the child their own lost virginities. At so many such 'cultural evenings', this would have been an act, a representation: in Sierra Leone, the performance was the reality – the loss they enacted, and the impossibility of its restoration, neither more nor less than bitter truth.

The next day, before two hundred of her fellow students and a crowd of local dignitaries and chiefs, parents and friends, Jemma told her story, of how, at the age of seven, she had been abducted with her older sister by the rebel leader Rambo. Aged fourteen when he died, she tried to escape, but was caught and would have been summarily executed, had not she been claimed as a wife by another leader. Then he, too, was killed and, with the war over, she finally returned home, to find her family wiped out and her village destroyed. She lived rough for nearly three years until found by the Red Cross, who brought her kicking and screaming into the rehabilitation project – a drugged, drunk troublemaker, who had lived by prostituting herself whenever the opportunity arose.

And yet there she stood, on graduation day, as neat as a pin in her school uniform, hair in tidy ringlets, eyes shining, as proud, strong and beautiful as could be. I came upon her a little later, sitting by herself with her certificate and the sewing machine she had been given to start her new career.

'Have a great life,' I told her.

'In Jesus' name,' she replied, smiling shyly.

I clapped my hands and thrust them towards her, palms out, a traditional local gesture of admiration and approval. In the customary manner, she 'caught' the feeling and clutched it to her heart.

In another of those strange conjunctions that happen in the Red Cross, I found myself, the following week, in ritzy Bermuda, addressing the assembled members of the international reinsurance industry at their annual conference about the response to disasters from the humanitarian perspective. In addition to establishing a possible fundraising opportunity with the industry, I was able to visit the Bermuda Red Cross, one of our 'overseas branches', which was conducting a modest range of typical community activities (first aid training, medical loan, etc.) and also raising not insubstantial sums of money on the island to contribute to our disaster response appeals.

Building on the experience of my visit to the Cayman Islands (another of our overseas branches) in 2004, I recognized once again the extreme vulnerability of small islands to catastrophic events like hurricanes or cruise ship disasters, and resolved to try and bring our eight overseas branches more closely into our general branch support network, rather than leave them, as we had done, pretty much to their own devices.

Then there was another Governing Board meeting to attend in Geneva, John's last as our 'nominated representative'. He had been popular with Board members, and his successful leadership of the *Federation of the Future* initiative guaranteed him a well-deserved fond farewell from the President.

The next two months were a whirl of overseas trips, to Turkey with Dr Hany's 'Humanitarian Forum'; to Belgium for a first meeting of European national societies to discuss opportunities for cooperation; and back to Pakistan for two days with the newly-married Prince of Wales and Duchess of Cornwall, their first working overseas visit together, flying by helicopter with them from Islamabad to Kashmir to see some of the amazing Red Cross earthquake recovery work; to Ukraine, another of our partner national societies at the time, for a conference of European national societies, to chair a working group; then straight on to Singapore to address the Asia-Pacific group of national societies about the change processes we had been going through at the British Red Cross; and finally, straight on from Singapore to two former branches of the British

Red Cross, Australia and New Zealand, to make speeches at the former's annual Assembly about current challenges for the Federation, and at the latter, to celebrate their 75th birthday (and independence from the 'mother ship').

I had one more visit that year, to another partner national society and one which was to absorb increasing amounts of our time in the years ahead – Syria. We had been working to build the disaster response capacity of the well-respected Syrian Arab Red Crescent for a couple of years already but, following a review, we intended to sign an MOU for a further three years, concentrating on risk reduction as well as response. They had been lobbying for a visit for some time and made me extremely welcome during a quick four-day 'in and out', which took in three of their fourteen branches – Homs, Aleppo and Damascus itself. I had several meetings with the wily but popular businessman President, Dr Attar, and met the British and EU ambassadors and two government ministers.

The country was beautiful and at peace, with no hint of the terrible fighting to come. With Marwan, the secretary general, I travelled first to Aleppo, virtually straight from the airport, pausing only for a quick canal-side lunch in Homs, and met the Branch leaders and their bright and buzzy young members.

In the morning we had breakfast at a busy local bean soup shop, then returned to Homs to address a gathering of dozens of youth members from all over Syria and tour the new Hospital for Burns Patients. Then it was time to return to Damascus for more formal meetings and the signing of the MOU, stopping off on the way at the hauntingly beautiful Crusader Castle Krak des Chevaliers. The next time I saw Syria, in 2013, half the country was in flames, Aleppo and Homs were in ruins, millions of civilians had fled to neighbouring Jordan or Lebanon and the national society was leading the humanitarian response, losing hundreds of its staff and volunteers killed in the fighting.

Chapter 8

A New Chairman, 2007

Tesco Charity of the Year – Handing over the keys –
Reviewing the UN – A summer of floods

This was set to be a year of solid progress and improvement. We agreed that we would focus on four main priorities: firstly, the ongoing build-up of our emergency response focus; second, the completion of a project to define the strategic framework for our short-term community crisis care services based on the concept of vulnerability; third, a look at our management practices and procedures with a view to working 'kinder and smarter'; and finally (and from my point of view, most excitingly) energizing the whole organization to make our Tesco Charity of the Year fundraising campaign a huge success. It was also James Cochrane's first year as Chair, so I devoted time to ensuring that he understood both the British Red Cross and the Movement as a whole.

We kicked off the year with the news that our work in 2006 had generated a £3m surplus, well above budget, and this gave us the confidence to tackle the Tesco partnership, which would be providing additional funds for new community-level projects in the UK, with gusto and enthusiasm. I had worked with Tesco before, at Macmillan, where we had raised a record amount in our 'Year', and earned sincere plaudits from the Tesco team as a great charity to work with. This was the second time at the Red Cross that we had applied to Tesco, and I was determined to beat the £2m Macmillan record, whilst being nervous (as I think Tesco were) that, whilst the Red Cross name was well known, its broad range of activities at home and abroad (though now significantly slimmed down) was not – shades of 'best known least understood' continued to haunt us.

I spent the first quarter concentrating on our UK work and getting to know James. We had a grand launch of the Tesco 'Charity of the Year' campaign at their flagship store in Kensington; started negotiations with the Olympics Organizing Committee about a first aid role for our

UK volunteers at the London Games; joined the COBRA-led national flu pandemic exercise 'Winter Willow'; and had discussions with the Highways Agency about offering a Red Cross emergency response service on the motorways for major incidents.

In the context of emergency response, it was particularly gratifying to see our volunteers and staff in Ipswich (my home town) providing the most superb 'emotional and practical support' service, in the streets and for days on end, to residents scared out of their wits by the five gruesome murders of female sex-workers, all of them young kids desperate to feed a heroin habit. The murders shocked the community, not just by their violence but by the sense of young lives needlessly squandered and the picture they revealed of urban and community decay and degradation. The Red Cross team did a wonderful job providing reassurance, a sense of cohesion and the potential for healing , which exactly personified our aims for the Red Cross as a whole.

In another significant piece of work we took on a 'Gateway' project in Norwich to provide reception and accommodation for sixty refugees from the violence in Congo, another sign of our growing influence and capacity in an area of work that had been relatively under-developed in the organization.

But all over the UK, volunteers and staff in the twenty Areas were growing and developing local services to meet local need, in accordance with our strategy, in remarkable ways. Every time I visited one of the four 'territories', met with the director and his or her territory team and visited some or all of the Areas in their patch, I came away excited and inspired by the passion and ingenuity they displayed. There was a new confidence throughout the organization, and I couldn't help but reflect upon how far we had come in six years – let alone the sixteen years since I had first joined the Red Cross.

All over England, the additional funds raised by Mark Astarita and his team were being invested in scaling up existing community services like our home from hospital schemes, or medical loan services; buying new emergency response vehicles and equipment to improve our support to the fire, police and (particularly in the winter) ambulance services; ambitiously bidding for local government funding for new activities or big public events where first aid cover was required; expanding our first aid training offer; and responding to the growing needs of an increasing number of refugees and asylum seekers.

In Scotland, Wales, and Northern Ireland, where the increasingly devolved administrations offered new and different opportunities to our directors to innovate and expand, the developments were at times even more exciting. In the three nations it was perhaps easier, given their size compared to England, to develop close working relationships with government, social services and other voluntary sector colleagues. Partnership working seemed at that time more embedded in the culture than in England, and our local teams responded magnificently.

We also had a major success in finally signing a three-year contract with the Foreign and Commonwealth Office to provide a psychosocial support team of specially-trained volunteers and staff on standby seven days a week to give emotional and practical assistance to British nationals affected by disasters and other traumatic events abroad. The Red Cross 'PST', as it was known, was to become a regular feature in the response to the plight of British citizens caught up in disasters and conflicts overseas and gave some of our volunteers valuable international experience, as well as the chance to work with colleagues overseas from other national societies. In the years to come, the PST (energetically led by Dr Sarah Davidson) was called out several times, including to the bombing of a nightclub in Bali, the attack on the Taj Hotel in Mumbai, the resettlement of British nationals from Zimbabwe (by air) and an emergency evacuation of British and other nationals from Libya (by sea on board HMS *Cumberland*) – and on many other occasions since.

The Federation Governing Board meeting in Ethiopia, James' first as our nominated representative on the Board and the first ever in Africa, was a moving and emotional meeting, as African national societies pleaded their case, successfully, for the Federation to adopt a coherent 'Global Programme on Africa', coupled with a fully-funded package of support for its implementation. It was inevitable that the outcomes of the meeting would be over-ambitious (as indeed they proved to be), but the dialogue was open and the debate good-hearted and sincere, and I think we all came away re-inspired with a sense of what could and might yet be. We finished with a private dinner to introduce James to three giants of the Red Cross in Africa, people who completely embodied the Red Cross spirit and gave visionary leadership to their national societies – Shimelis Adugna, Mandisa Kalako-Williams and Muctarr Jalloh, respectively Presidents in Ethiopia, South Africa and Sierra Leone.

In March, also as part of his induction, James and I went to Indonesia so that he could see our biggest and most risky overseas project, building 2,200 houses and providing livelihoods cash grants and support to over 3,000 individuals on one island and two mainland locations devastated by the Asian tsunami. I was relieved to see that we had made substantial progress and that the basic building programme was progressing more or less on time and budget, thanks to the excellent project and people management skills of the site manager Gabriel and his great team, who had achieved an enormous amount in extremely testing conditions.

Gabriel was worried about two problems. The first involved the plan for the provision of water and sanitation to a large block of new houses in Teunom which had failed to take account of the small size of the properties; whilst the second involved the timber for the door and window frames which had arrived in large quantities from New Zealand, but was mostly inadequately seasoned, and warped. These would have been a commonplace issues for an experienced house developer, but they were major and novel problems for us and involved lots of negotiations and discussion at head office level and with an unapologetic supplier in the New Zealand. We had a lot to learn.

The highlight of the trip, though, was a visit to Pulau Aceh, the devastated small island I had visited in 2005 with Ben Brown of the BBC. We were building 200-odd houses there, and it was a thrill to see many of them complete and their owners either picking up their old occupations (mostly fishing), or taking up new ones assisted by our livelihoods programme. As we were being shown round, I remembered my heart-rending meeting, two years previously, with the young woman Romaini (who had lost her husband to the waves) and our fruitless search for the remains of her house. I asked if she could be found and, just as I was clambering aboard the launch to motor back to the mainland, she pushed forward, her face a big grin from ear to ear. Not only did she have a new house, she told me, for herself and her two children, but we had also built her a small wooden kiosk and set her up in a tiny grocery business. The worries on the trip simply melted away as we hugged each other on the shoreline.

The bulk of the summer seemed to be about flooding in the UK. The floods wrought havoc across the country, destroying homes and livelihoods, and brought misery to hundreds of thousands of people. In one of our biggest ever peacetime operations, British Red Cross volunteers and staff from all over the country worked throughout June and July, from Scotland in the north, in Northern Ireland, through Yorkshire and the Midlands, down through South Wales and the Cotswolds, to Oxfordshire and the Thames Valley, during the wettest summer on record. Some areas received double the usual amount of rain, a month's worth in twenty-four hours in some places.

For the first time, on any significant scale, we were required to mount a co-ordinated nationwide response, with volunteers (and their transport and equipment) travelling as required from one Area to another to support their colleagues, including a 'swift-water rescue team' who travelled down from Scotland, the mobilization of our expert Logistics Emergency Response Unit (which had hitherto only ever worked overseas), and the utilization of our 'international' relief goods warehouse near Bristol for the provision of vast consignments of bottled water to people stuck in their homes and cut off from the mains.

We launched a national Floods Appeal, which raised over £3m in as many weeks, and set up a special committee chaired by Sir Stephen Lamport, the husband of Angela, one of our Board members and enthusiastic Surrey President and PST member, to distribute the funds to those most in need.

We ran emergency rest centres in a dozen locations; evacuated patients from hospitals and care homes; worked with fire crews to help evacuate residents by boat and secured empty properties; distributed over 300 tonnes of bottled water and thousands of food parcels and hygiene kits; provided blankets, duvets and pillows, wheelchairs, dry clothes and replacement clothing, warm refreshments, emotional support and practical advice and information to thousands; supported the ambulance service in counties all over the country; and used our 'Unimog' all-terrain vehicle to access flood areas which the emergency services couldn't reach.

It was the most remarkable nationwide response, which demonstrated the unique ability of the Red Cross to support the emergency services in a time of crisis professionally and comprehensively, moving resources from one side of the country to the other when needed, coordinated and supported nationally but managed locally and to a high standard. The value of our investment in emergency response capacity, training and practical experience (even through such relatively humdrum activities as the provision of first aid cover at local fetes and football matches) was vividly vindicated and demonstrated, and well-publicized in the media.

In many areas, it was encouraging to note, local authorities asked us to co-ordinate the efforts of other smaller voluntary organizations, and invited us furthermore to play a key role in what was often a lengthy recovery process for some of the worst-affected locations and individuals.

Having visited our teams in several flood areas, and accompanied them on some of their operations, I was delighted to be able to comment in my quarterly report to the Board of Trustees:

> It is not an exaggeration to say that this quarter has been one of the most successful periods for the British Red Cross for some considerable time. The whole organization, especially at the local level, performed great feats in response to the floods in the north and the west – a performance which met urgent need, established the Red Cross as a key player in responding to UK emergences, was watched by the world (quite literally – our operation was seen on TVs from Europe to the Antipodes) and made us all feel really proud of ourselves.

I hated tearing myself away, in early August, even though the worst was over by then, to visit the Indian Red Cross to talk about future opportunities for working together. Ironically, my counterpart, Dr Agarwal, had chosen to take me to Bihar in the north, India's poorest state, which had a population of 90m people and was at the time of my trip mostly under water itself after ten days of torrential monsoon rain. For two days we travelled extensively, frequently having to wade through knee-high flood waters to meet Red Cross teams toiling to help the millions of people who had been displaced as a result of the floods.

As a small treat at the end of a tiring trip, Dr Agarwal took me to Varanasi for a row on the Holy Ganges. As a huge orange moon slid from behind a vast black rain cloud, its edges highlighted by flashes of lightning, and with funeral pyres burning hot and red and the chants of worshippers to Shiva on shore filling the night, while cymbals clashed and acolytes waved burning torches above their heads, our boatman smiled at me and took a swig of muddy, mucky river water from his bottle.

'You see water,' he said. 'I see Mother.'

At home, the flood waters were subsiding, although we now found ourselves called upon to play on ongoing role in supporting many of the victims as they recovered from the mental, physical and financial shock. We found that thousands of families had had no insurance cover, and the help we were able to provide from our Floods Appeal, with advice on benefits, etc., was invaluable.

Internally, we had put ourselves through an internationally-renowned process of organizational audit, certification and validation run by Standard Global Services, in which we were benchmarked against other NGOs worldwide, and were delighted to score a 97 per cent rating, one of the highest achieved in our sector – a fitting tribute to David Causer and Helen Shirley-Quirk, respectively directors of finance and strategy and who sadly were both leaving: David had decided to retire from full-time employment, and Helen (a secondee) went back to her 'home' in the Department of Health. It always seemed to be the case during my time at the Red Cross that no sooner had you got on an even keel than something else happened to knock you off course.

I now had a bit of a 'break' from the British Red Cross (if not from floods), with two weeks in Pakistan, where I had been engaged by UNOCHA to lead a team of independent experts reviewing in real time the way the UN as a whole had responded to the flooding in Pakistan during June and July. The floods had inundated huge swathes of rural Sind and Balochistan provinces in the south of the country, destroying homes, crops and roads, and causing the temporary displacement of 2.5m people.

The reason why Pakistan had been chosen for the review was that it was a pilot country for the 'One UN' reforms, which aimed to make eighteen or more UN entities (UNICEF, WFP, FAO, UNHCR, UNOCHA, etc.) work together more like one organization, at least during a crisis. Pakistan had chaired the High Level UN Group that had proposed the reforms and was also chair of the G77 group of developing countries which would most benefit from the changes. It was also the only country where the relatively new UN 'cluster' system (for securing cooperation between UN and non-governmental organizations like the Red Cross, etc.) had been used twice – in Kashmir after the 2005 earthquake, and then again during the flooding.

The independent review was also prompted by a concern in New York that the UN's flood response had not gone well. The political sensitivities between the government of Pakistan, which as 'host' country had led the response on the ground, on the one hand, and the 'big beasts' of the UN system on the other, were substantial, and it was made clear to me in my initial briefing that there was a great deal riding on the outcome of the review.

'You are between a rock and a hard place,' I was told by one interviewee, and so it proved.

For me personally this was a fascinating opportunity to see at first-hand how the UN functioned in a politically sensitive environment like Pakistan, and to observe the workings of the 'cluster system' introduced by Jan Egeland (former head of the Norwegian Red Cross) when he was head of UNOCHA and in which the Federation had controversially decided to play a key role as lead for the shelter cluster two years previously.

I was given a great team, comprising two Pakistani nationals – Saba Khattak, a feisty, funny, feminist social development expert and campaigner, and Kaiser Bengali, an old sparring partner of hers, a very politically aware economist (who went on to become a senior government adviser). Lucia Elmi, a bright and bubbly emergency operations manager on loan from UNICEF, completed the team as manager/co-ordinator and link to the UN. When we weren't racing from one part of the country to another, or from one interview to the next, we spent most of our time teasing each other and laughing. It was a happy time on a high-stakes mission.

We travelled the length of the two Provinces, speaking to victims of the flooding, local and international NGOs, Army officers and provincial governors and politicians; and in Islamabad to the (ex-military) head of the Government's National Disaster Management Agency (NDMA), the leaders of all the UN agencies operating in Pakistan and, of course, the UN's Resident Coordinator (RC) and his team, who had led the response from the UN. Each day, we set out from our hotel in Quetta accompanied by a truck-load of policemen as guards, their rifles waving precariously in the air as we bounced along rural roads and tracks between meetings; and by a security service detail, heavily disguised as drivers or private motorists, who followed our every move at a discreet distance – and who flashed us sheepish smiles while pretending to wash their cars, as we waved a greeting to them every morning in the car park.

It was a gruelling trip. The muggy heat was intense; Ramadan was in full swing, so we had no alternative but to observe the dawn-to-dusk fast ourselves; there was rioting in the streets of Islamabad; and everyone we interviewed was out to defend the decisions they had made and the way they had co-operated (or not) with the other players in the humanitarian response.

As we highlighted in our report to Sir John Holmes, the newly-appointed head of UNOCHA, the issue at the heart of the findings was how the UN should react when it was working in a sovereign state with a strong government and an humanitarian crisis to which the humanitarian community felt impelled to respond, but where the government of the country (in this case because of political sensitivities in the Provinces concerned) does not wish to seek or receive international assistance at the level which the humanitarian community (and particularly the UN) believes is appropriate. This was a very big issue at the time, because it related so strongly to the 2005 UN doctrine of 'responsibility to protect' and the question of whether it was open to the UN, or to individual Member States, to intervene in the affairs of another member state, by force if necessary, in order to prevent genocide, war crimes, ethnic cleansing or crimes against humanity.

At the outset, the government of Pakistan, through the newly-created NDMA and with the help of the Army, launched a major relief operation. The UN, fresh from its successful response to the Kashmir earthquake and with other members of the international humanitarian community and local NGOs, swiftly set about mobilizing resources to help. The UN country team decided that it had to launch a full scale humanitarian response, sector-specific 'clusters' were set up and populated by representatives of all the agencies, an application for funds from the UN's central reserve was made and a special 'flash appeal' was launched.

Unfortunately, and for a variety of reasons, the Pakistan government was at best ambiguous in its response to these activities. It was proud of how it had dealt with the earthquake in Kashmir and felt quite capable of mounting its own response to the floods, run by the NDMA. Furthermore, Balochistan in particular was a politically sensitive part of Pakistan with a strong separatist movement, and access by non-Pakistan nationals was heavily restricted and unwelcome.

On the UN side, motivated as it was by the 'humanitarian imperative' to help, it seemed as if the reluctance of the government to accept external assistance was not fully understood or accepted, with the result that its appeal failed due, at least in part, to the lukewarm messages coming out of Islamabad and the confusion these caused amongst donor governments. Furthermore, the 'One UN' reforms and the 'cluster' system, both still being piloted, had not had time to bed down at the time the floods struck, and none of the participants really understood (or in some cases even accepted) their new co-operative mandates, roles and modes of operation. Persuading the leaders of massive global institutions like UNHCR or WFP to soften their sometimes competitive edges and accept compromise on their priorities is no easy task, particularly when the expectations of the crisis-affected population and other stakeholders are so high, and the cluster meetings we attended seemed cumbersome, time-consuming and lacking a decision-making focus.

The issue of the humanitarian imperative to intervene is a delicate and sensitive one and gives rise to fundamental issues of international law, as well as, in this case, to passions that ran deep on both sides of the argument. As I wrote in the concluding paragraphs of the report, written on the breezy roof of the review team's guest house in Islamabad, 'One person's imperative can easily become another's imperialism', and the task of reconciling the two requires careful negotiation and discussion and patient advocacy, based on good quality information and great sensitivity. In the heat of a humanitarian crisis, there isn't always the luxury of the time or accurate data that would enable such an approach. Sadly, the team felt that the UN's response to the Pakistan floods of 2007 had not adequately demonstrated this careful and sensitive approach.

Our further recommendations, made both in Pakistan and in person at the UN headquarters and based on what we had seen of the UN in operation in Pakistan, included more ongoing investment in the new cooperation structures; simpler UN and Cluster decision-making processes; greater clarity around the authority and resourcing of UNOCHA's role as the coordinator and convener of the UN system in time of emergency; and better sharing of information between governments and the UN, and between the UN organizations themselves inter se.

I was nervous that our report would not go down well in New York, but the letter I received from John Holmes, head of UNOCHA, spoke of a 'high-quality report while working to a very tight deadline and under difficult conditions … not least the complex political context'. The report was 'incisive and bold', the presentation of the findings in Pakistan, New York and Geneva 'masterful', and the findings were 'sensitive to the political setting and objective' and likely to attract 'broad support [which would be] extremely helpful as we think about the future direction of the humanitarian reforms and about how we work more generally'.

Later, and back at the British Red Cross, I went out to Indonesia, followed by the Maldives, to hand over completed houses to their new owners. Accompanied by Mark Astarita, who as fundraising director had done so much to make our projects achievable, I flew into Calang in the south-west of Indonesia's Aceh province, to see the 1,930 houses we had built, their red roofs clearly visible from our six-seater plane as we came in to land at Teunom. This was one of Aceh's worst-hit areas, with over 45 per cent of the houses flattened by the waves as they rolled in across the plain. In a moving little ceremony I handed the keys to Idris, the new owner of the last house to be built: he had lost his wife and two children and the fishing boat that was his livelihood, but he didn't want to go back to sea, preferring instead to scratch a living from a small patch of land nearby.

More of our houses had been built nearby, in a small riverside community hidden in the forest – we always aimed to work in hard-to-access areas where the needs were greatest. Here, the level of the water in the river was much higher than it had been before the tsunami, and floods were much more of a risk, so we had built all our houses on solid reinforced concrete pillars – all of them to a high standard of sturdy design and finish, earthquake-proof (in response to President Clinton's plea to 'build back better') and painted in pretty pastel colours. We met a mother and daughter who had both lost their husbands, and heard from our driver, who was from this community and who had had to walk for two weeks from the college where he had been studying, through the devastation of the tsunami, to reach his parents, only to find that they had both drowned.

The visit finished with another ceremony, this time to hand over the keys of the 100,000th house to be rebuilt after the tsunami (one of ours) to Pak Kuntoro, head of the Government's Aceh reconstruction agency. This was a great tribute to the British Red Cross team and its leader, Gabriel Constantine, whose houses Kuntoro said were the best he had seen. At our completion party that night, in an open-sided shelter in a jungle clearing, with the monsoon rain falling out of the sky around us, I paid tribute to Gabriel and our Philippino construction team, and had great pleasure in presenting him with a Red Cross 'Badge of Honour for Distinguished Service'.

My last words for the many local people who joined us at the party were: 'We can't fill the gap in your lives left by the death of your loved ones, but we will always carry in our hearts the memory of the people of Teunom, and we hope you will hold us in your hearts, too, and the friendships we have made with the houses we have built.'

As the rain tipped down, everyone gathered together to dance and sing along to the local superstar Rafli, who had risen from his sick bed with dengue fever to be there. The worries for us of the last three years, and the sadness of the locals, slipped away with the music.

Then it was home via the Maldives, to assess progress there on building 466 houses on five remote islands in the south of the 800-mile chain of tiny islands that make up the archipelago. No fewer than ten government ministers turned up for the meeting in the capital Malé to discuss progress; thankfully there was much to report, with the work on four islands complete and only Vilhufushi outstanding, awaiting completion of the government's ambitious project to triple the size of the island and raise it a metre in height, using coral sand dredged from a nearby reef.

After a late-night meeting with our buzzy team of 'community mobilizers', recruited to work on the islands to help with liaison, communication and advice to local people, we awoke the next morning to high winds and storm warnings, making the six-hour speedboat trip to Vilhufushi (uncomfortable at the best of times) totally unsafe. We hired an air taxi instead and flew through the storm, flying over the doughnut shape of the island, its original green core now surrounded by a huge ring of white coral sand, and landed inside the new harbour, narrowly missing the harbour wall.

In lashing rain we headed to a small hut for a briefing from the contractors, who had been slow bringing in labour and materials and were now running late. This was a very tough assignment, with literally every nail and brick having to be brought in by sea, and we couldn't afford things to slip much further. The living conditions were tough, too, with several hundred men on site from several different countries, no home comforts and nothing to do in the evenings. It all felt pretty grim, particularly after the celebrations in Indonesia, but work had started on every one of our 250 houses, and I was impressed with the plans for stepping up the pace whilst maintaining strict quality control.

Meanwhile, the former inhabitants were living as increasingly unwelcome visitors on the neighbouring island of Buruni and returned every few weeks with a barrage of questions and issues to discuss – When will the houses be ready? What colour will the walls be? Where will I smoke my fish? Can I have an extra bedroom? Can I live near my friend? Why aren't the windows bigger? Each one had to be answered carefully and sensitively, being accommodating where possible but avoiding dangerous cost overruns and recognizing that the people would be returning to what was effectively a new island, where they would be living much closer together than before and learning to cope with quite sophisticated power plants and sewage treatment systems that would be completely new to them.

Our team, supported by their colleagues in London, was doing a fantastic job in extremely challenging circumstances – but we were all going to be mighty relieved when the job was done.

I flew home just in time for Christmas – and the news that we were going to smash the Tesco Charity of the Year record with a cool £4.4m raised for work in the UK, over £1m more than the previous best. It had been a good year.

Chapter 9

Change and Challenges, 2008

China and the Olympics – Buckingham Palace in the rain –
Financial crash

We were in a good place, having well and truly recovered from the deficit, and were now moving forwards from a position of strength.

We were also busy promoting our capacity for helping to deal with emergencies to central and local authorities and to the emergency services, emphasizing that we had trained volunteers and staff, and ambulances and all-terrain vehicles, in every county and borough. All over the country, local 'resilience fora' were being set up by local authorities to coordinate the response to emergencies, and we were usually invited to join, both in our own right and often as representatives of the voluntary sector as a whole. We welcomed this opportunity and set out to be seen as convener and coordinator of the sector – which was regarded by the statutory services as fragmented and hard to engage with.

We still saw the provision of first aid cover at events large and small as a core part of our operational brand for emergencies, and I was always delighted to hear accounts of lives saved or of new and bigger duties being undertaken. We were subsidizing the activity, of course, because the 'market' (dominated as it was by St John and, increasingly, income-hungry NHS ambulance crews) rarely allowed us to charge the full cost, but the work kept skills fresh and teams sharp – and the Red Cross visible to the general public. Pop concerts and marathons were proliferating and brought us new opportunities to bid, and we responded with new equipment and vehicles and an enhanced set of standards for our teams to aspire to. Very often it was our first aid volunteers who filled the rotas for fire and emergency support services (many of them part-funded from the Tesco appeal) to help families caught up in the tragedy of a domestic fire; and they were frequently first on the scene at any major fire or flooding incident – the victims of these tragedies often ended up as Red Cross volunteers themselves.

I loved the first aiders' enthusiasm and often quite humbling dedication, not to mention their considerable technical first aid expertise, slightly bizarrely highlighted this year in 'plastinated' form at Gunther von Hagen's Body Worlds exhibition at the O2, where real human bodies impregnated with special resins were used to form extraordinary tableaux to demonstrate the wonders of life and movement and, in our case, first aid. Our first aid training business was growing, too, having now been centralized and moved to Manchester, and to some extent we were able to use it to promote volunteering opportunities in the organization as a whole.

Also developing rapidly were our 'care in the home' services, again part-funded from the Tesco money, which provided additional practical and emotional support for people coping in their own homes in the early stages of a return from hospital or with some rapid-onset disability or illness. It often seemed extraordinary, the extent to which it was left to the voluntary sector to do this work and usually to pay for it out of general funds, with little apparent understanding by state budget-holders for community services that this was simply not a sustainable model.

Our work with refugees and asylum-seekers was becoming ever more important, with new arrivals this year from Iraq in particular, and the continuation of our campaign to stop asylum seekers becoming destitute whilst waiting for their status to be determined. As part of this campaign I visited two like-minded national societies, Norway and Sweden, with Margaret Lally, who ran the UK service development team, to look particularly at their work with refugees and asylum-seekers; we were impressed with their central role and empathetic approach, not to mention the level of funding they got from their governments – our own government was cutting back its support to organizations like the Refugee Council, and we were increasingly having to step in to fill the breach.

On the way back, we had a meeting with the International Olympic Committee (IOC) in Geneva, hoping to persuade them that British Red Cross volunteers could and should play a significant and preferably high-profile role in keeping spectators and visitors safe during the London Olympics. The IOC representatives listened politely, but it was clear that the 'five rings' Olympics branding was sacrosanct, and that even if the Red Cross were to handle first aid, for example, there would be no opportunity for the Red Cross emblem to be prominently visible. We had further meetings planned that year with the London organizing committee for the Games, and a visit to China to see what preparations they had made immediately prior to the Beijing Games – but it wasn't looking promising.

That February, I took our new international trustee, David Fall (who, as the British Ambassador in Thailand when the tsunami struck, had done a sterling job with his team in supporting British victims) to Sri Lanka. We visited the tsunami-affected areas in the north-east, where our work had mostly been about rebuilding livelihoods amongst communities badly damaged by flooding, but which was also only slowly recovering from several years of fighting between government forces and the Tamil Tigers – not to mention occasional raids by marauding elephants looking for food.

We met lots of villagers delighted with the help they had received, often just a few hundred dollars to help them get back on their feet. It didn't seem much, but it was enough to buy seeds, a goat or two, a new boat, a sewing machine or, in one case, a new seine net for a group of fishermen. The impact on the local economy as a whole, and on prospects for the future, was substantial. In one village, the locals had asked us to rebuild their Red Cross centre; in another, the school; in another, a group of young women was using the money to build a dress-making business; and in yet another, a small group making chilli powder – known as the Red-Hot Chilli Ladies. It was all very participative, with each community carefully mapping its needs and identifying those who needed the most help. All we then had to do was to provide the wherewithal.

The trip with David was part of a mini-campaign to help trustees develop a more in-depth understanding of our work 'on the ground', featuring a programme of visits for individual and small groups of Board members to services and projects in the UK and overseas accompanied by directors or senior staff, and a 'twinning' of Board members with individual directors. Our new strategy director, Kate Lee, also instituted a system of regular briefings on the papers for forthcoming Board meetings for those trustees who wanted them. This ran in parallel with the development of a more detailed monitoring and reporting system for keeping the trustees and the senior management team updated on progress. In all this, we were responding to calls across the sector for increased accountability, but the challenge was always to try and ensure that accountability was accompanied by an appropriate level of understanding of the challenges and issues, often beyond our control, on the part of those demanding it.

Another trustee, Terrence Collis, who was communications director at the Food Standards Agency, came with me to China, along with the director of our London Branch and our head of volunteering, to see how the Chinese Red Cross was involved in the Beijing Games.

It was a fascinating trip. The Chinese Red Cross is enormous, with 25m members, 6,000 full-time staff, and branches in every province and prefecture in the country. Its independence was pretty theoretical, with all core costs being met by the Government, but the dynamic Secretary-General (who rapidly became a friend), though herself linked in to the Communist Party leadership, saw clearly the need for the Society to generate some of its own independent programme funding. It was the country's main emergency response agency, the only provider of first aid training and blood donor recruitment, and a big provider of ambulance services.

With only a hundred days to go, preparations for the Games seemed well in hand, with vast and beautiful new domestic and international airline terminals, new road and rail systems, exciting venues, massive luxury hotels, plush 'villages' for the athletes, new water supply and drainage systems, and acres of tree planting and pretty flowers all completed. The role of the Chinese Red Cross had been agreed early on – they were to train all 150,000 Olympics volunteers in first aid skills, provide some trained volunteers themselves and have emergency response teams ready for deployment as required. This massive contribution was regarded with huge pride within the organization and had been rewarded with an agreement that every single volunteer at the Games would be wearing a red cross on their uniform. We were dazzled and inspired. If only …

The trip comprised briefings and meetings at the Red Cross national headquarters and Beijing Branch, and a tour of a couple of the Olympics stadia, followed by a flight south to Qingdao, the venue for all sailing events. It was hard to imagine how Poole, in four years' time, was going to compete with the massive construction of breakwaters, piers and pontoons that had gone on in preparation for the sailing, let alone the high-rise athletes' village that was to become a five-star Intercontinental Hotel after the event.

We were made incredibly welcome wherever we went, particularly in Qingdao, where we took an early Sunday morning stroll along the promenade and watched family groups flying their kites, playing badminton, doing tai-chi or collecting seaweed and mussels for lunch. We stopped to watch a community sing-song in a large tented pavilion and were soon dragged up on stage to perform ourselves, struggling embarrassedly through a bizarre medley of *Edelweiss* and *Auld Lang Syne* to tumultuous and completely undeserved applause.

We were all staggered by the pace of change in China and the sheer scale of commercial development in the big cities at least, not to mention the splendour of preparations for the Olympics. Could London ever compete?

But I was feeling restless and, looking back, this was probably the time when, after seven years in the job, I should have moved on. Although I still loved the Red Cross, and hated the idea of leaving an organization to which I was so deeply committed, I felt ready for a new challenge and hoped that I might find it in Geneva, as Secretary-General of the Federation. Markku Niskala, the incumbent, had decided to step down, and I was excited by the prospect of putting my ideas about global Red Cross organizational development into action. Several Movement chums were kind enough to encourage my ambition. But it was not to be, and the job went to former politician and Federation regional director Bekele Geleta from Ethiopia. I had breakfast with Bekele the day after his appointment, and he seemed as surprised about his appointment as everyone else. I pledged to work closely with him as, of course, I continued to do.

I felt tired and unsettled, though, and thought seriously about looking for another job. The chairman and colleagues on the senior management team urged me to stay, and we talked about ways in which I could give myself more time to concentrate on overall strategy and external engagement, rather than day-to-day management. Various options were looked at, mainly focussed around reducing the number of directors reporting directly to me, but I hated the idea of appointing someone else to line-manage either the functional or the UK territory directors and losing my relationship with close colleagues and friends. I had always felt that the senior management team needed to reflect both geographical and functional concerns and interests – and that meant eleven direct reports. Eventually, some months later, I opted to ask Margaret Lally, Director of UK Service Development, to take on the extremely difficult and sensitive job of acting as *'primus inter pares'* with the four territory directors, who would nevertheless remain on the senior management team.

That summer, my focus switched to fundraising. We had a lively and dynamic fundraising team, which raised shedloads of money on a regular basis and were always fun to be with. Highlight of the year was the annual Christmas 'pod' decorating competition – our open plan offices were arranged in 'pods' of four or five staff, and the fundraisers used to vie with each other at Christmas to produce the most outrageous display, complete with themed fancy dress, glitter, snow and streamers galore, mini-pantomimes and musicals, and outrageous sketches. Mark Astarita and I were required to spend an enjoyable hour or so choosing the winner of the 'Golden Stuffed Turkey Award', which usually went to the pod that had offered us the best bribe in the shape of cake, alcohol or chocolate.

Red Cross Week in early May was another highlight, as we continued to try and raise the elusive £1m through street collections. The key was clearly 'bums on streets', as we tried, year after year, to get everyone out collecting, supported by a comms and social media blitz in our shops and elsewhere in the run up to our Week. I always enjoyed collecting – the challenge of raising a smile and preferably a donation from the most obdurate 'eyes down' commuters (who would sometimes veer yards out of their way to avoid a collector) was one that appealed to me, and colleagues in UK Office mostly joined in what was intended to be a fun few days, with cake bakes, sponsored activities of one sort and another in the office and a competition to find the best UK Office 'tin-rattler'. This was usually won by Naeem Khan, a member of the Comms team who, we were convinced, must have been a bank robber in a former existence, so extraordinary were his totals. I had always believed that successful fundraising at its heart was not just about going after big sums, but rather looking out for the pennies and the pounds – and they all add up.

It must have been about this time that the custom developed of organizing a 'village fete' in the square behind the office to raise money, complete with tombola, bottle and cake stalls and a rather good little staff band, whose professional performance I always managed to ruin with a solo spot, accompanied by members of an SMT backing group. This year, too, I was put in the stocks for a bout of wet sponge-hurling. But somehow, though we inched nearer, the magic million number eluded us for another year.

We had been awarded one of the fundraising 'season's' big set piece events, the Grosvenor House Art and Antiques Fair (organized by Maria Shammas), which raised over £1m for our work in Darfur. On one Lot, where there was in fact nothing to buy, I simply described the violence in the region and made an emotional appeal for straight donations. Our generous supporters coughed up nearly £250,000 – and then one guest offered to double it. I welled up at this amazing gesture.

I also had the privilege during the week of being guest of honour at Jersey's Liberation Day celebrations, when the Channel Islands remember the day the Red Cross ship *Vega* brought them their first fresh food after four years of Nazi occupation. This year, they were also celebrating the Island's amazing *Side by Side* campaign, which had raised over £3m for our tsunami recovery work in Sri Lanka, with a marvellous series of concerts on the harbour wall.

It was just as well that our fundraisers were in good form; these were troubled times in the financial markets, as the global effects of the sub-prime mortgage crisis in America became clearer. Undaunted, our fundraising went from strength to strength, with special appeals for the Sichuan earthquake in China, for the terrible flooding in Myanmar and South Africa, and for recovery work after wide-scale post-election rioting in Kenya all running at the same time and generating extra funds now – and names and addresses we could tap (in those pre-GDPR days) for help with future efforts.

We had 235,000 regular givers signed up at this stage, worth over £23m each year, and every appeal enabled us to add a few more to the list, chasing Oxfam's total of 600,000. We were doing record amounts of door-to-door and face-to-face street fundraising, too, as Mark Astarita's annual 'Scores on the Doors' results promotions showed, and he and I spent a fascinating afternoon in Moorgate trying our hand at this difficult art. In three hours of wearing our brightest smiles and giving our cheeriest greetings, neither of us signed up a single donor.

Former British
Red Cross offices
in Grosvenor
Crescent.

(L to R) John Gray
(fundraiser), Mike Whitlam
(CEO), Lady Limerick
(Chair of Trustees) at the
launch of the Simple Truth
Appeal, 1991.

PAs Sheila Ashbourn and
Paula Collier, 2001

Earthquake damage,
Gujarat, India, 2001.

Cyclone shelter,
India, 2001.

Great North Run, 2005

Volunteers being briefed.

First Aid facility.

Inside the First Aid tent.

Nelson Mandela and ICRC delegate on Robben Island, London 2003.

Chair of Trustees John McClure, 2001–2006.

Baghdad, 2003
– wrecked ICRC
vehicle.

Temporary camp
beside a road in
Bam, Iran.

The remains
of the Citadel
at Bam, 2004.

Aceh, Indonesia after the 2004 tsunami.

The remains of Romaini's island village, just off the coast of Aceh, 2005.

Romaini's new house and shop, 2007.

Balakot, Kashmir, just after the earthquake in 2005.

ICRC supply convoy, Kashmir.

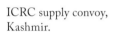

Kashmir – ruined hillside hamlet.

ICRC supply helicopter in the hills of Kashmir.

Auld Lang Syne farewell in Kashmir.

Distribution of building materials, Kashmir.

Senior management team, 2006.

James Cochrane,
Chair of Trustees,
2007–2012.

Red Cross flood rescue vehicle, UK floods, 2007.

Sixty Land Rovers at Buckingham Palace, 2008.

I owe my life, saved by a Red Cross first aid volunteer – Maddie Sparrow and family.

Homeless family, Gaza, 2009.

Palestine Red Crescent leader Younis al Qatib in front of bombed-out Red Crescent building, 2009.

Red Cross emergency response team, Haiti, 2010.

Red Cross earthquake relief camp, Haiti, 2010.

Dzud relief yurt, Mongolia, 2010.

A Mongolian toast – in fermented mare's milk.

Queen's Badge of
Honour, 2013.

Author's family
with HRH Prince
of Wales, 2013.

Buckingham Palace
Garden Party, 2014,
author with the
Prince and David
Bernstein, Chair of
Trustees.

Damascus, Syria, burning, 2013.

Syrian Arab Red Crescent volunteers loading supplies, 2013.

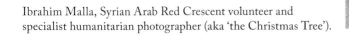

Ibrahim Malla, Syrian Arab Red Crescent volunteer and specialist humanitarian photographer (aka 'the Christmas Tree').

Author as 'Morecambe', with Angela Rippon, National Assembly, 2013.

'This must have been your worst afternoon ever,' I remarked to the Team Leader as I handed back my clipboard.

He pushed his jaunty little cap back on his head:

'Well, no actually – I've signed up ten, and Gill over there [who to show her dedication even had a red cross tattooed on her ankle] has a dozen. You've just got to have the knack.'

We felt suitably chastened as we trailed back to the office.

The shops were doing well, too, generating £22m after a period in the doldrums, a nationwide programme of rebranding and improvement and the closure of the less successful performers. I always tried to visit the local Red Cross shop on my visits to our work around the UK, loved to see the donated goods all neatly displayed and enjoyed the cheery atmosphere created by the manager and volunteers. I usually returned home laden with unnecessary purchases.

It was a wet summer, though, which rather depressed the spirits of the first aid teams from all over Europe who descended on Liverpool for the four-yearly European First Aid Competition. We had laid on a testing set of accident and injury scenarios, against which the teams were to test their skills in a large park, with impressive amounts of fake blood oozing from realistic-looking gashes on the bodies of our 'casualty simulation' volunteers, whilst ghastly broken bones protruded from a dozen injured limbs. But on the day it poured with rain, as bedraggled teams plodded around the course, a gaudy array of brightly-coloured national uniforms hidden under plastic ponchos, whilst shivering 'casualties' risked adding real exposure and pneumonia to the list of ailments the teams were supposed to look out for. The city of the Beatles gave them a good time, though, with a lively awards ceremony and dance to warm them all up.

The sun was shining again in June, however, and we all started to look forward to a very rare highlight indeed – a Buckingham Palace Garden Party solely for the Red Cross. With Her Majesty the Queen as our Patron, the Prince of Wales as our President and Princess Alexandra as a very loyal and regular supporter, we enjoyed generous Royal patronage, and it was my own rather cheeky request to Prince Charles one day that had resulted in this particular treat. With room for 7,500 guests, we would have ample opportunity to thank our wonderful volunteers and donors, as well as numerous corporate supporters and friends in other national societies, and to entertain some of the people we had been helping. We had been planning the day for nine months or more, greatly encouraged by major sponsors Land Rover, who had offered us no fewer than sixty brand new vehicles to celebrate their sixtieth birthday. We hoped to make the front pages the following day with an iconic photo, taken by helicopter, of the all-white vehicles drawn up around a red carpet in the shape of a red cross in the courtyard of the Palace. A Red Arrows flyover, in 'red cross' formation, was to be the dramatic finale of the afternoon.

I woke that morning to the sound of rain falling from the sky and wasted no time in contacting the event mastermind , Mark Astarita.

'Mark, we need plastic ponchos, thousands of them.'

'Already on it,' he said.

There was no other wet weather plan, and nowhere else to go.

As the morning wore on, and the rain poured down, our overseas guests were flying in, and from all over the country volunteers and supporters, many of their names drawn at random from our database, descended on London – and the phones started ringing.

'Yes,' we explained, 'the party is still going ahead, and no, it will not be moved inside. Just come in your finery, bring a brolly and hope for the best.'

As I arrived at the Palace, lines of drenched invitees were queuing at the gates waiting to be admitted, as cheery policemen scrutinised their tickets, dished out see-through plastic ponchos and ushered them through to the gardens. Inside, small groups gathered around tables, dainty cakes and sandwiches afloat on wilting cardboard plates, and clutched warming cups of tea. Neither the helicopter nor the Red Arrows could take off, so bang went our iconic front-page photos; the Queen could only watch from an upstairs window with the corgis; and the Prince, the Duchess of Cornwall and Princess Alexandra dutifully trudged round shaking hands with our pre-arranged groups of 'special guests' sheltering under large umbrellas.

But of course, as ever on such occasions, the weather seemed to bother no one. Everyone had come for a great day out in a spectacular setting and they were determined to enjoy it in Red Cross style – we did disasters and crises all day long; who cared about a bit of rain? As the gardens emptied at the end of the afternoon, I spotted in the distance an elderly lady pushing her mother in a wheelchair perilously close to the muddy edge of the lake, and raced across to rescue them.

'Oh, Nick,' trilled the pusher, 'what a wonderful afternoon. Thank you so much for inviting us. We will never forget it, will we, Mum?'

'No, dear, we certainly won't,' came the imperious response from under a brolly. 'Now hurry up, or we'll miss our train.'

That evening, we hosted a glittering dinner at a London club for our overseas guests, most of whom had nipped back to their hotels first to dry out. As I took the mic around the room after dinner, introducing guests and inviting them to say a few words, it was clear that they too had had a great time. Buckingham Palace had worked its magic, and as for the weather, well, what can you expect from an English summer?

The Federation's Governing Board in September debated a somewhat vexed topic for the Red Cross – the question of the extent to which it was appropriate for an organization that listed impartiality and neutrality amongst its fundamental principles to engage in activities or campaigns aimed at shifting public and political opinion on specific issues, or on behalf of particular groups of people in need. There were still some in the Movement who argued that speaking out publicly was not our job and that it would put in jeopardy our unique ability to work with and help all sides in a conflict. Others, whilst accepting that great care was needed during a conflict, felt that in 'normal times' it was absolutely vital for the Red Cross to use its voice as well as its actions, backed by years of experience and expertise, on behalf of people in need.

This was certainly the conclusion we were coming to in the British Red Cross, with a new 'advocacy' policy already in draft, and we were pleased that, in spite of the nervousness, we were not alone in believing that the Red Cross had something to say, a duty to say it and a belief that people would listen.

Because Heli was being treated for breast cancer around this time, I was making only short overseas trips at this point, one to Jamaica (another former British Red Cross branch) to make a speech at the celebrations marking their 60th birthday, and then on to an existing branch, Turks and Caicos, to see what we could do to help in the aftermath of Tropical Storm Hanna and Hurricane Ike.

In Turks and Caicos, where they still had no mains water or electricity one month after the hurricane, I spent a day driving around the island (in a new Land Rover, part of the company's generous birthday gift to the

Red Cross) with Cynthia, the formidable grande dame of the local Red Cross. We saw hardly a house left untouched by the 150mph winds. Many, particularly the fragile illegal shacks of a group of Haitian migrants, were completely flattened and bore the Government's pink cross mark, to denote that they were to be pulled down and their inhabitants rehoused.

As we drove around, the bright sun and tranquil turquoise sea contrasted jarringly with the sad piles of 'Ike debris', the forlorn tents and flapping tarpaulins, the tipping telegraph poles and trees stripped of leaves and leaning at crazy angles. We talked to Henry, a garbage collector, sitting on an armchair in the awning of his tent. His family had gone to his sister's house, leaving him to guard what was left. There wasn't much, he had no insurance and, as he gazed into the distance, it was clear that he had no idea what, if anything, was to be done for him. As I walked away I stooped to pick up a tattered book lying in the sand – it was *Chantes d'Esperance ('Songs of Hope')*.

And there was a little, hope that is. I attended and spoke briefly at a Government-hosted event that evening with the local Chamber of Commerce, where the Governor and two ministers outlined their optimistic-sounding recovery plans. There was little or nothing, though, for the uninsured or those Haitian migrants, and my remarks sparked what I hoped would be a gentle but persistent campaign of humanitarian advocacy on their behalf by Cynthia and her friends. As it was, the Red Cross Thrift Shop on the island was their only source of assistance, and I saw once again the fragility of small islands against the might of the weather, and the vital role that even a small group of Red Cross volunteers could play in bringing help and comfort to the most vulnerable.

The second brief visit was to South Africa with Kate Lee, to conduct a short review of our long-term partnership with South African Red Cross (SARCS), and visit a pilot HIV-AIDS project in KwaZulu-Natal funded by one of our major donors. The Secretary-General, Mandisa, was one of the great 'warriors' of the Red Cross Movement, a passionate speaker with a bubbling sense of humour, and it was always exciting and inspiring to spend time with her. She had stepped down as President of SARCS in order to lead the Society in troubled financial times as SG, and I was determined to give her as much support as possible. The problem was that, for all our many years of supporting the organization, it had never shown signs of becoming self-financing, and now the businessman donor, who was pouring large amounts of money into Kwa-Zulu Natal, was insisting upon a promise of sustainability for his project within three years – which on projections at the time would soon dwarf the rest of SARCS' work.

As I had found so often before, even brilliant commercial minds found it difficult to comprehend the economic practicalities and challenges of fundraising; and in this case,the donor refused to sanction a small portion of his grant going to fund a dedicated fundraiser post for the project. The upshot was that we had to shoulder the fundraising burden ourselves, and thereafter Mark Astarita and his team were effectively in charge of raising money both in the UK and South Africa.

South Africa was an early demonstration of what a challenge I had taken on, leading the Federation's national society development project. National societies in the north were literally streets ahead of most of their southern counterparts in terms of fundraising, an art (or a science, depending on your point of view) which, though by no means impossible for a small charity in a developing country, was nevertheless much harder and required committed investment and expertise from outside before it stood a chance of replacing northern generosity as the main or even a substantial source of income. For a couple of years now Mark had been inviting our overseas partners to his annual fundraisers' 'skill share' conference, astonishingly the first time that any concerted effort had been made in the Movement to spread these skills around, and South Africa (where the potential was considerable) would prove a good testing ground.

By this time, the global financial crisis was in full flow with the collapse of Lehman Brothers in the States, and our own financial position, though more than secure for now, was by no means so certain for the future. We set a cautious budget for 2009, and wondered what the impact might be on our next five-year plan, work on which was progressing well.

I made one further quick overseas trip in 2008, to Yemen as vice-chairman of Dr Hany's 'Humanitarian Forum' initiative to build voluntary sector capacity in Muslim countries, and attended one more external engagement, to Wales to review the performance of the Welsh Assembly Government as part of a small team set up by Gus O'Donnell, head of the Civil Service. Both, in their very different ways, were extremely moving.

In Sana'a, capital of Yemen and one of the oldest continuously-inhabited cities in the world, we held a conference of voluntary organizations eager to learn and desperate to grow during what was a relatively peaceful period in the country's troubled history. At night, a group of us roamed the labyrinthine Old City, with its many-storeyed mud brick tower-houses decorated with extraordinary geometric patterns, whilst during the day we spoke of government restrictions and best volunteer-management practices and fundraising, and (weirdly) extolled the virtues of the Charity Commission.

In Wales, the Performance Review Group, comprising an academic, a senior civil servant and me, toured the principality for a fortnight, roamed the corridors of the Welsh Assembly, met Rhodri Morgan and his ministers and interviewed anyone who would talk to us about the ten-year-old Welsh Assembly Government. We found, to our surprise after the close-call referendum that led to its creation, a significant degree of enthusiasm, and a fetching modesty about the scale of their substantial achievements. It emerged during our research that they had all been so nervous of failing, in the light of the referendum result, that they had deliberately pursued a kind of 'under-the-radar', low-profile approach that had in fact served them well. They still struggled to be heard in Westminster, but we were delighted to commend their achievements in our final report, and encouraged them to take full credit for what they had done.

Chapter 10

Saving Lives Changing Lives, 2009

A new strategy – Speaking up and speaking out –
Gaza – Bangladesh – Liberia and Sierra Leone

We spent a great deal of time in 2008 debating the new corporate strategy that was to replace *Across the World and Around the Corner* in 2010. The aim was to spend 2009 promoting it to the whole organization and externally so that by the end of the year it could form the basis of the annual planning process for 2010 onwards. These processes always seemed to involve huge amounts of time and effort in the Red Cross, partly because there were so many different strands of activity which had somehow to be knitted together into a coherent and manageable whole; partly because the organization rightly valued consultation and ownership, particularly at the local level; and partly because we all somehow felt a particular responsibility, it being 'The Red Cross', to get it right. It was all too easy to lose sight of the wood for the trees, and we tried to keep things 'light-touch'.

We had started with a brave attempt to look 10–15 years into the future and pick the key trends that would impact upon our work as, primarily, an emergency response organization. We could see that climate change and conflicts over resources would increase global vulnerabilities; that increasing urbanization would mean that natural disasters would affect far more people and have far greater impact, whilst global recession, unemployment and government spending cuts would hamper the effectiveness of response mechanisms; and finally, we foresaw an increase in global health crises like HIV/AIDS and pandemic diseases. Writing this in 2021, fifteen months into a global shutdown due to Covid-19, it is clear that, whilst we might have predicted the event, we certainly failed to predict the seriousness of its impact, and did nowhere near enough to prepare for it.

As a further piece of preparatory work, we commissioned Kate Lee and her Strategy team to carry out a thorough evaluation of *Across the*

World and Around the Corner. This was hampered by the fact that, in 2004 when the strategy had been produced, we lacked the systems to capture and quantify exactly what the Red Cross was doing at the local level; so, in 2009 we had no proper baseline against which performance and progress might be judged. Though it was some comfort that our improving data-collection and management systems meant that we were now able to measure just about everything, it was disappointing that we could not show exactly how far we had travelled in the five years – from an organization stuck in a dark and dusty old headquarters building, struggling to overcome a big financial deficit and an even bigger collapse in morale and confidence, newly and drastically restructured and still traumatized by the public relations disasters of Archer and the *Simple Truth*, 'banning Christmas' and Sangatte. We tended to beat ourselves up when things went wrong (or even when they went right) – I used to call it 'Red Crucifixion' – and I hoped that better data collection would help us redress that tendency.

Despite the lack of data in some areas, the Evaluation celebrated the 'significant achievements and major contributions' made by the British Red Cross over the past five years, and the 'major inroads' made into realizing our three main operational priorities in the UK: of enhancing emergency response capacity, short term crisis care and fundraising.

We had also clearly moved much closer to being the 'dynamic, modern and responsive organization' we wanted to become, and had increased fundraising income by an impressive 61 per cent (largely thanks to Mark Astarita's direct marketing efforts to increase regular giving). Brand recognition and media coverage had improved markedly, we were working more collaboratively both internally and externally and we had made positive strides towards becoming a 'learning organization'.

I always fretted that we could and should have done more, but it was good to hear one Board member (Angela Lamport, our Surrey President), comment:

When I originally did fundraising tin collections a few years back, people were attacking me about Christmas and what a rotten organization we were … and this year I just couldn't believe it. People were coming up to me and saying, 'Where would we be without the Red Cross?'

But we weren't complacent. The global financial crisis that had begun in the US in 2008 had already impacted every aspect of our work, both in terms of increasing need and in reducing the resources available to meet it, and the new strategy was written on the assumption that we might, at least in the short to medium term, have little or no additional funding available. We also recognized that we worked in a crowded UK charity market place, where competition for the donor pound was fierce and where the Press was increasingly assuming a critical role in holding charities to account for what they did and how they did it – and where any adverse media coverage could have an immediate impact on the bottom line. We set up a 'major expenditure panel' to review all spending and recommend cuts and cost-savings, and drafted a detailed contingency plan showing how and when we could make deeper cuts if and as our income was adversely affected.

Internationally, it was also clear that competition for funding was becoming intense, and that government funding departments like DFID were setting ever higher standards in terms of value for money. Operationally, too, there was a threat, since conflict situations were becoming ever more complex with the increasing involvement of 'non-state actors' (like Al Quaeda), whilst the growth of militant Islam was resulting in growing political polarization in some countries – and this put the lives of aid agency workers, often caught in the middle, at risk.

The final result of the whole year-long debate was the approval by the Trustees of a new strategy, *Saving Lives Changing Lives,* a title that sought to reflect a focus not just on the drama of the immediate response to emergencies and conflict, but also on the vital longer-term task of building capacity and resilience in individuals and communities to be able to stand up to shocks for themselves and recover from them more easily. This shift, not a sudden one, towards both preparedness and recovery, embraced not just our work on the ground in the UK and internationally, but also organizationally a sharper focus on the very nature of vulnerability, advocacy on behalf of vulnerable groups, risk management, the volunteer experience and collaboration with other organizations.

Our recently enunciated organizational values – 'inclusive, compassionate, courageous and dynamic' – had proved to be a thought-provoking mirror in which to see ourselves, and the new strategy was a first step in breathing life into them, as we began to understand better the behaviours which those values implied. Inclusion, for example, implied not just a push for greater diversity, but also doing things in partnership with people and organizations; compassion meant real comprehension of the issues people faced; courage meant taking decisions or saying things that were right, even if they were unpopular; dynamism meant growing and learning at every stage and in every area of our work.

We set ourselves four service delivery priorities, with each of them covering both UK and international work, and four 'enabling' priorities (covering human resources, promotion, fundraising, and organisational development), with clear measures and targets for each.

As far as delivery was concerned, emergency response was still our top priority, with an emphasis on our core expertise in logistics, mass sanitation, shelter and cash/household economic security (an area where we were rapidly becoming globally-acknowledged leaders), and an acknowledgement that there were many disasters that never hit the headlines but where Red Cross assistance was also needed. Next as a priority came resilience, which included the promotion and development of first aid skills, as well as disaster-preparedness training and projects and recognition of the centrality of humanitarian principles as a way to spur the involvement of young people.

In health and social care, vulnerability was the key concept, with a commitment to grow our short-term care in the home services both in number and in depth, by including strands around advocacy and signposting to other agencies. Finally came a renewed commitment to support the Movement through the sharing of expertise and resources – this was unusual at a time when the stronger and richer national societies were becoming less and less inclined to support the Federation and the ICRC as a whole, and ever more inclined to work bilaterally or even unilaterally.

This was a very ambitious agenda, looking back, with several new or newish strands of work which would require extra resources and time to bed in, and achievement of the four 'enabling priorities' would be vital to our success. At the top came our volunteers and staff, recognizing that the Red Cross, like every great organization, has to be all about people. We wanted to make volunteering in the Red Cross the 'best experience that money couldn't buy', and to make the Red Cross the kind of organization that everyone wanted to work in. As early indicators that we meant what we said, we launched a talent management programme for young 'high flyers', and a nationwide award scheme for innovative new programmes, leading up to the presentation of 'Excellence Awards' at the national assembly as the prelude to rolling out some of the new ideas across the country.

Another key part of the new strategy was to invest more in positioning and promotion – not only to attract more financial support, but also as a means of attracting more volunteers, and making sure that people in need knew what help we had to offer and how to access it. The organization had accepted advocacy for change as a key weapon in our armoury of help for vulnerable people, though it would take a while yet for everyone to become comfortable with the sometimes very uncomfortable experience of 'speaking up and speaking out' on controversial issues. The Federation had gone a bit further, calling its own new ten-year strategy *Saving Lives Changing Minds*, but we expressed doubts about this, sceptical at the feasibility of promoting global messages from Geneva that would resonate in every country, and fearful that they might conflict with national messaging or politics.

We were full of confidence and belief in ourselves and what we had achieved over the previous five years, and the enthusiastic response to the proposals from volunteers and staff when we launched them at the National Assembly and then took them out to a dozen or more 'roadshows' all over the country was a great tonic. I went on every one of those roadshows, leading a varying presentation team of directors and trustees each time, and loved every minute. I was never happier than when out in the field, in the UK or overseas, feeling the passion, dedication and commitment of 'our people'; it made every late working evening and busy weekend worthwhile.

In the midst of all the planning activity we launched three new appeals in support of sister national societies, one for the Italian Red Cross response to the L'Aquila earthquake, and another for the Australian Red Cross and its work after the bushfires in the south-east of the country. I launched the latter at a raucous Aussie Club for expats in London with the Australian High Commissioner, John Dauth, who was so enthused by the partnership that he later became a trustee. The third appeal was more problematic, involving as it did the destruction wrought in Gaza following three weeks of fighting between Palestinian paramilitary groups and the Israeli Defence Forces, after Israel entered the territory in response to Hamas rocket attacks on Israel and allegations of arms smuggling into the Gaza strip.

After the Israeli Operation Cast Lead, there were allegations of indiscriminate attacks on civilians and civilian homes and infrastructure by the IDF, and there was a humanitarian crisis in the densely populated and impoverished strip of land that is Gaza. Well over a thousand people lost their lives, most of them said to be civilians and overwhelmingly Palestinian. We launched our appeal early in the New Year, closely followed by the DEC, whose appeal the BBC controversially refused to promote because it failed to mention the (comparatively minor) Israeli losses. Veteran Labour politician Tony Benn came to the rescue in a masterly interview with John Humphrys on the BBC *Today* programme, in which he insisted on giving out the full details of the Appeal, in spite of Humphrys' half-hearted attempts to stop him.

I travelled to Palestine via Israel in early February, one month after the end of the fighting, mainly to do a peak-time interview with ITN on the spot. It was a grim trip. I was met on the tarmac at Tel Aviv by a security officer, who whisked me off for questioning about my passport (stamped, of course, in several Muslim countries) and the purpose of my visit. I then drove through the Israeli security 'fence' to Ramallah, where I met up with my old friend Younis al Khatib, President of the Palestine Red Crescent. The ICRC had been able to arrange for Younis to go to Gaza with me (his first visit since the start of the fighting) in an ICRC vehicle, and we drove together to the heavily fortified Erez crossing, then the only access point.

It appeared that we were not welcome. Younis was ordered out of the vehicle and required to enter via a foot tunnel. Our ICRC colleague protested, to no avail, whereupon I got out of the car and made to accompany Younis on foot. The border guards immediately trained their weapons on me and ordered me back into the vehicle, which was then directed to an enclosed area, where we had to get out whilst a lengthy search was conducted before we were allowed to resume our trip.

Inside Gaza the destruction was substantial. There was rubble everywhere, and the headquarters of the Palestine Red Crescent and its large Al Quds Hospital had both been largely destroyed by shells sometimes, it appeared, packed with phosphorus. We stopped and talked to families crouched in the shattered mess of their houses and heard their tales of loss and misery, and listened to surviving members of the extended Saloumi family, who described houses and shelters bombed, a brother run over by a tank and a mother decapitated by a shell while hugging her daughter at her side. It was estimated that 10,000 houses would have to be rebuilt, but no building materials were being allowed in, and we saw dozens of trucks smashed and lying on their sides, Israeli tank tracks still visible in the sand around them.

My interview was an unusually outspoken one but, such were the political sensitivities, much of it was cut, and I returned home despairing at any prospect of peace for the tortured souls on all sides in the Middle East.

We spent a lot of time in 2009, following the adoption of our *Saving Lives* strategy, looking again at the question of whether our management structures needed to change in order to support the organization's continued and successful growth, and to reflect our new objectives around 'humanitarian advocacy' and support to the Movement. As has already been noted, the senior management team was quite large, and it was generally agreed (including by our external consultants) that if I was to spend more time facing outwards I would have to do less day-to-day management.

Whilst excited by the idea that the balance of my job would change, I was also nervous, and quite sad. I had a lovely, loyal and cohesive team, and I hated the idea that our strong and friendly spirit might somehow become diluted or threatened by significant structural changes. My instinct was always that people (and their passions) and relationships were far more important than structures and wiring diagrams and crude attempts to judge efficiency, so I was wary of some of the more radical options put forward.

What was eventually agreed with the trustees was that the six operational divisions – UK service development, the four territories and international – would together form a semi-separate unit under a new 'Director of Operations', whilst Kate Lee as Director of Strategy and Corporate Performance would have a much more hands-on role and authority, effectively as my deputy, to manage the implementation of our new strategy and to run my desk whenever I was away. Nevertheless, all the directors of the original operational divisions, whilst reporting to a new colleague, would continue as full members of and attend all senior management meetings, thereby ensuring that we remained together as a team and fully plugged in at all times to the operational heart and reality of our work on the ground.

It was amusing to hear an echo of this thinking at the Federation Governing Board meeting in Paris that May, when the French Foreign Minister Bernard Kouchner (founder of Médecins sans Frontières and a former Red Crosser) chided us all for becoming 'too professional, and thus lacking in passion and idealism'. It is a difficult balance to get right, and having been myself part of a new generation of career charity managers who came into the sector in the 1980s, I could see both sides of the argument – but for me, passion always came first.

I went virtually straight from Paris to Bangladesh with our new Finance Director Rohan Hewavisenti, to inspect a recovery programme we had funded in the wake of Cyclone Sidr in 2007, and to advise (at the request of the Bangladesh Red Crescent leadership) on governance/management relations – problematic at that time in Bangladesh because there was little or no separation of function between the two.

At the start of our £2m programme we had looked for the most vulnerable victims of the cyclone and had identified a large fishing community squatting on a beach on the seaward side of a protective embankment. They had no land, no shelter, no hope. Our first task was to find them some land; with a population of 150m, set to grow to 230m by 2030, and a landmass that was slowly disappearing under water due to the effects of climate change, land in Bangladesh was precious, and its ownership often hotly contested. We found some pockets of *khas* (or 'royal') common land, but every time we stuck a flag on it, a local 'landowner' would appear to make a rival claim. This turned into a Robin Hood-type struggle, complete with pantomime baddies, saintly local government officials, benign judges and flash mobs of local villagers rushing to occupy every inch of threatened land. Remarkably, we ended up with 784 small plots and were able to hand tokens of ownership to the landless fishing families.

In close collaboration with the families, our team had designed simple wood and corrugated iron shelters strong enough to withstand winds up to 150mph, and then given each family a small grant of £300 and some business counselling/training to enable them to develop an existing small business or start a new one. The aim was to create a more diverse local economy and to build resilience and independence. It was a wonderfully comprehensive programme, overseen by a 'New Awakening' local committee, who described to me how we had helped them achieve something that was beyond their wildest dreams. Was she happy, I asked one woman.

'Yes,' she said, uncertainly, 'but I do wish I had asked for two doors!'

Our other ongoing project in Bangladesh was about building disaster-preparedness capacity in eighty-five rural communities which were subject to a high risk of flooding. The starting point in each community was the setting up of a local inclusive and democratically elected committee to mobilize and organize the local effort. After some basic training, the committee would then organize a vulnerability assessment of their area to map hazards and identify the resources and equipment required to mitigate the risks. One big issue was the 2,000-odd cyclone shelters built (many of them by the British Red Cross) in the 1990s. Most of these large, round, two-storey, reinforced-concrete buildings had not been maintained and, although they still served a useful life-saving purpose and gave protection for dozens of families from the floods, they all needed substantial repair and proper facilities for women, children and people with disabilities. I discussed the issue with the in-country DFID team and the British High Commissioner over dinner, but none of us had ready answers for the financial and practical challenges.

The year ended, after a long string of conferences, and speeches both in the UK and overseas, with a long overdue visit to two of our partner national societies, Sierra Leone and Liberia. I had become very fond of these two small West African countries, both recovering slowly and with determination from brutal civil wars and both blessed with well-led Red Cross societies which had greatly valued our (quite generous) support over several years, listened to and implemented the advice we had given them and made good use of every penny they had received. I felt very proud of the contribution we had made.

Unfortunately, both countries shared the distinction of having just about the worst roads in the world – mile upon mile of mud and potholes at this time of year, making internal trade extremely difficult and economic development problematic. Only a year after major back surgery, it was also a slightly nerve-racking trip for me as we bucketed around both countries in Toyota Landcruisers or Land Rovers at the height of the rainy season.

Over fourteen years of conflict (1989–2003) had totally destroyed Liberia's infrastructure, and many people had fled to the capital Monrovia, which remained in Government hands, to escape the fighting. One third of an estimated population of 3m now lived there, many of them in frightful slum accommodation with little or no access to sanitation, safe water or health facilities. The global financial crisis had reduced remittances from Liberians with jobs overseas, and a 50 per cent drop in the price of rubber had resulted in an official unemployment rate of 85 per cent; some massive social problems and community violence to add to the country's economic woes. In Monrovia there were posters everywhere – 'Real Men Don't Rape' and 'She Could Be YOUR Mother'.

Liberia was one of the four 'ONS' in the '8NS Initiative', a project which we had suggested to a group of national societies as a means of learning together what worked in terms of organizational development. Four developing societies were to meet regularly with their four partner 'PNS' to share plans, successes and failures, and to exchange notes – so this was a timely opportunity for me to see what Liberia was doing before a meeting of the whole 8NS group, which we were due to host in Windsor the following year.

My guide was another of my Red Cross heroines – Theresa Sherman, the Liberia Red Cross (LRC) President and formidable leader of the country's Women's Movement. We spent the first day jouncing along flooded tracks between small towns dotted around Monrovia, past countless trucks that had subsided into ditches, their axles smashed by the potholes and their crews banging hopelessly with spanners on the wheels, whilst the locals looked on and tried to sell them things. We met dozens of local volunteers and heard about their community health schemes (which we had funded).

Within earshot of our final destination, a tiny hamlet on the edge of a rubber forest, a log bridge over a stream collapsed as we drove across it, leaving the other three vehicles in our convoy on the other side. As we stood disconsolately in the pouring rain wondering what to do, the sound of singing filtered through the trees, and we were carried off for an ecstatic welcome from the local girls, who whooped and stamped around us as we ran for cover under the bamboo shelter they had erected for the occasion. Coconuts to drink from and generous homemade gifts followed, then a few speeches – then it was down the road in the evening gloom for the two-hour drive back to Monrovia.

After a quiet supper with Theresa, hearing her awful tales of the civil war – her house stripped at gunpoint, the secretarial college she owned ransacked five times, friends who had died or fled overseas – the next day was a complete contrast, spent with the management team talking me through their detailed quarterly reports for each department. I have always found it quite difficult to get excited about power point slides and spreadsheets filled with little boxes crammed with data; but the significance they attached to proof of the progress they were making, their deep concern about failures and shortcomings, and their transparency and willingness to be held accountable, were deeply impressive and very moving. They were mortified to have to reveal, right at the end of a seven-hour day of reports, that they were facing a substantial deficit, but this led to a useful discussion about core costs and a debate about community fundraising – one of my pet themes.

I had long been convinced that even the poorest of ONS could actually raise money for themselves, with some training, some support and some early investment; perhaps not much, but enough to help, and enough to enable them to feel that they weren't entirely reliant on handouts from other national societies. Part of the problem was that the Federation did little to help its poorer members with their fundraising challenges, and most PNS gave no thought to the topic even as they poured money in. Hoping to inspire them, I told them about the famous Macmillan Coffee Morning which, having been started by a group of friends in the 1980s, had now become an almost breathtakingly simple annual nationwide fundraising effort that brought people together for an hour or so one morning and raised millions. Slightly tongue-in-cheek, I told them how taken I had been on the previous day by the welcome dances that had greeted us everywhere we visited, and I suggested that maybe they could raise money in Liberia with a yearly 'Dance for Humanity'.

The final day in Liberia involved meetings with the ICRC and the Minister of Internal Affairs, who promised to take a Red Cross First Aid course himself as part of the local campaign to persuade all car drivers to learn the skills – starting with the Cabinet. Then we drove to a nearby rehabilitation centre for child soldiers, very similar to the one I had visited in neighbouring Sierra Leone a few years earlier. In the evening there was a formal dinner, with guests, speeches, gifts, and a spectacular local dance troupe. Then Daniel, the Secretary-General, stood up and, with a smile on his face, announced the arrival of the band and dancing.

'There's only one thing,' he said, looking at me. 'Our friend Nick set us a challenge yesterday, to raise money ourselves for the Liberia Red Cross. So tonight, if you want to dance, you'll have to pay!'

Hours later, the band was still playing, the dance floor was full, and they raised nearly $2,000 for the Red Cross. I had a tear in my eye as I said my goodnights in the early hours.

Before making another bone-shaking drive, to the border with Sierra Leone, we had one more engagement. Theresa Sherman had been to university with the President of the country, Ellen Johnson Sirleaf, the first elected female head of state in Africa, and she was determined that I should meet her and try to persuade her to invest more in disaster management, first aid training and support for the LRC's fledgling fundraising efforts. We had a great meeting, casual and full of laughter, and came away with promises of help with all the work we had mentioned – the President was even going to do the first aid course herself. She was to continue as President for another ten transformational years, receiving the Nobel Peace Prize in 2011 for her efforts to bring women into the peacekeeping process in her country.

Once over the border, with Emmanuel Tommy, the new, popular young Secretary-General of the Sierra Leone Red Cross, I was in for another four hours negotiating potholes and mud as we wound our way that evening through rain forest and rubber plantations, the gloom broken only by an occasional huddle of huts, hurricane lamps and waving children, as we scurried by in the rain. This was the main road from the border to Kenema, one of the largest cities in the country and the nearest to the border. When we finally reached journey's end, there was just time to stretch my stiff back and pour a bucket of cold water over my head before dinner with the Board – and more speeches.

I was woken early by a large black bird flopping around above my head on the corrugated-iron roof of the guest house, so I went for a walk around the area, already busy with stallholders setting out their wares in the cool of the morning. I got warm smiles from all as I headed back for breakfast and then another ghastly drive to a lovely Red Cross centre in Bandajamo (the Island of Bananas), where I was treated to an exuberant welcome from the massed Red Cross volunteers and a tour of the immaculate community health and sanitary facilities. At a delicious lunch of rice and sweet potato leaves they begged me to stay the night – I told them it was all so lovely, I might even retire there.

Then on to Bo for a second excited, chanting, rocking welcome at the branch office, followed by a series of skits about HIV from the skilled young 'peer educator' group, the girls at one point delightedly pulling fake penises from the boys' trousers in order to demonstrate how to put on a condom – a great way to break down stigma and encourage open discussion about the disease. The hilarity which this stunt generated only increased when the local reverend spotted a gang of young children peering wide-eyed through the open window and hurtled out to chase them away. I spent the evening quietly with Emmanuel and the local branch chair, as they told me their stories of the civil war. They had both had to flee with their families into the bush, past piles of dead bodies, and endure months in hiding, terrified of Charles Taylor's rebel troops, the 'comojos'.

'Those were the years,' they said, 'when you never felt safe – shops would close in an instant if they heard that the comojos had hit town. You could be shot for the slightest wrong move, or for no reason at all. You just kept well out of the way and prayed.'

The next day in Pujahon, which I had visited before, the welcome hit new heights, with a lengthy parade through town led by the police band and accompanied by more masked dancing devils and frantic waving and clapping. Then we adjourned to a small, packed and steamy hut for speeches, as ancient craggy faces gazed, tough and muscly ex-fighters stared, young kids jostled boisterously for a good view in at the window and the girls chattered over the teacups. Every so often there was a burst of song and maracas, and the mood shifted. I felt quite choked actually, and tried to explain, without sounding pious or pompous, that there was nothing to thank us for – they were the brave ones, doing it all themselves.

After a lunch of chewy meat and plantain we set off on what turned out to be a triumphal tour around two local communities, who had clearly been waiting for hours in the sun for our little convoy to arrive. More dancing, more devils, more speeches and clever presentations about their work by local volunteers. I had a go at pounding freshly-picked rice in a large wooden pestle, and everyone laughed warmly at my pathetic efforts.

'Have you harvested enough to feed your family?' I asked.

'Only till December,' a young woman shrugged and smiled.

There was no fresh water source nearby – only the river a mile or so away, which flooded regularly. I was the first white person they had seen, I was told as we walked around the village.

We drove back to Bo in the gentle evening light, children playing with their simple toys in the dust, smoke from a cooking fire drifting across the road and momentarily filling the Land Cruiser with the smell of roasting meat or corn. People walking, walking, walking, bowls or bundles on their heads, flip-flops or nothing at all on their feet, striding purposefully across the vast continent. I breathed deeply. Africa.

I thought of all the tense discussions there had been about management structure back home that year, and budgets and board meetings and the like, and a weight seemed to drop from my shoulders – none of it mattered a damn beside the help we were giving these people, little enough as it was, and the joy and the energy and the confidence it had engendered.

Freetown, the capital, the next day was an appalling, teeming, crazy mess of people and cars and baked red mud. Selling was the name of the game here, as the Land Cruiser ground its way forward and children and beggars knocked on the windows with stuff to sell or open hands held out. Driving down Kissy Road, the scene of so much violence when the rebels stormed the town before they were driven back by Nigerian ECOMOG forces, we saw the tell-tale signs of burnt out buildings and shambling amputees that told the story with stark and silent eloquence.

That night, another farewell dinner, more speeches, and Emmanuel told a joke, at my expense as I recall. Everyone laughed.

'Haha!' he said, 'that'll cost each of you a dollar' – and 'Laugh for Humanity' was born.

At the end of 2009 we celebrated the last of our maximum of eight years as members of the Federation's Governing Board. This was a significant moment. There were two Board meetings a year, each lasting four or five full days (mostly spent in an airless, smelly, basement meeting room in Geneva without natural light), and they took up a great deal of my time in terms of both attendance in support of the Chairman (who was our 'nominated representative'), preparation and follow-up, and involvement in discussions in the months between. It was a real privilege to have been actively involved in the governance of one of the world's great humanitarian institutions, becoming friendly in the process with peers and colleagues from all over the world and from many different cultures and creeds.

But it had also been at times frustrating. The Board was large, with thirty or so members (plus an even greater number of 'accompanying persons', three or four from some societies) seated in a horseshoe facing the chair, vice-chairs and secretary-general, all of us plugged into microphones and headphones for simultaneous translation from a bank of interpreters in a gallery above us.

The President (and therefore Chairman of the Board) during our eight years, Juan Manual Suarez del Toro Rivero from the Canary Islands, had been elected on a pledge, long overdue, to reduce the perceived 'northern and European' dominance of the Movement's institutions. As a result, his style in chairing the meetings was to encourage everyone to speak on every topic, whether or not they had much to say, in the hope of achieving consensus whether through a meeting of minds, compromise or sheer exhaustion. This did not lead to snappy decision-making.

Nevertheless, we were sorry to be standing down, at a time when key issues upon which we had taken a lead were just beginning to gain traction. The new Federation strategy *Saving Lives Changing Minds* (with James as a member of the working group) was adopted at this meeting for formal approval by the forthcoming General Assembly; there had at last been a realization, prompted partly by the global financial crisis, but also by the sense that organizations like Oxfam were much better at it, that the Federation needed to up its game on fundraising; national society development was now seen as a core part of the agenda; and even branding was being recognized as a matter which no one could take for granted, even the Red Cross. We had played a leading part on all these issues, and it would be much harder to push them forward if we were no longer on the Board.

Then it was on to Nairobi for the biennial meeting of the Federation and its members, and with the ICRC. The meetings were notable for the exuberant and generous hospitality of the Kenya Red Cross (easily the strongest national society on the continent, largely thanks to its dynamic and outspoken secretary-general, Abbas Gullet), which coped with an influx of 1,500 delegates with grace and style. We were meeting in Africa for the first time, and it proved a great opportunity both to engage with the humanitarian challenges and to acknowledge Africa's capacities and potential, whilst celebrating its riches in culture and heritage.

After a hard-fought election campaign against some worthy contenders, Tadateru Konoe, President of the Japanese Red Cross and scion of the royal family, was elected as the new President of the Federation. I had come to know him well since the Donor Forum meeting on Mount Fuji, and I was touched when he asked me to his room for advice on his big campaign speech to the Assembly the night before the voting. He was a quiet, painfully polite and rather shy man, with an admirable sense of duty coupled with personal humility, but I struggled rather to imagine him making a barnstorming election pitch. Then I remembered his extraordinary karaoke rendering of 'Mona Lisa', when he had seemed to put his very soul into the love song, and that was what I told him – 'Remember Mona Lisa, Mr Konoe, remember Mona Lisa.' And he did, his speech a lovely, heart-felt hymn of praise for the Red Cross and its work around the world and a moving glimpse into his dreams for the future.

The historic Assembly in Africa ended in a mood of unity and some inspiration as we flew home pondering how we would adjust to our new role as 'ordinary members'. I would certainly miss the friendships across countries and cultures around the world, and the sense of being at the centre of things in an extraordinary global humanitarian movement.

Chapter 11

Haiti Earthquake, 2010

Iceland's volcano – Mongolian steppes – Nepal

Early in the New Year, I made a short courtesy trip to the American Red Cross in Washington with the Chairman. The American Red Cross is huge – half a million volunteers, 35,000 staff, 700 local chapters and an annual income of well over $1 billion, most of it spent in the US rather than overseas. First aid was a big area of activity, and James was delighted to spot a special first aid kit for dogs. The American Red Cross runs a major chunk of the country's blood service and is the main provider of domestic disaster relief, as well as providing a wide range of health and safety educational programmes and community services.

The so-called 'special relationship' had always seemed to have relevance in the Red Cross, and we had often found ourselves in agreement with the Americans at Governing Board meetings on key issues. They were going through a major internal restructuring at the time and were keen to hear about our own experiences, as well as to talk about how to further our mutual interest in progressing initiatives on global resource mobilization, humanitarian diplomacy and national society development.

They also wanted to promote their extraordinary Tiffany Circle fundraising group of wealthy and sociable female supporters, named after the beautiful stained-glass windows in their headquarters which had been paid for by the jewellery family, and suggested that we should form a similar group in Britain – which we duly did, though a little doubtful if the American model of philanthropy would translate to the UK. The ever-enthusiastic Angela Lamport, ably assisted by the extraordinarily well-networked Pinky Lilani, founder of the Asian Women of Achievement and Women of the Future award and networking schemes, agreed to act as ambassadors and were soon recruiting our first 'Tiffanettes', as I used to call them. The Tiffany Circle turned into a very generous and dynamic fundraising force, and I used to enjoy attending their meetings.

Our trip took in meetings at the Headquarters in Washington, at chapters in New York and Miami (often affected by the same hurricanes that regularly blasted some of our Overseas Branches) and at both the Federation and ICRC offices at the UN. As we arrived in New York we saw on TV screens in the airport the first report of a massive earthquake in Haiti, an event that was to dominate all our lives in the months ahead.

By the time we returned to a snow-bound UK, with Red Cross ambulances and volunteers supporting the NHS in a dozen counties, we had already deployed twenty of our expert disaster response, water and mass sanitation delegates to Haiti, and our logistics team was installed at the nearest functioning airport, in the adjoining Dominican Republic. The earthquake had caused devastation in the capital Port-au-Prince and several other cities, towns and villages, with early death-toll estimates ranging from 100,00 to over 300,000 – all in one of the world's most poverty-stricken countries. Nearly 3m people lost their homes in a few minutes. As dozens of aftershocks rocked the city, the only safe place for our delegates to sleep was in tents alongside the runway of the town's defunct airport.

I made a fleeting visit to Port-au-Prince in March, the airport now functioning after a fashion, its arrivals lounge replaced by a large temporary corrugated-iron hangar, superheated in the baking midday sun and filled with incoming aid workers clamouring for their rucksacks and cases, which had been shoved onto the floor through a hole in the wall. After a short drive past chaotic piles of rubble and ramshackle tents huddled on every yard of empty space, we had a quick soup in the central Red Cross base camp, home now to hundreds of delegates from around the world, then set off for Automeca and La Piste, the two encampments where British Red Cross had taken responsibility for organizing the sanitation for 12,000 and 48,000 people respectively.

Automeca was a clean, lively place, a collection of blue plastic tents and makeshift huts and shelters built on some waste ground beside the main road. It seemed calm and quite cheerful on a Sunday afternoon, the residents taking their weekend ease, squatting in shady doorways a few feet from their neighbours. The latrines, run by a committee of inhabitants, were spotless though in constant use, one latrine for over 200 people. A gleeful gang of small children danced around two clowns, chanting (in French) the refrain, 'After a poo, I wash my hands'. Two laughing boys flew a kite, a ragged tangle of sticks, scrubby plastic and string; up and away it went above the camp.

By contrast, La Piste was a cramped, edgy place, the wind scurrying busily around the shacks, all built of tarpaulins and wood from fallen homes and offices and stretched out across a windswept expanse of tarmac. They leant on each other at crazy angles: here a small shop, there a bar, now a guy beating out some sheet metal. The camp looked as if it had been there for years and would still be there in a few years' time. For some Haitians, these were the best living conditions they had ever had; access to fresh water, health care and sanitation was a distant dream for most in the slums of Port-au-Prince. As we were to find in the coming months, as fast as we moved people out of their temporary shelters and into better accommodation, so their places were rapidly filled by others desperate to escape the slums. It was a grim place, and you could sense that the relatively relaxed weekend atmosphere could shift in an instant, the tension just waiting for a spark to ignite trouble. They had reason to be angry, the unlucky people of Haiti.

In the evening there was a security briefing, a sign of the danger to our teams of violence erupting in the 600-odd camps, despite the 6.00pm curfew on the island. It started raining, sheets of solid water sluicing from a coal-black sky, as we sat for a while under an awning, before shrugging our shoulders and trudging back to our tents, soaked through. The approaching rainy season was to inflict yet more misery on the camps, the prospect of rebuilding whole sectors of the city a remote one. The Federation team was already planning for what was to be effectively a second disaster response once the rains started in earnest.

The problem in Haiti – well, one of the many problems in Haiti – was land. There wasn't enough of it, and efforts to free up privately-owned space were making little progress. Every vacant square inch was filled with tents or piled high with rubble. In a four-hour drive across the city I saw not a street untouched by the earthquake, from the shattered Presidential Palace, to the heap of dust that had been the Tax Office and the mangled wreck of the local Red Cross HQ, to the meanest of the shanty towns. Barely 40 per cent of the houses in the city were still habitable, the Government was seen as corrupt and incompetent, supplies of wood and materials for rebuilding were virtually non-existent, there was no plan, no capacity and nowhere near enough money. In the absence of a massive UN-led and -sponsored relief effort, there was no hope either.

I flew home depressed and worried. Responding to the Haiti earthquake was clearly going to be another very tough challenge. The member agencies of the DEC alone raised well over £100m, and we were planning to spend £17.5m in 2010, but with more than 70 per cent of the population living on less than $1 per day, and 86 per cent of people living in crowded slums, in tightly packed, poorly constructed and crumbling buildings, the needs were enormous. There was half a city and several towns needing to be completely rebuilt, and before that, 19m cubic tons of rubble had to be cleared away, with nowhere near enough diggers and lorries on the island to do it. The relief and recovery effort was going to take a long time. It rapidly became clear that conditions for delegates would be poor, meaning that turnover would be high, sickness a problem and recruitment difficult. Feelings were running high amongst the population, too, and media scrutiny was intense in a location only an hour's flight from Miami. At a Federation coordination meeting in New York in April it became clear that we weren't the only society worrying about scaling up our response.

Back at home, our determined and thorough approach to implementing the new strategy was gaining momentum. We had decided to change to a two-year budgeting cycle, to iron out problems caused by the normal annual cycle, and I met with the Area Directors to listen to concerns and try and address issues; we felt that the appointment of a new Director of Operations to oversee all our work and services both in the UK and overseas would help ensure that this ongoing investment process was well-coordinated and prioritized – no easy job in an organization with as many diverse services as our own.

We were also delighted that our successful campaign to include the voluntary sector in the Civil Contingencies Act had resulted in a higher profile for the Red Cross as a significant contributor of capacity and resources in any major emergency in the UK. Our Area teams were being called out increasingly often to help with local emergencies, setting up rest centres and helplines, supporting the Ambulance Service, providing emotional and practical support to those affected, and we had established a reputation for reliability and professionalism. Furthermore, our role as chair and secretary of the newly-formed Voluntary Sector Protection Forum, set up after the Act to identify and maximize the voluntary sector's contribution to UK civil protection arrangements, gave us a seat at the table of some key government working groups. Even within the voluntary sector, where we all guarded our independence jealously, our convening role was being seen as helpful rather than threatening.

In April the Chairman led a party of trustees and directors to Vienna for a four-yearly conference of all the national societies in Europe which was looking at the then hot topic of ageing, and the pressures that a growing proportion of older people was likely to place on Red Cross services. The conference ended in disarray as flights all over the world were halted by the eruption in Iceland of a volcano that few had heard of and even fewer could pronounce or spell. I caught the news item relatively early and managed to grab the last flight to Paris, where the following day I met up with Kate Lee, who had also fled Vienna, and we came back to London by Eurostar. Kate had recently announced her departure for pastures new, after eighteen years or so in the Red Cross, and I spent half the journey trying, sadly unsuccessfully, to persuade her to stay. We were quite a close-knit management team, and it was always unsettling when we lost popular key members.

I appointed, as the new Director of Operations, Mike Adamson, with whom I had worked early on in my time as CEO when he was Strategy Director, before leaving for a job in the NHS and then RNID. We had had quite a strong field for an attractive job, but it was a relief to be able to appoint someone who knew the organization already and with whom I had worked well before. He would go on to become my successor after I stood down. Very soon after he started, I took him to Shanghai for a meeting of the Donor Forum hosted by the Chinese Red Cross where he could meet some of the Movement's senior executives. I then flew on via Seoul for a visit to Mongolia, another of our partner national societies in the region.

This huge landlocked country the size of Western Europe had a population of just 2.7m, about half of whom lived in the capital Ulaanbaatar, whilst many of the rest lived a semi-nomadic lifestyle as herders/farmers. It's baking hot in the summer and bitterly cold in the winter, with temperatures sometimes down around -50°C. During the previous winter there had been a bitterly cold snap called a *dzud* with prolonged heavy snow that had resulted in the death of nearly a quarter of the cattle, sheep and goats that formed the basis of the rural economy, and forced over 100,000 people to abandon their rural lifestyle and head for the cities, where they were now living a meagre existence in shacks, or circular tents called *gers*.

Our programmes in the country were all focussed on these *ger* encampments, providing a mix of health education, home care assistance and livelihoods support through small volunteer-staffed social care centres. The methodologies around working out exactly who needed help, budgeting, record-keeping and reporting were impressive, and (with some advice from our fundraisers) they had started to expand the programme by generating their own funds through small-scale ventures like a bakery and a small dairy.

The Mongolian Red Cross was run by the jovial, rather roguish Samdan Ravdav, who dressed in long capacious Mongolian robes and carried a pretty carved snuff bottle hidden in a pocket which he would offer lovingly in greeting to fellow snuff-takers in exchange for their own bottles; both would then indulge in a friendly little ritual of sniffing, removing the coral stopper and scooping out a dose of snuff with a tiny carved spoon attached to the stopper: another sniff, a sneeze, a smile and then the bottles were passed caressingly back. The author of an apparently popular book on wolves, Samdan was a larger than life character in his cowboy 'ten gallon hat', and I enjoyed his good-humoured company and warm hospitality.

I passed the morning with Samdan's team, and then we set off for what became a kind of royal progress around the country, visiting first our programmes on the outskirts of the capital, where I was presented by the Mayor with a locally made shirt and a badge as 'Honourable Citizen' and entertained with a display of dancing and then tai-chi, followed by the captivating reindeer dance and two love songs. After a talk with some of the volunteers and the people they were helping, I was hauled off for a formal dinner with a government minister, at which we had long and rather laboured discussions about the economy, football and the English weather, and then had to give lengthy speeches of mutual admiration and respect. He described Samdan as the 'humanitarian successor to the national hero Genghis (or Chinggis) Khan'. At regular intervals the proceedings were interrupted by formal toasting – of each other, of our respective countries, of the Red Cross, of any handy subject that came to mind – each toast followed by a collective emptying and then refilling of vodka glasses. It was a long night.

It was a leisurely start, thank goodness, the next day, with a trip in convoy to the nearby modern industrial city of Baganuur, passing on the way an extraordinary stainless steel monument to Chinggis Khan on his horse, glinting in the sun and towering 50 metres above the surrounding plain. We see Chinggis as the blood-soaked villain of legend, but in Mongolia he is revered as a wily, thoughtful leader, who successfully integrated the lands he conquered into his vast empire. Clambering up dozens of steps through the white marble base of the monument, you find yourself on the horse's mane, looking at the statue's enormous head high above with, closer at hand, a massive gloved fist resting magisterially on the hilt of a sword.

We were met at the city boundary, under a magnificent Soviet-style triumphal arch, by the Red Cross branch chairman and the director resplendent in a bright red dress, accompanied by a colleague in a traditional blue outfit bearing a bowl of warm milk to refresh the travellers. We each had to collect three small stones and then, circling a pile of rocks surmounted by a pole and draped in blue plastic bags filled with food and other offerings, we threw our offerings onto the heap in a gesture of gratitude for a safe arrival and set off with a police escort for lunch – which was accompanied, as usual I soon gathered, by more vodka toasts.

After a greeting from the local Governor and the Speaker of the local parliament, and a ceremony at which I was presented with a certificate and large gold badge as Honorary Citizen No. 92 and a model of the town's triumphal arch, we visited the local Red Cross Care Centre to be greeted by another delightful round of love songs and dancing, followed by stories from local people about how the Red Cross had helped them.

By now the sun was beginning to set, as we raced 40 kilometres along a desert track, bouncing from rock to rock, to meet a herder and his family in their *ger*. Just before dark, we found him with his thousand-strong herd of sheep, goats and horses on a windswept plain near a bend in a steely-grey river. Shivering in the biting cold, we were glad to be invited inside the *ger*, where our beaming, ruddy-cheeked host quickly changed into a long robe of brilliant blue and gold, set off by a chest-full of medals and a bowler hat. It was supper time for him and his family, who pressed on us bowls of frothy, milky, cheesy, curdy drinks, followed by two vast steaming piles of glistening, fatty sheep meat, which everyone set upon with murderous-looking knives. As the meat was 'rare', you might say, I poked about nervously with my knife looking for bits that might be slightly more cooked, whilst gratefully acknowledging the efforts of my hostess, the herder's wife, to load my plate with the choicest morsels of fat. The meal ended after an hour or so with a bowl of fermented mare's milk, its oily surface garnished with a few knobs of melting yellow butter. I smiled and gulped and my stomach heaved, but honour was satisfied and no offence was given. Then we sang songs, my hosts leading with a kind of throaty, nasal keening that combined well with the howling of the wind outside. As it was turn and turn about, I gamely essayed a couple of Seekers numbers, to warm if slightly puzzled applause. They sounded weak and weedy in comparison with the muscly tone of the local style, but generated considerable discussion in the tent – so perhaps there's a future for a Seekers revival in Mongolia after all.

Soon it was time to go, speeding through the black night to a small encampment of *gers*, miles from anywhere and grouped around a kind of hostel. I was allocated my own *ger*, sharing with our interpreter (who I was sure was some kind of undercover policeman). We spent a while trying to get the metal stove to work and, just as it was starting to produce a trickle of heat to penetrate the icy cold, we were summoned up to the hostel for a late 'snack' of salami and cheese, more singing, and – vodka. Back in the *ger* some time later, we eventually rekindled the meagre stove and I spent a fitful night stoking it, in between trips through the snow to the loo. I was up long before dawn, desperate for tea.

The nearby Red Cross branch was based in one of Mongolia's many huge open-cast coalmines. This one was 17 kilometres long, and had been running for thirty years at full throttle – with another sixty to go before the seam was exhausted, the manager said. After a talk to the volunteers about their work with the herders, we returned to Ulaanbaatar and a visit to another branch (more wonderfully energetic and entertaining volunteers regaling us with stories of their work). All too soon, we were hurried away to a draughty village hall for more traditional singing and dancing, including Mongolian nose music and an extraordinary young female contortionist.

This was followed, to my dismay (I was feeling a touch weary by this time), by another formal dinner, this time in the headquarters of the Mongolian Border Guards. As I willed myself to rise energetically to the occasion, we toured their museum (lots of guns and pictures of guard posts), sat through a lengthy performance by two famous musicians on saxophone and guitar accompanied by Red Cross volunteers on mandolins, ate a lot of food, were required to drink more vodka and exchanged long speeches of mutual love and respect. The evening ended with my being presented with a full set of beautiful Mongolian robes by Samdan, in return for which I was required to perform 'Yesterday' with a backing group of two young female volunteers, who seemed to know some of the words, if not the tune.

In hot sun the next day we drove to the third city Darkhan to view a large Disaster Response competition for young Red Cross members. Maga, the guitarist from the previous night, came too, and we passed the five-hour drive singing and humming melodies to each other, trying to find something we both knew. Sadly, Mongolia was so isolated during its seven decades of Soviet 'alignment' that our respective musical histories and styles had little in common. It was fun, though, and we arrived in time to see the final stages of the competition – first aid, casualty evacuation, ambulance driving around obstacles and, somewhat unusually, walking blindfold through a minefield. I had to give out the prizes, including a special award to a group from a nearby province who had insisted on dancing and singing their way through each test. Then it was lunch, with Robbie Williams at Knebworth by way of loudspeaker accompaniment, followed by a very moving visit to a local father and his young son, who had been left only with the use of his arm after a road traffic accident. I kept thinking of my own son Tom's injuries after his awful road accident in 2003 and was relieved when we left.

We visited another branch on the way to our nearby hotel, full again of the most irrepressibly enthusiastic social care volunteers, and then had an hour or so to prepare for … another formal banquet. This time, we had high-pitched, rather squeaky singing, rather than growly nasal stuff, then more throat-singing, then some music from a curious instrument with horse-hair strings, then some Chinese pop songs, then an exhibition of national dances. Then we all had to have a go, after a few more rounds of toasting, and I had to delve once more into my 1960s back catalogue for inspiration. Before we left, I was presented with a bottle of much-prized Chinggis gold label vodka, in case I got thirsty in my room overnight.

The following day, we returned to the branch for a film show about local Red Cross activities, then a visit to the Red Cross bakery, before getting in our cars for the return to the capital – stopping, of course, on the way for the ritual snacks, speeches and stone-throwing on the city boundary. Samdan threw his fourth glass of vodka (tradition apparently says that, once opened, a bottle has to be finished) high in the air and onto the pile of stones, and we were off. The drive back across the hills and plains of central Mongolia had a mercifully soporific effect on all of us and, after crawling back through the heavy Sunday afternoon traffic, I was able to persuade my generous hosts that we all needed an early night. As I was up at the crack for the flight home, this was a mighty relief.

It was a busy autumn, as the organization continued to flourish and grow in new directions, with fringe meetings at all the Party conferences, several speeches at external events and various TV and radio interviews pursuant to our new determination to speak out more, and a seat on the new Foreign Secretary's Human Rights Panel.

In December I travelled to Nepal, where we had been investing significant sums in the Nepal Red Cross and its capacity and preparedness to respond to an expected and long overdue major earthquake. All the predictions were that, if the quake struck the capital Kathmandu, it would be devastated, because so little had been done over decades to make the buildings in its maze-like alleyways and streets to any extent quake-proof. Located as it is in a huge valley surrounded by mountains, access for rescue and supplies would be problematic, and a major humanitarian disaster for its million inhabitants was clearly on the cards.

Luckily, we had an excellent partner to work with in the Nepal Red Cross, under the leadership of veteran Secretary-General Dev Dhakwa. After many years of political instability caused by a long row over the country's constitution and an attempted Maoist revolution, the 'caretaker' government was weak, and the need for a capable Red Cross to play a major role in any response to a natural disaster or health emergency was correspondingly strong. With 85 per cent of Nepal's 29m people living in remote rural settings, and 30 per cent below the poverty line, the task for the Red Cross was significant. Nevertheless, like so many other 'operating' national societies, the Nepal Red Cross met only about 15 per cent of its 'core costs' from its own local fundraising efforts – the rest, and all of its programme costs, were funded by international donors such as other Red Cross societies, other NGOs or the UN.

We had been working for many years to support the headquarters in Kathmandu in building up its strategic and operational emergency response capacity but, with some 60 per cent of the buildings in the capital threatened with collapse during a big earthquake, there was a limit to what the national society could be expected to do. With the government's own resources in disarray after the years of political upheaval, massive support from the UN and/or from individual other governments was obviously going to be necessary, and it was encouraging to hear from the British Ambassador that a £100m investment by DFID was confidently expected.

I landed at Kathmandu's vast confection of an international airport late in the afternoon and trekked across acres of empty marble to a warm welcome reception, complete with marigold garlands, from the Nepalis and our local delegate, followed by a two-hour crawl along the two miles to the hotel in the bright evening sunshine. The evening was spent in a briefing over supper near Durbar Square in nearby Patan, in front of the old Royal Palace and surrounded by several historic temples (many of them to be tragically flattened by the earthquake which devastated so much of the city in 2015).

The next morning and part of the afternoon was spent in a series of meetings with Dev and his managers and a tour of the offices and their large warehouse, filled with supplies against the anticipated disaster. Then there were a couple of hours free, before a formal dinner in the evening, to visit the Boudhanath or Great Stupa, 36 metres high, situated in the north-eastern outskirts of Kathmandu on an ancient trade route through the valley. The gold-topped stupa dominated the small square around it, which was filled with little shops and stalls to serve the crowd of pilgrims and tourists surging clockwise around the base of the stupa and twirling as they went hundreds of prayer wheels set into the base. From each corner of the square hundreds of prayer flags flapped and waved from long wires stretching right up to the very top of the stupa where, on each side, two painted, angry-looking, beady eyes gazed unblinkingly and with seeming disapproval at the crowds below. We clambered up to a rooftop café and just sat and watched the extraordinary timeless spectacle, before struggling back through the grinding traffic for a rather morose formal dinner completely dominated by a loud and tuneless local band.

The next day, much delayed by heavy fog, we flew to Bhadrapur, in the far south-east of Nepal, just glimpsing on the way the tops of Everest and the Himalayan range as they emerged from the clouds. After a quick visit to the District HQ and its alarmingly ramshackle blood transfusion and processing centre, we drove in convoy along miles of winding, potholed tracks to a remote riverine community, where we had been training a cadre of 'community mobilizers'. Their job was to motivate and assist the local villages in their efforts to mitigate and counteract the impact of flooding from two nearby rivers which had regularly burst their banks in recent years during the snow-melting season.

In the gathering gloom we were surrounded by dozens of chanting locals, who smeared our foreheads with vermilion pigment, loaded us down with garlands and welcomed us with lengthy speeches, before taking us on a torch-lit route march down to the muddy river bank so that we could see for ourselves the scale of the problem. We eventually tore ourselves away and trekked back to a filthy hotel in the town centre, where we forced down a dubious dish of something or other and went to bed for a night of plaintive howling from the town's multitude of street dogs.

Relieved to be up early and away, we set off for another visit to a riverine community, where again there was a delightful and tumultuous welcome in store and more long speeches, interrupted and enlivened this time by a fire which broke out in some neighbouring huts. After an initial panic, it turned out that the fire had been laid on for our benefit, as a means for the local Red Cross volunteers to demonstrate their disaster response skills, the show spoiled only by the fact that, in their enthusiasm and excitement, the fire had been started too early and was actually threatening to destroy half the village. They did a great job putting it out, however, and the speeches soon restarted once the wounded (mostly simulated) had been carted off for medical attention.

For an encore, I was escorted to the nearby snakebite clinic where the proprietor, an intense, weedy chap with impossibly black hair, treated me to a chilling lecture about various snakes and the effect of their bites, and a tour around the shelves of his clinic, which was crowded with jars and vials of unpleasant-looking serums and antidotes, before revealing his plans for a big extension and giving me the hard sell.

'It's only a million rupees,' he wheedled, before my hosts hustled me out of the door and back to the airport.

Chapter 12

Progress in the Federation, 2011

Murder of ICRC colleague – Pakistan with the UN again –
Haiti – South Sudan and Independence – Kyrgyzstan – Kenya

After a short break over Christmas and the New Year, I flew to Pakistan on 4 January on another mission for the UN, to work with Dr Hafiz Pasha, a development economist and former national finance minister, to help the provincial government of Sindh put together its rehabilitation and reconstruction strategy in the wake of the previous summer's flooding. Nearly 2m homes were washed away or partially destroyed along the length of the Indus River, from the north-west frontier with Afghanistan right down to the delta at Karachi. The cost of reconstruction was estimated at over $10 billion, of which less than a third had been forthcoming from international donors.

The poverty-stricken southern province of Sindh, which has Karachi as its capital, caught the worst of the damage – nearly half of the national total. The flood waters breached the poorly maintained Tori Bund at Sukkur, 500km to the north-east of Karachi, and the resulting huge and unexpected outflow of water towards the west caused the flooding of nearly 20 per cent of Sindh's landmass. By the time this disaster struck, most of the major response agencies were already committed in tackling the flooding further north, and Sindh was largely left to struggle on alone.

When Dr Pasha and I arrived to commence our review, there were still 500,000 acres under water, and nearly 100,000 families were still in need of emergency food and medical assistance, many of them still living in temporary relief camps around the edge of the flooded areas. This explained why recovery operations had barely started, and highlighted the importance for the provincial government of putting in place a reconstruction strategy as soon as possible, before international attention turned elsewhere and all chance of obtaining international funding had gone.

Our first task was to make a speedy assessment of the scale of the damage and the size of the reconstruction effort required. Before focussing on the numbers, we wanted to see for ourselves, so we flew north over the flooded areas and along the Indus valley in an ancient Army helicopter, to see the damage from the air. As far as the eye could see, stagnant muddy water covered the land, for mile after mile. Everywhere there were families camped in flimsy white tents perched along raised dykes, like teeth in a jawbone. What remained of mud brick and wood dwellings poked out of the water, the dispossessed family camping alongside or within sight of their home for fear of losing their tenuous purchase on the space. In the whole day we saw just two diggers at work on the deep drifts of silt and the crumbled irrigation systems, and my heart ached for the families we talked to wherever we landed.

The next few days was a blur of meetings: with the provincial governor (my old friend Kaiser Bengali from my last UN mission in 2007); all his ministers and their senior civil servants; the UN Cluster leads in Hyderabad and Islamabad; the Asia Development Bank; the National Disaster Management Authority (many of whose responsibilities had recently been dumped on the provinces, without the benefit of funding to meet them), the representatives of three donor governments; the EU; the UN Special Envoy; many national and international NGOs; the Pakistan Red Crescent; the ICRC and the Federation; representatives of the private sector; numerous UN staff and local officials; and many affected families.

Whilst Dr Pasha was focussed on the job of rebuilding or repairing 800,000 houses, 8,000km of road, hundreds of kilometres of flood-protection structures, irrigation and water supply systems, 11,000 villages, 5,000 schools, and so on, my task (with John English, one of our recovery specialists) was to draft the humanitarian section of the overall strategy. We had to consider how, in recovering from this tragedy, the government of Sindh should deal with livelihoods, food and nutrition, shelter, health (physical and mental), water and sanitation, education, protection (from all forms of abuse); what the priorities should be in each sector; how and what to communicate with the myriad affected communities and how to manage their expectations; how to manage and coordinate the humanitarian effort and the numerous actors whose help would be needed; what the risks were and how to mitigate them; and what principles and values should underlie the entire process.

It sounds monumental – as indeed it was, though of course in essence not very different to the recovery effort that is required after every major disaster. The elephant in the room in Sindh, however, was money. There simply wasn't any. The government of Sindh had already spent $23m on the relief effort (over 5 per cent of its entire annual budget), and was now in deficit. The Federal Government had no money either and was in fact cutting back its already inadequate funding to the provinces, whilst at the same time denying them the right to approach international donors direct. The UN's intervention in 2007 may have been problematic, but its funding was missed this time.

Governor Bengali's only hope was that he would be able to persuade the central government to agree to a special Donor and Investors Conference (putatively in March). We discussed this idea with various government representatives, who all nodded their heads sympathetically but then made clear that current national policy was to say that no international help was needed, and that anything actually given had to be paid into a controversial and poorly-administered central scheme of cash disbursements to affected individuals using a cash card (the *watan* card), to which the provinces themselves had to contribute half of the cost.

We worked eighteen hours a day for twelve days and produced a thoughtful and comprehensive paper for Hafiz Pasha's overall report, but left gloomy at the prospect that Sindh would be able to come anywhere near 'building back as bad as it was before' let alone be able to 'build back better', Clinton's aspirational goal for the *tsunami* response. Moreover, the Indus often floods in July – and indeed it did again in 2011, with inevitable results for the many families who had yet to recover from the earlier disaster.

No sooner back from Pakistan (with the usual tummy bug) than I was off again to another disaster, Haiti one year on. The Federation had called a meeting to agree a recovery strategy for the Red Cross, now that the initial relief phase was more or less over. It was my second visit and, whilst it was encouraging to see signs that life in Port-au-Prince was beginning to return to some semblance of normality – smiling people, busy streets, traffic jams, markets and shops open – the central areas were still clogged with rubble and dominated by the large tented encampments that occupied every open space. Port-au-Prince was not really recovering, but rather learning to live with the aftermath of the earthquake. Only 5 per cent of the rubble had been removed, and 800,000 people were still living in the tented camps that were beginning to look depressingly permanent. Around them, life was going on in an irrepressible Haitian way: as the Prime Minister himself admitted, 'Nobody knows quite how it all works, it just does.' After a fashion.

Before the meeting began, we visited our own team of twenty ex-pats and around seventy local staff in their 'container offices' on the large Red Cross base camp near the airport. As living accommodation, I was pleased to see that we had found them a reasonable flat away from the worst-affected areas. I was always watchful to ensure that our delegates were living in safe, clean and secure billets, because the problems they were dealing with day in day out in a disaster area were difficult enough, and it was important for them to be able to get away in the evenings and refresh. On the other hand, it was vital that the people we were there to help felt confidence that we were 'sharing their pain' and, as we were using money given to us by generous supporters, we also had to keep such overhead costs as low as was reasonably possible.

We had made a conscious decision to concentrate our efforts in Port-au-Prince itself, because that was where the most urgent needs were. Of course, the earthquake had affected towns and communities outside the capital, too, and in some respects these were a little easier to work in because they were less crowded and more relaxed in atmosphere – but the case was clear for us to stay in town, so we did.

The first project we visited was our Cholera Treatment Centre in the huge La Piste camp. This terrible disease had been eradicated nearly a century previously in Haiti, but it returned in October 2010, nine months after the earthquake, and rapidly became endemic, with high levels of morbidity and mortality. Many suspected that it had been reintroduced into the country by UN troops brought in to help soon after the quake, but it spread rapidly, due to terrible sanitation, and by the time of my visit had already killed over 4,000 people and hospitalized thousands more.

The Centre was like a field hospital with two or three tented wards, and sealed off from the rest of La Piste by a rigorous infection control measures such as disinfectant foot baths, careful screening and distancing, protective equipment for the staff and volunteers and stiff rules around personal hygiene. The ward I visited had about twenty patients, down from around sixty earlier in the year, each lying on their basic cot, plugged into life-saving drips to replace the fluids leaking out of them in acute watery diarrhoea into the buckets beneath their beds. A cleaner constantly swabbed the floor, a child crouched wide-eyed on a bed; the early morning sun seemed almost insultingly cheerful, but the staff were full of smiles, very conscious of the vital role they were playing in keeping the disease at bay. This was so different, they said, to the early days of the disease, when there was panic in the streets and a desperate scramble to get ahead of the spread before it could establish a stranglehold. The manager described how he had rescued one sufferer, lying in her own excrement in the street, from a rampaging, fearful mob and carried her to the Centre.

After the Centre, we went into the camp itself, with its shifting, edgy population of 50,000 souls crammed onto the windswept tarmac of what had once been a sports park. Last year, when I visited, this was a scary place, with a tinderbox air of menace and grindingly unsettling poverty. It was no less scary now – fifty rapes each month by one estimate, and the air of menace was hardly dispelled by the armed UN security patrols who drove rather smugly around during daylight hours. But the camp was calmer now, and cleaner. As one of the very few humanitarian agencies still working there, the onus was on us to continue supporting the local coordinating committee to keep the banks of latrines (which we had built) hygienic, the showers working and the supply of fresh water maintained. Lack of funds would mean that we would have to hand over our responsibilities within a few months, but it was by no means clear who was going to step into our place.

Next was Delmas 19, one of the worst slum areas in Port-au-Prince. It was effectively a mass squat on a swamp. Concrete and wood shacks nudged and shoved against each other, two or three families to each. Tiny alleyways, barely wide enough to squeeze through, wriggled past doorways and around corners, rivulets of dirty water and worse trickling underfoot. The earthquake had picked haphazardly through this mess, reducing some houses to dust, cracking some asunder, missing others altogether.

Our team were surveying the shacks block by block, trying to work out what needed to be pulled down and what could be repaired, negotiating family by family to identify a suitable building strategy for each. As we threaded our way warily through the maze, they chatted and joked with the locals – one wanted two storeys (not affordable); another needed three rooms (maybe); a third was told that her house had to come down and could she move out by Friday; another had to face the fact that the repairs he had carried out himself were unsafe. Each family needed a separate water and sanitation solution, a revolutionary concept in Delmas, where there has never been a drainage system, and each will have a livelihoods assessment and the chance of a small grant to get them back on their feet again.

This was incredibly intricate, careful and exhausting work. In time it would transform this tiny, forgotten corner of the capital, which would begin to thrive as people were enabled to return to their shattered homes from the social jungle of the camps. The problem we were already seeing, however, was that as fast as we moved people out of the camps and back into their homes, the vacant tents would fill up again with people from other slum areas unaffected by the earthquake, for whom life in the hell of La Piste, with its promise of fresh water, sanitation and medical facilities, looked like heaven compared to where they had been living.

When we got together with our colleagues from other national societies to discuss the Federation strategy going forward, we were delighted to find our painstaking approach endorsed as the 'gold standard'. Several other national societies had concentrated their efforts and resources on building thousands of 'temporary' or transitional shelters; these had the advantage of offering virtually-immediate accommodation solutions in bulk, but the downside certainty (in Haiti) was that they would rapidly become just another unsustainable and earthquake-prone slum. Although building new houses was a viable alternative in more rural areas (where several other big NGOs were working), this strategy could not work in Port-au-Prince because there was virtually no vacant (or affordable) land, and what there was was still covered with rubble – so the only answer was in fact the Delmas model of slow and detailed repair and reconstruction.

It was just such a daunting task. Each phase of the operation brought gut-wrenching new challenges and dilemmas, and it was all too easy to forget the successes of what had gone before – over 2m litres of fresh water delivered daily, 300,000 people reached with basic sanitation and health care facilities, 172,000 families provided with emergency shelter, thousands already rehoused and receiving livelihoods grants. But for now, each day brought another mountain to climb, and more agonizing decisions about priorities and what we could or couldn't afford to do.

Back at home, various issues were bubbling away. The organizing committee for the London Olympics had made it clear some time previously that the Games would have its own cadre of first aiders and that, even if some of them were Red Crossers, they would not be permitted to display our emblem – nothing must diminish or dilute the branding supremacy of the Olympic rings. This was disappointing, but as there was to be an Olympics event or training camp in nearly all of our operational Areas, we were in active discussions with the emergency services about how best we could support or supplement their activities in dealing with the expected crowds. The anticipated influx of tourists into London was also causing the Greater London Authority some concern, and we offered to recruit volunteers to provide information and support to visitors, with volunteers on hand at transport hubs and other potential trouble spots to provide first aid, emotional and practical support, and extra on-the-spot assistance in the event of a major incident.

The issue of our Emblem, and how to promote and protect it, was a constant source of concern and sometimes exasperation internally and externally. This year, the pantomime season was the surprising cause of the hoo-ha. It so happened that the Pavilion Theatre in Glasgow was putting on *The Magical Adventures of Robin Hood* over Christmas, and the script required a male actor in drag to play the part of Nurse Poltis to minister to the Merry Men in Sherwood Forest. Although nurses in the UK had not worn red crosses on their uniforms since before the war, the costume department saw fit to emblazon the character's ample padded frontage with a very large one.

A serious-minded volunteer reported this apparent breach of the Geneva Conventions Act 1957 to Michael Meyer, our renowned and respected Head of International Humanitarian Law who, pursuant to his agreement with the Ministry of Defence (which, under the Act, owns the Emblem) fired off a standard 'cease and desist' letter to the theatre over the misuse of the Emblem, arguing that their abuse of it could put lives at risk on the battlefield. Inevitably, Nurse Poltis and the theatre management were affronted, and they released the correspondence to the local newspaper, which had a field day at our expense and to hilarious effect, swiftly followed by the nationals. It all blew over eventually, and no lasting damage was done. Nurse Poltis carried on her onstage humanitarian activities in Glasgow with a green cross on her chest to replace the red one.

But the issue had come up many times before, in one form or another, often in connection with fundraising activities, and poor Michael was frequently on the receiving end of aggrieved complaints from people who genuinely thought they were doing their job or trying to help us, but who had been told they could not use the Emblem. Businesses also tried sometimes to use a red cross to boost their takings or positioning, and they too would complain bitterly, either that they 'didn't know' or that 'they couldn't see what harm it could possibly do'.

Meanwhile, the new Coalition Government was having a long and hard look at humanitarian aid with its Humanitarian Emergency Response Review, which sought to analyse HMG's response to sudden onset emergencies, to see if it could be more effective, timelier and better value for money. Since a proportion of DFID's budget was spent not via foreign governments or the UN, but through NGOs like Oxfam and Save the Children, and also through the Red Cross system, we put a great deal of effort into demonstrating for the benefit of the Review not only our financial cost-effectiveness and probity, but also the added value that funding for the Red Cross brought – a global institution with a Red Cross or Red Crescent Society active, volunteers on the ground in virtually every community, a clear set of values and principles and a reputation that was second to none. 'You have nothing to worry about,' we were assured, but we did anyway.

What we did not know at the time was that the Review was a prelude to the Prime Minister's announcement in 2012 that henceforth the UK would regard itself as fully bound to achieve the target set in 1970 for donor countries to contribute 0.7 per cent of their gross national income as overseas development assistance – which would amount to a large increase in DFID's budget to around £12 billion each year from 2013 and would set a powerful example to other developed countries.

There was so much going on. Just in March 2011, my diary shows that we were involved in discussions about all of the issues mentioned above, plus a massive proposed ('yet another') reform of the NHS to create 'clinical commissioning groups' and a new body to be called Public Health England; possible changes in the UK's approach to human rights; the disbanding of the Government's 'Third Sector Advisory Body', of which I had been a member; ongoing roadshows promoting the *Saving Lives Changing Lives* strategy; launching a new movement for young Red Cross volunteers; supporting the development of a department of Health Flu Pandemic response strategy; appeals for the Christchurch earthquake in New Zealand, the terrible earthquake in Japan and ensuing tsunami, flooding in Colombia and Panama, polio in the Congo; the evacuation of British nationals from Egypt and Libya in the wake of the 'Arab Spring' uprisings; water distribution in Northern Ireland after disruption caused by snow and flooding; an application for accreditation as an independent ambulance provider; the expansion of our Home from Hospital service as an adjunct to a Government campaign to avoid unnecessary admission to hospital; the loss to a private contractor of a big contract for the provision of medical equipment in Leicester (which we had held for fifty years); the controversial closure of a Red Cross day centre; a DFID grant of £1.6m to help with our organizational development work with Red Cross partners; a leading role in the development of a new global resource-mobilization strategy for the Federation; a fundraiser seconded to No. 10 to advise on the development of payroll giving; involvement in the EU/UN Year of Volunteering; a big push to develop our links with universities; the development of new IT systems … etc., etc. All of these issues, and more, floated across the CEO's desk at some point that month, and I don't even have a memory of it as a particularly busy one.

The so-called 'Arab Spring' in early 2011 generated a great deal of interest and speculation, and I co-chaired a conference in Cairo organized by the Humanitarian Forum (of which I was vice-chair), the League of Arab States and the Organization of the Islamic Conference, to discuss the humanitarian consequences. In the Humanitarian Forum, my friend Dr Hany El-Banna's organization, we saw it as an opportunity to promote the growth and development of civil society actors in some Muslim countries where governments had been less than encouraging and supportive, and we hoped that the US and UK Treasury authorities might loosen their tight restrictions on the movement of funds by Islamic NGOs, introduced in the often-mistaken belief that the money was being used to support terrorist activities.

Our own emergency response capacity was continuing, meanwhile, on its exciting upwards trajectory, with volunteer numbers up (for several months in succession) to just under 35,000, and increasing involvement for our local teams in responses to emergencies by the statutory services and in the local resilience fora that had been mandated across the country. At the national level, we were invited onto the Steering Group that was advising the Cabinet Office Civil Contingencies Secretariat on the development of its community resilience programme and the guidance notes and toolkits that were being distributed to local authorities. I attended the annual training weekend for our Psychological Support Team, which was now being used quite regularly by the FCO, and enjoyed spending time with a very enthusiastic bunch of volunteers and their special guest, Terry Waite, who gave a fascinating and moving lecture about how he coped during his long years as a hostage in Lebanon.

Allied to this, we celebrated the moment at which sales of smart phones exceeded sales of PCs in the UK by launching the first ever First Aid app, offering life-saving advice right there on the phone in your pocket, and soon started receiving calls from people who had used it to save the life of someone often in their immediate circle of family or friends. It was exciting to see 1,000 UK cinemas that summer promoting the app to young people during screenings of one of the Harry Potter films, and to have a Big Red Bus travelling the country with first aid messages and volunteer recruitment materials. There was the launch, too, of a new website for our popular first aid training courses for companies and businesses, and a UK-wide pricing structure to replace the mishmash of local offers that had previously been in place.

We also launched that summer a new campaign urging people to look beyond the stereotypical 'refugee' label and highlighting the positive contribution made by people who were refugees, including working as volunteers themselves in our growing number of local asylum-seeker and refugee advice and support centres. We gave powerful evidence, too, at a Home Affairs Select Committee review of the Borders Agency, arguing the urgent need to reform the asylum process based on principles of fairness and good and timely decision-making.

This was a good example of our developing 'humanitarian advocacy' agenda and positioning, as was our leadership of a voluntary sector meeting to discuss and debate the opportunities and issues for the sector arising out of the Prime Minister's 'Big Society' initiative, and the evidence we presented to an NHS review about the need for greater integration between health and social services – a rallying cry for reformers for thirty years, and one which remains unfulfilled to this day.

Tragedy struck in May. Angela Hoyt, who had worked for the ICRC in London in their offices on the top floor of our building, was murdered by a former boyfriend at her flat in Hertfordshire. She was a very bright and popular member of staff who worked closely with her British Red Cross colleagues on communications issues, and her death cast a shadow over the office for the whole summer. Geoff Loane, her boss, a mild and softly-spoken Irishman, was devastated, and I did my best to console him as we worked through the issues surrounding her death. Angela's family, including her twin sister Ami, came over from Canada and kindly came to talk to her many friends in the office after the inquest. It was a sad time, and a tragic waste.

Finally, in a busy summer before I set off for visits to South Sudan (via Kenya for a meeting with the African national societies) and Kyrgyzstan, we were able to celebrate Mark Astarita's election as President of the Institute of Fundraisers, Comms Director Phil Talbot's nomination for a communications award and my own receipt of the Civil Society Award for Outstanding Leadership – plus an appointment to the Government's National Honours Committee for the local government, community and voluntary sectors.

South Sudan had changed a lot since my last visit six years previously, when a peace agreement had just been signed to end thirty years of civil war, on the day the charismatic John Garang, leader of the revolt, was killed. Then, the capital Juba was a one-horse little place, with a handful of scraggy shops and virtually no made roads. Now, with just two weeks to go before independence, the town was buzzing – tarmac laid, a new airport terminal almost complete, roads being frantically swept clean, holes dug for street lights and some trees, shops and restaurants busy. I was there to talk with the new national society, also now to be independent of Khartoum, about the support that it might need.

The staff and volunteers seemed tired and listless, though, and I sensed exhaustion at the scale of the task ahead of them. Their 78-year-old secretary general, the dedicated and dignified Arthur Poole, was hesitant about handing over the new society to his more energetic deputy, John Labor. Talking about what the future held for the new country, it was hard not to feel deflated. The government in the north, no doubt still smarting that it had 'lost' the referendum on independence, had closed the border and was exerting all kinds of pressure on the south, mainly to strengthen its hand in negotiations over oil, which had been found only in the south but could be sold only through pipelines that ran north. There were constant disputes and rows, the latest threat being that half a million people of southern origin but living and working in the north would be pushed back over the border any day.

In the south, there were still no roads, no industry or organized agriculture, no health service, no agreed constitution – not much of anything really. Politicians in the south weren't even agreed amongst themselves, and there was real fear that ethnic violence and civil war could break out after independence (as indeed it did, two years later). It was not surprising that the UN, the World Bank and our own DFID rated the chances of success for the new country as low.

The new national society was in a similar state. The northern Sudanese Red Crescent had done little to help it financially or otherwise, the Federation had yet to appoint a country representative and those few 'PNS' working in the country had not so far been able to put together a coordinated plan of organizational development or support. Expectations of the new society would no doubt be high, and the needs would be enormous – but there was no money, no constitution and no management team. We had money to offer to get them going, but we were pushing to see a short-to-medium-term development plan in place first.

My one visit outside the capital was to Mangala, the old colonial headquarters about 70km from Juba, along a dire and dusty dirt road. The town was no more than a collection of straw huts and collapsed concrete blockhouses in a clearing on the banks of the White Nile. Any colonial buildings remaining were flattened during the civil war, leaving a sense of brooding grievance and muggy, drowsy heat. The new health centre, the object of our visit, was two years old but already cracked and falling apart, its dusty rooms piled from floor to ceiling with upside-down boxes filled with a random assortment of date-expired drugs. The medical assistant, who had put up a security fence to stop pilfering after all the door locks were stolen, told a dismal tale of distressed but doubting patients and an uninterested committee, which disliked the assistant because he came from a different tribe.

I spent the last precious hour or so of an inconclusive trip chatting in the fading light to Arthur Poole in the Red Cross compound, as he reminisced about his soldier father in the British Army, of the visit by Lady Limerick (a previous British Red Cross chair) in 1970, and the 'good days' of colonial rule. As we talked, a long-awaited supply of brand new Red Cross T-shirts arrived, proudly emblazoned with the new society's logo, and were brought to him by an excited volunteer. He brushed them quietly aside and went back to the past.

I drove out to the airport, past the new clock counting down the minutes and seconds to the brave new world of independence.

Soon after returning from Juba, I travelled to Kyrgyzstan with Vicky Peterkin, one of our Board members, at the request of the secretary-general Ravza (or Rosa) Shaiahmetova, who was having difficulties with her President (and Board) following a complaint from one of the branches. The local branch of PWC had been called in to investigate the complaint, and Vicky and I were to conduct a joint workshop for the Board and the management team, based on our own experiences at home. The workshop went well, although it was ominous that the President pulled out at the last minute; but Rosa felt that we had 'touched their souls' and seemed hopeful that the matter would soon be resolved.

The visit was a happy one, though, with Vicky obviously revelling in her first overseas mission for the Red Cross and charming everyone with her gentle good humour. Rosa organized a very full programme for us which, as with many countries in the former Soviet Union, involved several large meals (including one memorable feast cooked by Rosa and her daughters in their home) and a great deal of toasting – which, if you can avoid the vodka, is a great excuse for saying nice things about people or just changing the subject of conversation. The Red Crescent in Kyrgyzstan seemed to be run mostly by able and powerful women, so often I was the only man at the table, which led Vicky kindly to nominate me as an honorary member of the sisterhood for the duration of the trip. The Parliament, after a very public campaign by the national society, had very recently voted to end the pernicious practice of bride kidnap and the granting of 'informal marriage certificates' by some religious authorities, so they had plenty to celebrate.

We travelled a lot around the large, mountainous, landlocked and thinly populated Asian republic, from the capital Bishkek in the north to Jalalabad in the south. There had been serious inter-community violence in the south in recent months, with more than a thousand deaths and severe damage to thousands of properties, and the national society felt that it had a lot to learn about how best to deal with it. As so often in such situations, the national society either reflected within its ranks the societal divisions, or else was biased, or perceived to be biased, towards one side or the other – either way, it was difficult in those circumstances to demonstrate neutrality and impartiality, and often, as here, it was best to bring in the ICRC to lead the response.

The country was badly affected by TB and HIV and, with our assistance, the national society had been focussing its efforts on community-based healthcare and highly cost-effective peer education and awareness-raising campaigns with vulnerable groups such as the internally-displaced (as a result of ethnic violence), truck and taxi drivers, drug abusers and others with chaotic lifestyles. Many of those helped by the society had become in their turn volunteers, and we had one emotional encounter with an elderly man recently recovered from TB who, grasping my hand in his finger-crunching fist, waggled his prayer beads and bawled out his advice for our benefit, before bursting into tears of gratitude.

Vicky was particularly taken by the women's programme, again funded by British Red Cross, which sought to combine healthy lifestyle messages with vocational skills for women from the target groups. We talked to some amazingly passionate people, who spoke movingly about the small businesses and self-help groups which they had been enabled to set up, with a little financial assistance from us, via the national society. One of the dressmakers expertly sized Vicky up and produced as a parting gift a beautiful frock which is no doubt still one of Vicky's proudest possessions. Later that day, Vicky made an impromptu visit to a group of young female sex workers who were receiving regular advice on health issues from a Red Crescent volunteer, a fine example of the lengths this small and ill-funded society was going to in order to seek out the most vulnerable for assistance.

Much of the rest of the year was taken up with Federation business. The most significant event was the first meeting of the 'Secretary-Generals' Panel on National Society Development', which I was to chair. This meeting of twenty-five or so secretary-generals from around the world with the Federation and the ICRC, which took place in London, was the first attempt within the Movement to agree a strategy for developing the capacity of national societies. I was very excited that this long-debated idea had finally got off the ground and, as British Red Cross was also providing the secretariat for the group, we would have every opportunity to ensure that its work was focussed and productive.

It was well-timed too because, as a result of its review of humanitarian aid policy, DFID had resolved to enter into longer-term funding agreements with key partners like the Red Cross. We had already been informed of a small longer-term grant to help with our national society development work, and we had lobbied hard on behalf of both the ICRC and the Federation. We were successful on both fronts, but the Federation's award of a £28m grant over five years for helping other national societies with their development (music to my ears) and improved coordination came with strings attached. DFID expected to see results and, at a Donor Forum meeting in Montreal, the Director of Security and Humanitarian Affairs at DFID told us all that improvements in accountability, financial reporting and a stronger network of national societies were expected of the Federation. We immediately suggested to the secretary-general, Bekele Geleta, that we work together with him and his team to draw up and monitor a plan of action to achieve the required results.

Our Federation colleagues were much preoccupied at the time with a food security crisis in the Horn of Africa, caused by what was said to be the worst drought in sixty years, which affected more than 9m people in Somalia, Djibouti, Sudan and South Sudan, Uganda, Ethiopia and Kenya, and led to a massive flight of refugees from Somalia into Kenya and Ethiopia, after the UN declared a famine in southern Somalia. Deaths were variously estimated at 50,000–260,000 people. A DEC appeal, of which we were of course part, raised a whopping £57m.

As we debated our response strategy, which we wanted to focus not just on the short-term (great though the immediate need was) but also on recovery and resilience-building for the future, I flew with our international director, David Peppiatt, to Kenya to discuss the possibilities with my counterpart, Abbas Gullet, and the President of the Somali Red Crescent, the quietly-spoken Dr Ahmed Hassan.

Our intention had been to include a visit to the massive Dadaab refugee camp in eastern Kenya, close to the Somali border, now home to half a million refugees, many of whom had been there for twenty years or more as a result of the long-running civil war in Somalia. Abbas had recently offered to take over the running of the enormous and troubled camp from UNHCR, and we were amongst several national societies very concerned on his behalf about this great security and reputational risk. The visit was ruled out at the last minute due to the kidnapping of two Spanish aid workers, which rather highlighted the concerns we were expressing. Abbas was undaunted, and showed us instead what the Kenya Red Cross had achieved in a nearby dusty desert camp, a desolate place with thousands of once-white tents shielding disconsolate families from a continuous, flogging wind that constantly whipped shreds of fading plastic litter against the wired fences of this purgatorial prison of the soul.

The crisis in the Horn was complex, comprising as it did a drought (not so very different from similar droughts in the area in 2000, 2001, 2005, 2006, 2008 and 2009); a twenty-year civil war in Somalia in which the rebel group Al Shabaab (linked to Al Qaeda) refused to allow western aid to people in the areas which it held; and the resulting inflow of refugees to Kenya. While we were there, Kenyan troops invaded Somalia, intent on wiping out Al Shabaab, protecting the border, building a buffer zone and setting up a new semi-autonomous Somali region – thereby potentially making the crisis a great deal worse.

Meanwhile, several national societies were parachuting people and supplies into Somalia unbidden, with little apparent regard for safety or security considerations – as was promptly demonstrated when a suicide bomber attacked the Iranian Red Crescent team in Mogadishu. We decided to spend half of our funds in support of a comprehensive ICRC feeding programme in Somalia, and the rest helping Kenya Red Cross with its work in Dadaab, plus an investment in the society's efforts to improve irrigation and cultivation in some of the worst-affected areas. As ever, there was far too much need, and far too little money.

In London, the new government was conducting various policy reviews, and we spent hours preparing to advocate for improvements – particularly to the Health and Social Care Bill, which threatened to reduce local social care budgets still further, making it ever harder to achieve sustainability for schemes like our cost-effective and NHS bed-saving 'home from hospital' schemes. DFID was also producing a new humanitarian policy which looked destined to dilute DFID's laudable focus on real humanitarian need in favour of a focus that had more to do with the UK's own commercial and security interests. Perhaps this was the inevitable result of the government's choice of 'austerity' as its answer to the 2008 global financial crash, but the 'double whammy' of increased need and decreased cash was clearly destined to hit the voluntary sector hard in the coming years.

It was encouraging then, in a sense, to be going to the Red Cross international meetings in November with two strong sets of proposals – one for a new worldwide fundraising strategy which I was to present, and the other for the development of the global Red Cross Red Crescent brand, where again I was very energetically and enthusiastically engaged.

The Federation had never really had an effective income-generation policy, either for its own benefit or, much more importantly, as a vital support tool for its member national societies. Hitherto, the Federation had relied for funding upon the membership fee (or *barème*) paid by its member societies on a sliding scale according to their own relative wealth and the share of UN costs borne by their own government, and on grants from donor governments. This amounted to a rather hand-to-mouth existence for such an important international institution, and resulted in endless internal arguments about the *barème*, from often cash-strapped national societies who wanted to prioritize their own work over support to the Federation as a whole; and arguments about approaches made by the Federation to national governments which, it was argued, should be the exclusive preserve of the relevant local Red Cross.

I hated this inward-looking focus and, strongly supported by Mark Astarita and his team, argued that if we all worked together we could do – and raise – so much more, for the good of the whole, with a detailed fundraising strategy showing how it could be done. Approaches to specific governments, major corporations, wealthy individuals and trusts would be coordinated through Geneva but in cooperation with those national societies that were prepared to share expertise, experience and resource, in return for a share of the proceeds. For national societies (the majority, sadly) that lacked the wherewithal or know-how to fundraise in their own country there would be a central team, backed by capable national societies to 'spread the word'. We knew that this could work because of our experience with the '8NS initiative', which had had fundraising and income-generation at its core.

At home, I had found that the idea that we were 'all fundraisers in the British Red Cross' had struck a chord, and decided to give it a go in Geneva with my thousand or so fellow delegates. I rattled though my presentation, waving my arms about and making a lot of noise as usual, but feeling somewhat lonely onstage in front of some rather staid national society representatives, who were used to a more sober even sombre style. As I neared the end I paused and looked out across the huge conference hall.

'Where are the fundraisers?' I bellowed.

Nobody stirred.

'Come on,' I said. 'There must be one or two fundraisers here.'

People looked about them, and a couple of hands went up.

I shook my head, hands on hips.

'No,' I yelled. 'You haven't got it. We're ALL fundraisers in the Red Cross! Everybody up, out of your seats. Wave your arms around. Where are the fundraisers?'

There was a moment of stunned silence – this was new. A few got up, grinning nervously.

'Mr Konoe,' I said, looking at the President, my Japanese friend of *Mona Lisa* fame. 'You're a fundraiser, aren't you?'

Dear man, he leapt to his feet, and then everyone had to follow suit. The place was a mass of waving arms and smiling faces – we were all fundraisers in the Red Cross after all.

The brand development proposal went down well, too, and it was agreed that a working group should be set up to oversee a set of work streams that would look at how to strengthen our global positioning, reputation and influence.

Why did I put all this personal effort into these Federation initiatives (demanding the same of British Red Cross colleagues), when so many national society peers did much less? I was often asked this question, and it certainly cost me dear in terms of time and energy, as well as being inevitably a distraction for my senior management colleagues. But the fact is that we all believed passionately that the Red Cross Red Crescent

Movement as a whole, for all that it was already doing, could do, and needed to do, so very much more, and that the initiative for it to do so had to come from its member national societies. Knowing as we did how lucky we were, in our smug, rich western world, it was time for us to step up, to put our shoulders to a collective wheel and push to show an increasingly-divided world that the spirit of Henri Dunant was still alive and abroad on the battlefields of humanitarian need.

The Movement also debated and adopted a resolution calling on states to prohibit and eliminate nuclear weapons through a binding international agreement. The Movement had never before taken such a high-profile stance on the issue, and the (minority of) national societies whose governments actually possessed nuclear weapons (including, of course, our own) tended, whilst recognizing the unarguable moral point, to advocate nevertheless for a more nuanced approach, which took into account the reality that, whilst such weapons remained in existence, deterrence also had its place.

Chapter 13

A Kidnapping in Pakistan, 2012

The Olympics – Azerbaijan – Lesotho – Haiti again

The most traumatic three months of my time at the Red Cross started on 5 January, when our international director David Peppiatt called to say that Khalil Dale, one of our delegates but seconded to the ICRC, had been kidnapped on his way home from work, in a clearly-marked Red Cross vehicle, in Quetta. For several days we heard nothing, as the ICRC tried desperately to find out who had taken him and why, whilst we linked up with the Foreign and Commonwealth Office and established contact with Khalil's family and friends.

Khalil was a brave and totally committed humanitarian who had worked, mostly for the Red Cross, as a nurse and general aid worker in trouble spots like Sudan, Somalia, Afghanistan and Iraq, for thirty years. He seemed drawn to danger, judging no assignment off-limits in his determination to make the world a better place, single-handedly if he had to. Born in York in 1951, Ken (as he then was) Dale followed his mother and brother Ian into the nursing profession. Qualifying in 1974 and moving with the family to Dumfries, he soon took a job as a nurse with an American shipping company and got his first taste of what he would have regarded as adventure as one of 400 foreigners held under house arrest for two weeks after the 1979 revolution in Iran.

After a short spell on an oil rig in the North Sea, and then in Libya with the oil industry, he 'saw the light' and trained in tropical diseases, before taking his first Red Cross deployment in 1981 to Kenya, where he led a small team setting up feeding centres for drought-stricken people in Turkana in the north, often beset by attacks from Ugandan cattle-raiders armed with machine guns. He converted to Islam the same year, deeply inspired by his time living with a Muslim family in Kenya and their simple, peaceful way of life.

His next assignment was in Sudan, where he was responsible for food distribution, healthcare and development projects in the Red Sea Hills, a semi-desert region inhabited mostly by nomadic tribes, most of them suffering from malnutrition. He became a familiar sight travelling around his area with his two camels, Kipling and Paddington – one for himself and one for supplies. Challenges followed him everywhere, from a burst water-skin which necessitated an eight-hour return trip in 53°C with no water, to a fall followed by a two-day trek nursing a severely strained back, to a sword fight between two furious tribesmen which he sought to break up.

Then came war-torn Somalia, where he was running relief flights across the battle lines to communities cut off by the fighting, and Afghanistan, then racked by violence as warlords battled for post-Soviet supremacy – efforts for which he was awarded the MBE. With his strong sense of duty and responsibility, he gave up his life of humanitarian adventure in 1998 to return home to Dumfries to look after his terminally-ill mother, working first as a nurse at the Dumfries and Galloway Royal Infirmary, and then for the charity Turning Point – until 2007, after his mother's death, when he took up a posting as a programme manager for the Danish Refugee Council, again in Somalia.

Finally came Quetta in 2011, working on an ICRC programme to improve access to healthcare and physical rehabilitation for people wounded in local conflicts. He was happy there, doing the work he loved, amongst people he liked and respected and who felt the same about him.

Then he was taken. For a month we heard nothing and focussed our own efforts on supporting the family, spread all over the world, and Khalil's friends, encouraging them to help us keep the story out of the media, since FCO experience suggested that once a hostage story got into the press, it became much harder to negotiate a successful release. We set up a special self-contained team to manage this intensely personal saga, led by International Director David Peppiatt, and waited nervously for news. Eventually it came, in the form of a 'proof of life' video from the kidnappers (or the people then holding him), and we knew at last that at least there was hope, and the ICRC were able to redouble their efforts to establish contact with those responsible.

But we all knew that the prospects were grim. For some time, ever since the US-led invasions of Afghanistan and Iraq, it had been clear that aid workers were seen by some as valid and even useful targets for politically motivated attacks and kidnapping, partly for the publicity and propaganda value, partly perhaps for their implied complicity in 'Western aggression', partly of course as potential income-generators for terrorist groups. Only a few years previously, the civil engineer Ken Bigley and the Care delegate Margaret Hassan had been taken hostage and savagely murdered in Iraq, and since then the number of attacks had increased each year, to around a hundred in 2012, for example. Nevertheless, whilst we believed that the job of the Red Cross was to continue to try to help and protect the innocent whatever the circumstances, we also had a very clear and well-known policy that ransoms would never be paid, so the risks were high, and everyone knew that.

The weeks dragged by, punctuated by regular meetings with the FCO and nameless individuals, presumably from the security services, conferences with our ICRC colleagues and briefings for the family and key friends. I held regular 'all staff' gatherings, partly to share whatever limited information we could, partly to give individuals the opportunity to express their concerns, partly to keep up morale and show, in the ongoing media silence, that Khalil was by no means forgotten and that we were doing everything we could to get him back. Two more 'proof of life' videos were received, Khalil looking ever more wretched; ICRC reported a shadowy link to the people who were holding him and the possibility of a discussion of some kind – and then, on 29 April, a headless body was found beside the road out to the airport in Quetta. Our friend and colleague was dead.

We never found out who had taken him, or why. There were reports that it might have been members of a terrorist group based in the north-west of the country, bordering Afghanistan. Unsubstantiated rumours surfaced that Khalil had been involved in some kind of dispute in Quetta, or that perhaps he had been suspected of working for British Intelligence. It was all very vague, and the most likely explanation was that a heroic, dedicated and innocent humanitarian had simply been in the wrong place at the wrong time and had paid the price.

As I said in a press release at the time:

Khalil Dale has been a committed member of the Red Cross Red Crescent family for the last thirty years. He was a gentle, kind person, who devoted his life to helping others, including some of the world's most vulnerable people.

We condemn his abduction and murder in the strongest possible terms. It not only robs him of his life, and his family and co-workers of their loved ones and friend – it robs the people he was helping of the expert care they need. Care workers like Khalil, and his colleagues in dangerous places all over the world, should be allowed to work free from threats of abduction and violence.

Khalil's kidnapping and murder was a devastating start to the year. The death of a respected colleague is a traumatic event in any organization, particularly one like the Red Cross, where people do come to feel as if they are part of a family, and where we were all very conscious that we had other colleagues (in the British Red Cross and in other national societies) working in similar situations facing similar dangers all over the world. The pressure and emotional burden on David Peppiatt and his team, particularly Cathy Fitzgibbon, who all did a magnificent job of liaising with his family and friends, had been intense, and the mood was subdued and depressed. It had been a terribly difficult time for everybody.

I found myself questioning, not for the first time, whether it was right for us to send delegates to work in areas or contexts where their safety could not be guaranteed. My own personal conviction was that the work and mission of the Red Cross demanded that we place ourselves in dangerous locations, precisely so that we could be in a position to help innocent victims – but it was easy for me, in my peaceful office in London, to take that view; although I had several times placed myself in harm's way I had never had to live with the fear and risk day in day out as some of our colleagues did – with no security guards, no bullet-proof vests, and only common sense and the Red Cross Emblem to protect them. We reviewed our processes, procedures, training and mission briefings yet again – but our hearts were heavy.

Mike Adamson was acting up as CEO during the first two months of the year, as I was in hospital having two new knees fitted, and he did a great job. It was a tricky time, with escalating community violence and the start of the civil war in Syria affecting both our colleagues in the Syrian Arab Red Crescent and our own delegates; a looming food crisis in the Sahel; heavy snow across the UK with frequent call-outs for our volunteers; a recent Government-commissioned report recommending deregulation of commercial first aid training (which was likely to have a serious impact on an income-generating core activity); supporting the team through the Khalil crisis; leading negotiations for the transfer of the long-established and much-loved Red Cross 'cosmetic camouflage' activity to Changing Faces, the organization for people with facial disfigurements run by the inspirational James Partridge (himself severely marked following a tragic road accident as a young man, and now sadly deceased), where we felt it would be able to flourish and grow far better than if it stayed with us.

On the horizon later that summer was the Olympics, but before then I was committed to visit Azerbaijan on the Caspian Sea, where we had a big livelihoods programme running for the extremely vulnerable families in the area of Azerbaijan that borders the region of Nagorno-Karabakh (NK), which had been occupied by neighbouring Armenia twenty years previously.

It was a complicated story. In 1991, following the collapse of the Soviet Union, the predominantly Armenian population of the NK region attempted to secede, backed by Armenia, war broke out and the Armenians of NK took control of the region and surrounding territory. A ceasefire was agreed in 1994, and this left about one seventh of Azerbaijan's territory occupied effectively by Armenia. Some 600,000 native Azerbaijanis fled the area, many of them choosing to remain along the 'line of contact' between their own country and Armenian-occupied NK, within sight of the mountains and forests of their homeland. They lived in terrible conditions, neglected even by their own government, with little opportunity to work and subject to frequent incursions and shooting across the line of contact which had left many dead.

We were working in partnership with the ICRC and the Azerbaijan Red Crescent, providing cash grants (by now one of our established and recognized areas of special expertise) for about 900 families – money to help buy a cow, start a small business, pay the medical bills for a family member – plus financial assistance to whole communities for special projects like the construction of earth walls to shield them from bullets, a borehole to provide fresh water, or money (in one case) to provide a communal tent for village ceremonies such as weddings or funerals.

My visit started in the capital Baku, its stylish seaside boulevard thronged with families and lovers enjoying the warm evening breeze, or sipping cold drinks and eating ice cream in the shady open-air restaurants along the front. In the distance, across the bay, was the vast Crystal Hall conference and concert hall, built at a cost of millions for an Engelbert Humperdinck concert (he was big there, for some reason) and itself dwarfed by what was claimed to be the largest flag in the world, flying gaudily from the top of a newly-constructed hillock. Baku was Oil Town, its wealth concentrated in the hands of politicians and a few oligarchs.

I met the Deputy Prime Minister, who fulminated about the iniquities of the Armenian occupation of NK but seemed little interested in the needs of his fellow countrymen and women who used to call it home. I was delighted to see how patiently the ICRC worked at persuading him to assist them by focussing not on the big issue, but on individual cases where they thought some pressure from the central government might help.

When we set off the next day for the five-hour drive across a flat sun-baked landscape for the line of control, I was able to see for myself the disconnect between the politicians in Oil Town and their people. I met a dozen or more families, both permanent residents and 'internally displaced persons', living in simple wooden shacks in tiny rural hamlets, sometimes with a little land at the back, almost all of them struggling to make any kind of living at all in an area completely poisoned by war and the sense of powerlessness it induces in its victims. Tragically, there seemed to be very little community spirit, each family bleakly isolated, wound up in its own problems and still fixated in a deep-rooted mistrust of politicians and the fear of a return to Soviet-style collectivization.

We saw bullet holes in walls and fences, the barricades families had built for protection, the cows they had been given, the sparse crops they were growing for family consumption and survival – no sign of a cooperative approach to agriculture or of any market to sell their produce in. Our programme was providing some help and comfort, much appreciated by the residents, and it was forcing the Government to take some notice, but it wasn't providing much real hope for the longer-term future of the homeless Azerbaijanis of Nagorno-Karabakh, and it wasn't going to bring those distant hills and forests of home any closer.

We met a woman living with her daughter and elderly mother in a battered, bullet-holed old farm cottage. We had given her a cow.

'Will you sell it?' I asked, interested to discover her 'business plan'.

'No,' she said, 'not yet. I will wait until my mother dies, then it will pay for the funeral.'

She shrugged. The old lady peered into the distance. The daughter looked at the floor. The sense of helplessness was palpable.

More than a thousand staff and volunteers from every part of the UK were involved in providing first aid support to the Olympics and the Paralympics that summer. As the country basked in sunshine and the pride and excitement engendered by the Games, we treated over a thousand casualties at the main train stations and other key tourist spots in London, and at the sailing in Weymouth, where we ran a joint operation with St John Ambulance. We were disappointed, of course, not to be the main providers of first aid cover to the Games as a whole, but we did our bit to keep the capital safe and felt confident that the cover arrangements that we had made with the London Ambulance Service and other statutory providers would have worked well, if the much-feared terrorist attack had materialized.

It was a good summer for first aiders, as volunteers provided cover at the usual plethora of local and national events, including several marathons and half marathons, and dozens of fetes, gymkhanas and concerts, in all weathers and all over the UK. We won contracts to cover two major golf tournaments (including the Ryder Cup in 2014), and saw more than 300,000 downloads of our first aid app, which we had now started releasing for use by other national societies – including America, where it was downloaded more than a million times in the first month, and China, where I was invited to deliver a speech on first aid learning at a large regional Red Cross conference. We also received a request from Prince Charles to send a first aid trainer to his summer holiday retreat at Birkhall, so that he and his wife could brush up their first aid skills.

But internationally, the threat of violence to healthcare workers that had dominated our thoughts at the start of the year continued, with an ICRC colleague killed in crossfire in the Yemen, another colleague taken hostage (later released), and five volunteers of the Syrian Arab Red Crescent and its secretary-general killed in the spiralling violence in Syria. In Libya, the ICRC had been forced to suspend operations in Misrata and Benghazi following attacks on their offices, and had more than halved its staff in Pakistan. The ICRC had launched a global campaign called Healthcare in Danger, and I made a keynote speech at the London launch, trying to highlight the issue for British policymakers, and followed it up with letters to major newspapers – but the problem was that there was little anyone could do to stop the attacks, in the context of increasing tension between the US and Islamist groups, with aid workers and of course innocent civilians very much caught in the middle.

It was quite a relief to travel to a country where violence to healthcare workers was not an issue. Lesotho, a tiny, mountainous, landlocked and hauntingly beautiful country in the middle of South Africa, has a population of just over 2m peaceful, friendly and generous people. It also had one of the highest rates of HIV in the world – 23 per cent in 2009, with around 290,000 people living with the illness and over 150,000 children orphaned by it. Although the economy was growing, fuelled partly by the kind of Chinese investment in infrastructure that was happening all over Africa, the country still had to import nearly 70 per cent of its food, because most of its landmass is either mountainous or barren and because recent bad weather had massively reduced agricultural output.

Lesotho was another of our partner national societies, having started life as the Basutoland Branch of the British Red Cross. With the engaging and energetic secretary-general, I quickly set out on a cross-country odyssey, starting with a ninety-minute drive to Mafeteng, past fields parched and barren during a rainless planting season. The landscape in the lowlands was a lovely patchwork of brown ploughed fields sculpted to the contours as we drove out of the plains and into the rocky foothills. We saw an occasional ancient rusty tractor, but most of the ploughing was done with cattle or even, occasionally, by hand. A few years ago, the land would have been brilliant green at this time of year, but now the only reminder of better times was an occasional flash of shimmering young willow clinging to the bank of a shrivelled stream.

After a brief courtesy visit to the Acting District Administrator, up to his ears in preparations for a forthcoming visit by the King, we stopped at a small clinic, where a single male nurse was working his way slowly through a queue of sixty or so pregnant women, with their babies and small children, who were waiting for his advice and an HIV test. Those who tested positive were referred to the local Red Cross and became part of the Home-Based Care Project for advice on preventing mother to child transmission of HIV, which we were funding. The poor male nurse seemed overwhelmed by the scale of his daily task and had little time to speak, so we edged our way out through the gloomy sunless waiting room, past the hordes of wide-eyed and nervous-looking mothers, and set off again in the Land Cruisers.

The destination this time was Thaba-Morena, a long bone-shaking drive up into the hills and mountains, along a track punctuated by enough startling double bends and switchback ascents and descents to give the phrase 'the middle of nowhere' a new meaning. Suddenly, three small boys on donkeys appeared, quickly followed by a troop of men on small tough-looking ponies who raced about in front of the Land Cruisers, blowing whistles and shrieking out their greetings. This was clearly the welcoming posse, come to guide us in. Two miles further on, perched on a hilltop amidst a looming range of rock-strewn slopes and baking fields, was a scattering of huts and straw-roofed houses – the village. Chasing out to meet us came a horde of waving, dancing, ululating, chanting, clapping, screaming locals. Just like a visit to one of our own branches, I joked.

The parade eventually wound its way through the village and fetched up at a large tent where, led by the Chief, we were entertained for an hour or more of speeches, singing and dancing, followed by an enormous feast of maize, beans, lamb, bread and spinach, all washed down by bowls of cold, grey fermented sorghum. The generosity, warmth and friendliness of the gathering was extraordinary. I was soon decked out in a personalized Chief's blanket, hat and special stick and, as sunset approached, we abandoned the thought of going anywhere else that night.

In the morning, after more rattling along rutted tracks, we arrived in Kena, its rural community spread across a range of small hills and valleys, with a soon-to-be-completed health centre at its centre – and not much else. There was no electricity, no shop, no road, no reason to be there. We prided ourselves in the Red Cross on our ability to deliver services in 'the last mile' – but this was the last mile beyond the last mile. We had been funding the training and management of a cohort of volunteer care facilitators, gardeners and maternity supporters, to provide help for the 300 people living with HIV in this community of about

5,000 souls, and more than 200 AIDS orphans. The project was about home visits to deliver and administer anti-retrovirals, basic care support and advice on nutrition, aided by the construction of ingenious small 'keyhole'-shaped gardens to grow fresh vegetables. The transformation in this small village had been dramatic – stigma had decreased and the whole community had taken on the tasks of caring for its HIV-infected brethren and limiting future infection. It was a great example of how a simple, integrated, hands-on, community-based solution could change the world in the remotest of places, with minimal investment of money; it just takes people, knowledge and time.

The cost of HIV was enormous and heart-breaking. Shwe-shwe, a 15-year-old orphan, lived in a little brick bungalow. Her name means flower. Inside, her house was dark, cool, spotlessly clean, achingly neat. She was tall and thin, dressed in pink shirt and slacks, and reading *Tom Sawyer* in English. She was completely alone. Her father had died of AIDS three years earlier, her mother worked as a cleaner in South Africa and occasionally sent her a little money via an uncle. Her grandmother lived in a distant valley. Day by day, week by week, she barely knew where her next meal would come from, dependent on the Red Cross care worker and her neighbours, all of whom had their own family troubles and many other orphans to look out for. It was always the same: one personal story said more than whole pages of statistics.

The autumn was always a busy time. It felt like the start of the new school year, with detailed planning and budgeting meetings with each director, a new round of local roadshows – and this year, the task of finding a new Chair to replace James, who was coming to the end of his maximum six-year term. There was also a donor forum meeting in Oslo and a Pan-African Conference in Ethiopia to fit in.

Then came a return to Haiti, nearly three years after the earthquake, to see how well we had spent the money we had raised. The transformation in Port-au-Prince was immediately visible around the airport – no corrugated iron sheds, but a proper terminal, a new car park, smooth tarmacked roads, working roundabouts. No tents.

No tents – that was the difference. On my first visit, just a couple of months after the earthquake had killed 220,000 people and made half a city homeless, it had seemed that most of the population was living under blue plastic sheets and in rickety wooden shelters. Every spare inch of space along every road was covered with either tents or rubble. Now it was a different place, with busy roads, thriving shops and market stalls – it looked like business as usual.

But you didn't have to look far to find the tell-tale signs that there was still a long way to go. Red Cross Base Camp was still there, for example, close to the airport. Then it had been home to hundreds of Red Cross Red Crescent workers, from more than thirty different countries, all there to support the relief effort and the tiny Haitian Red Cross. Now it had become the headquarters of the reborn national society, plus a dozen or so other Red Cross organizations (including our own) that were still working in the country with large-scale rebuilding, health and livelihood support programmes. These programmes were due to continue into 2015 – it takes time to rebuild a city, and the Red Cross share of that task was substantial, and difficult.

You could see why in Delmas 19, the area of 30-year-old slum dwellings built on a swamp near the centre of Port-au-Prince that we had undertaken to rebuild as part of our £22m earthquake response programme. There were no streets, for example. This was a rickety patch of concrete-block, wood and corrugated-iron hovels, where 2,500 adults and children eked out a minimal subsistence in conditions of really quite heart-breaking squalor. It was dark, gloomy and smelly. The alleyways, some no wider than a person's shoulders, threaded between the shacks. Rancid grey water ran underfoot.

People lived in the alleyways. Everywhere, people were washing themselves, eating, tending crying children, pushing wheelbarrows of goods or building materials through the mire, carrying buckets of water on their heads, smiling and joking far more cheerfully than the conditions warranted. Each of the 500 or so families who lived in Delmas 19 owned or rented a house that had either collapsed completely or suffered from multiple cracks. One by one, we had inspected and assessed them all: 200 were habitable, just about, 60 were repairable, 330 had to be pulled down and rebuilt.

Of course, a commercial developer would have bulldozed the lot and started again. The trouble was that Delmas, like all the other slums in Port-au-Prince, was a legal patchwork of rentals and ownerships which had grown up haphazardly over time and to no set plan. Some shacks were bigger than others, or had a better outlook, or were closer to the entrance; some occupiers had a title, others didn't; some were landlords of adjoining properties too; some were owned by distant landlords; many were just squatters, with no rights at all. Negotiating a fresh start that was fair to all with that lot would have taken decades, and anyway we could not have afforded to do it. So we had decided that every single new house would be rebuilt on its original plot, preserving the extraordinary intimacy of this small community, with all that meant in terms of access, health risk and convenience – or the lack of it.

But even this limited rebuilding was beyond our means, so the plan was to train Delmas inhabitants as masons and help them build a reinforced-concrete earthquake-resistant floor plate for each house and put up frames for the walls and roof, with the occupiers filling in the rest themselves. The task of explaining and indeed 'selling' all this to the local community (who of course had ideas of their own about what they wanted) rested with a team of twelve British Red Cross 'community mobilizers', whose job it was to be our eyes, ears and mouthpiece with local people. They had, first and foremost, to hear and understand what the people affected by the earthquake wanted, then explain, in due time and very patiently, what it was we could do and why.

The other part of their job was to initiate a carefully integrated livelihoods programme, using a mix of grants and loans to twenty-five small/medium-sized local enterprises (in partnership with a local social enterprise consultancy), and setting up a network of neighbourhood mutual support groups and small loan clubs to help individuals rebuild their lives sustainably.

It was great to meet with them. They spent every day deep in the community, encouraging, assessing, talking and listening – a link with the local people that was of a depth and quality that we had never attempted before. I talked to Richardson, a young Haitian who had been working with us for six months, his eyes shining as he described his work.

'It's really important for us,' he said, ' to be close to the local residents, and to understand their dreams for the future. We can help them build that future themselves.'

In the building yard, right in the centre of the slum, was our team office, where Gabriel, the Project Manager (the same Gabriel who did such a brilliant job in Aceh after the tsunami), watched the work progress like a hawk, interrupted by a constant stream of visitors, craftsmen, suppliers and the people whose homes we were rebuilding. He was in his element. Sadly, he died soon after completing the project.

The main work in hand was the construction of a covered market for the thirty or so stallholders who used to sell their meat, vegetables, fruit and other produce outside in the muddy street. One chap was working the cement mixer; three teams were laying blocks for the foundations; another group was soldering supports for the roof. Gabriel was everywhere – an encouraging nod, a smile as he checked a level, a warning shout as the aggregate lorry dumped its load at the feet of a stallholder. He had trained every one of his workers, and they followed his guidance carefully – they all knew that the eyes of the community were on them, and they were keen to show what they could do with their newly-learned skills.

Nearby, a raised walkway carried a stream of curious passers-by. This was Gabriel's pride and joy – once a grim, putrid watercourse that carried a poisonous brew of sewage, rotting food and vegetation, old car tyres and wreckage of every sort from the community up the hill, down through Delmas 19 and out, eventually, to the sea. When this 'canal' flooded, as it did several times every rainy season, the flow of refuse increased, and every house within fifty yards received a generous helping of muck. It would be hard to imagine a more disgusting, dangerous or life-threatening amenity.

Not anymore. Gabriel had encased the canal for its full journey through the area in a two-metre-deep reinforced concrete channel, topped with a paved and tiled walkway. I could have sat there for hours, watching kids play hopscotch, mothers chatting, lovers strolling, the whole life of a vibrant community now playing out on a simple yellow brick road through a once forsaken stew of humanity that had been helped to find a new way. I remembered Clinton's exhortation after the tsunami that we should be aiming to 'build back better', and breathed a sigh of relief and pride that, here in Delmas 19, we were doing just that.

I came home to the final Board meeting of the year, James's last as Chair, and was amazed and deeply delighted when he announced that I was to receive the 'Queen's Badge of Honour', the Society's highest award and one that was in the sole gift of the Sovereign, our Patron. He and I had not seen eye to eye all the time, but then not many chairs and chief executives do, and a degree of creative tension is inherent and often desirable in the two roles. We parted on good terms, and remain so to this day.

Chapter 14

Another New Chairman, 2013

Syria agony – Kenya and Somalia – Myanmar –
Orkney and the Western Isles – North Korea

The new chairman was Sir Charles Allen, a former chief executive of Granada and ITV and, at the time of his appointment, chairman of Global Radio (amongst other things). He had been knighted in 2012 for services to the Olympics and Paralympics. He was also chairman of the executive board of the Labour party, and there had been some concern about whether his political links might put the perception of Red Cross neutrality at risk. The Board had decided that the role was sufficiently low-profile and non-political in its nature as to cause little problem in terms of his otherwise impeccable credentials; they also liked his slogan that trustees and senior management should be 'one team', albeit with distinct roles, but mutually supportive and working well together. He was a bright and energetic Scotsman, with a brisk mind teeming with ideas and energy, and he quickly made a good impression on his fellow trustees, staff and volunteers alike – as I saw on an early visit together to some of our Home from Hospital and other work in South Wales, where he engaged quickly and warmly with everyone he met.

As part of an ongoing drive to cut costs and increase efficiency, we had decided to take advantage of the retirement of the Territory Director in the south by reducing the number of Territories to three, dividing England into two, north and south, and putting the three other countries, Scotland, Wales and Northern Ireland, into one – under the three remaining experienced directors Jean Henderson, Annie Bibbings and Norman McKinley respectively. We were keen to encourage more consistent ways of working across the UK and to support knowledge-sharing on issues specific to devolved governments and commissioning structures. At the same time, the Territory communications teams were integrated more closely into the communications division at UK Office, to ensure greater consistency of messaging across the organization. Change is always unsettling, particularly in a voluntary organization where the feeling of being 'part of a family' is strong, but the change was handled well by Mike Adamson and the three directors concerned.

The newspapers at the time were completely dominated by the dire situation in Syria. What had started in 2011 as 'Arab Spring' protests against Bashar al-Assad's regime and demands for democratic reform had turned alarmingly quickly into a full-scale civil war, fuelled by the rapid rise of armed opposition militias across Syria which eventually coalesced into the Free Syrian Army. An UN-mediated ceasefire in 2012 failed, and rebel forces began attacking towns and cities in the north of the country and eventually Damascus itself. The Government's response was brutal and, as far as its own citizens were concerned, indiscriminate; millions left their homes and fled south away from the worst of the fighting, or into neighbouring Turkey, Jordan and Lebanon.

We had been investing in the emergency response capacity of the Syrian Arab Red Crescent (SARC), another of our partner national societies, for some years. I had last visited in 2006, spending time with the Society in Damascus, before travelling up to Homs (the country's second city) and the beautiful ancient town of Aleppo. Then, the country had been peaceful and apparently content – now, as I stepped across the border from Jordan on a visit that had already been postponed several times because of security concerns or visa refusals, it was a war zone.

I was met, on a chill February morning, by Ibrahim, a former SARC volunteer and now living with his Italian wife in Milan. His mother was still in Damascus, and he was pleased to have the opportunity to return as our photographer, charged with recording the visit and helping me to tell the story of what was happening in Syria for the British media and public. He was festooned in cameras, lenses, badges, first aid equipment and identity cards as he stepped out of the Land Cruiser to greet me, garbed in a violent vermilion boiler suit and cap, each covered in red crosses and crescents.

'My goodness,' I said, as we shook hands, 'you look just like a Christmas Tree.'

He roared with laughter, and we became friends immediately. He told me that he was fearful for his mother's safety, despite her determination to remain, and worried about the changes he would find in his beloved homeland.

Negotiating the border took time and patience, and all Ibrahim's skills as an interpreter and diplomat. The border guards were jumpy and stressed, and it took a while to convince them that my visit had a bona fide humanitarian purpose. As we drove into the city, the streets, normally thronged in mid-morning, were eerily silent, the skyline punctuated by plumes of smoke rising from bombed out buildings. The midday call to prayer was interrupted by the rolling boom of mortar and artillery attacks and the shriek of warplanes overhead.

The volunteers and staff of SARC had been doing a remarkable job. Every day, in virtually every part of the country, they were leading convoys filled with food and medical supplies for communities beleaguered by the fighting or hosts of people forced to flee their homes. They had to run the gauntlet along roads fought over by conflicting forces, won and lost by one side or the other, changing hands daily, sometimes more often. Along the roads, checkpoints every few kilometres caused lengthy delays, and constant fear.

'Who are you? Where are you from? Where are you going? Why? What's in the truck?' The volunteers never really knew which 'side' (of which there were several) was manning the checkpoint, or how the fighters would respond to their answers. Sometimes they weren't fighters at all but criminal gangs or hostage-takers, their activities unchecked by the security forces, just another manifestation of the lawless chaos that had overwhelmed the country. At each checkpoint, they had to explain all over again the role of the Red Cross Red Crescent, and its neutrality and impartiality – the same explanations that I had had to give back in 2003 when the *Daily Mail* had accused us of 'banning Christmas', but this time there really were lives at stake, and a less-than-convincing story could mean death at the hands of a nervous soldier. They could carry no mobile phones, in case a contact or an incautious comment in a text gave them away as being somehow 'on the other side'. Several volunteers had been captured or taken hostage; some had been killed. Each day was a nightmare.

'Come with me. Leave your vehicle.' These were the words everyone dreaded. Many times, SARC volunteers had been stopped and held for questioning. Half a dozen or so including, while we were there, the coordinator of the Idlib Branch, had been arrested and imprisoned.

We called first at the SARC ambulance control centre in Damascus, which at that time was the main provider of emergency aid for the civilian population. Every day, crews were sent out to dozens of fires, bombed buildings and car crashes, each trip requiring a dangerous drive through battle-scarred streets. The manager told me how he hated sending out his young volunteers on these dreadful missions, never knowing if they would return safely. Already, in the first two months of the year, eight volunteers had died, mostly caught in crossfire. His wife was one of the volunteers, and I asked how he felt about deploying her, in such dangerous circumstances.

'Oh,' he replied. 'I have given instructions that I am not to be told which vehicle she is on.'

One of the controllers, Razan, told me she was a librarian, but the library had closed months before and she had no job. She was living on her savings and volunteering for SARC seven days a week. She and her team had wept together as friends and colleagues died.

'We are trying to do our best,' she said, with a tired smile, 'with everything we have.'

The President of SARC, the widely-respected Dr Attar, told me that not long ago, before the fighting, Razan had been suspended for insubordination, but 'now, she is one of our treasures.' Outside, a kilometre or so away, a column of grey smoke drifted into the sky.

Later, we talked to a young doctor in a SARC clinic. He seemed drained and subdued.

'My wife has already left,' he said. 'Now I must decide whether I should follow her. Many, many doctors have already gone. Many hospitals and clinics have been bombed. We are suspected by the Government of assisting the rebels: by the rebels of informing on them to the Government. A week ago, I got home to find that a sniper had fired a bullet through my window: it destroyed a suit I had left hanging on the wardrobe door. Yesterday, a sniper killed a man in that caravan over there, just outside the window.'

He pointed across the parking lot, a few yards away.

'We are getting over 1,000 patients a week now. We are running out of medicine. I wake up in the night, I can't stop crying. I feel I should go. But who will take my place …?'

As we left the clinic, a woman came down the steps towards us.

'He is wonderful, that doctor. He is a saviour. They are all wonderful here.'

Food was in short supply, with bread hard to find outside Damascus, and medicines almost unobtainable after many pharmaceutical factories were destroyed or damaged in the fighting around Aleppo. The UN was estimating that there were 4m people on the move inside Syria, desperately trying to get away from the fighting, camping with family or friends or living in school halls or community centres. Another million, mostly poor and with nothing to lose, had fled across borders into neighbouring countries. The rich had fled to Dubai, Saudi Arabia or other countries, to sit it out.

Early the next morning, we went to one of the SARC distribution centres, where food aid shipments were being divided up and loaded onto lorries, which were then formed into convoys for the precarious journeys north. SARC had been appointed by the Government as the lead facilitator and coordinator of the aid effort, and the UN and all other agencies were expected to coordinate their work with and through SARC. This placed an enormous extra burden of responsibility on the organization, a burden made worse by the suspicion in some quarters that SARC was, as a result, in the pocket of the Government and therefore not to be trusted to distribute the aid impartially. Every shipment of aid through the docks in Latakia had to be registered with SARC, brought down to the main warehouse in Tartous and then, from there, trucked to one of SARC's distribution centres in its fourteen branches all over the country.

The compound was buzzing and noisy as porters heaved bundles onto lorries, whilst volunteers bustled about with checklists and the drivers lounged against their trucks smoking in the early morning sunshine. Rice, oil, sugar, jam, cooking equipment, soap, toothpaste, toilet paper and towels, a few medicines – all had to be logged, checked in and out and despatched to the next destination on the list. '*Yalla, yalla* – it's time to go!' was the cry, as the lorries revved their engines, ground their gears and trundled out into the street. I longed to join them, intoxicated by the air of excitement, urgent purpose and the smell of diesel, but it was impossible of course, and would have put their lives as well as my own at risk. I talked to Khaled, another volunteer. He had been shot at several times on the convoys. Last week, a passenger had died in his arms.

After a lengthy meeting with Dr Attar, planning a forthcoming trip to London to talk to DFID and address a committee of MPs, we headed out of town, back towards the border. I had thought I might feel relieved to be going home, but instead I felt sad, depressed, even guilty. I wanted to stay – we all did. It was like leaving your family behind to face an uncertain future. Ibrahim talked about his mother. He had gone to see her one evening, blagging his way past several checkpoints in the dark, empty suburban streets. He could hear mortar fire and machine guns. His mother had been afraid – afraid to stay, afraid to go, afraid she might never return.

'But Mamma, unless you go, my brothers and sisters must stay too, to look after you.'

That morning, as we drove towards the border, he phoned her.

'I will go,' she told him.

Ibrahim, a sunny, funny, friendly man, still festooned in red, with his wife and his life ahead of him in Italy, sat quiet, tugged back towards the country of his heart as we sped away. Another plume of grey smoke spiralled upwards.

Dr Attar and a delegation from SARC came over to London in March, and we had a working meeting at DFID, a useful discussion with DEC colleagues, a visit to see our work with refugees in Peterborough and a session with our trustees and senior management team. Dr Attar was a moving and compelling speaker, and when I took him to meet the Foreign Office minister Alan Duncan, Attar ended up in tears, as did Duncan. It was really important for us to impress on ministers that SARC was completely neutral and as independent of the Government of Syria as it was possible to be, and it was a relief to hear that more funding for their work might be forthcoming.

The visit was also a useful opportunity to impress on DFID how important it was to ensure that humanitarian work and military activity were to be kept strictly separate – it had recently been announced that a larger proportion of DFID's funds were to be used for 'stabilization/ military purposes' in countries affected by conflict, and we were concerned that this might lead to a further blurring of the lines between security issues and true humanitarian activity, thereby putting at further risk the safety of our teams in the field. In the case of the Red Cross, the problem was compounded by the fact that the military also used the red cross emblem to denote and protect medical personnel and facilities, which could also cause confusion on the battlefield.

Our new strapline *'refusing to ignore people in crisis'* was proving a surprising success, and we had been using it on a series of TV ads since October which had resulted in a significant spike in the public's awareness of our work. The brilliant but spooky ads, tagged 'I am a crisis', featured a spiky young woman in a hoodie representing many different types of domestic emergency – 'I am the reason you need a wheelchair, the flood that leaves you stranded, the empty house when you return from hospital, the sweet stuck in your child's throat' – and finished with the scary line, 'I am a crisis, and I don't care who you are …' The ads were very powerful and were timed to coincide with a new first aid app for mothers and babies which enjoyed a correspondingly high take-up.

I was always sensitive to the charge of 'wasting charity money' on advertising campaigns, particularly if they didn't directly ask for money or promote specific services. But at Macmillan Cancer Relief I had seen how effective a sustained and high-quality awareness-raising campaign could be in preparing the ground for local appeals or other fundraising activities and promoting a general willingness to give, and it felt like a breakthrough to be able to afford to do one at the Red Cross, albeit on a much smaller scale. It also supported our raised profile as an advocacy organization, with something to say on key issues that were relevant to our work.

We celebrated this media success with our usual *joie de vivre* at the National Assembly, for about a thousand volunteers and staff in Brighton. This was always a deliberately feel-good affair, the aim being to send volunteers and staff, from all over the UK, home with a good feeling about the organization and its plans, in the hope and belief that they would spread the word amongst their colleagues, supported by clips from the event and key messages put out on our intranet. This year, our guest of honour was long-time supporter and vice president, the broadcaster Angela Rippon. Good sport that she is, we persuaded her to recreate on stage the famous Morecambe and Wise sketch in which she revealed not only her skills as a trained dancer but also her shapely legs, hitherto always hidden behind the news desk. True to her word, she went at it with great gusto, with me playing Eric to Mark Astarita's Ernie, and ended up dancing me completely off my feet.

'You look as if you need a first aider,' she remarked, to rousing applause and laughter at the end.

Early in the summer, I was invited again by the Kenya Red Cross to see how they were getting on running Dadaab on the border with Somalia, the largest refugee camp in the world, with a shifting population of around half a million people, some of whom had been there for twenty years. My previous attempt to visit, eighteen months earlier, was called off after the two Spanish aid workers were kidnapped; they had still not been released.

It was a windswept, lawless place, with rows of tattered tents cowering behind razor-wire fences, a poor shield for the families sheltering from the burning sun and the harsh world outside. They had few other options, having fled violence in neighbouring Somalia, where fighting between the Al Shabaab rebel group and a series of weak Somali governments had turned their home into a war-ravaged nightmare. The rebels had been defeated in some parts of the country, and some families were keen to go home – but when was 'the right time'? A new government was in place but still finding its feet, and whilst an estimated 50,000 had returned, many others played a kind of hopscotch to and fro across the border, a deadly game of wait and see.

But it was no game – Dadaab was a dangerous place, too, home to Al Shabaab sympathizers and hardened criminal gangs, who thought nothing of preying upon these frightened and vulnerable people; the womenfolk in particular were prone to assaults of every kind every time they ventured out for firewood or fresh water.

I had shared the concern of many that Kenya Red Cross should have taken on responsibility for the camp but, as usual, they had done an excellent job, their volunteers and staff living right in the middle of the camp, sharing it with the refugees and relying for protection on the reputation they had built up and their rapport with the refugee community. They had built up a network of health and immunization clinics; provided feeding programmes that had cut malnutrition from around 40 per cent to less than 15 per cent; built a magnificent 100-bed hospital; provided counselling and support for victims of violence; constructed new boreholes for clean water and a latrine for every family; organized camp security and dispute resolution – the list was endless and impressive.

Nothing could dispel the sense, though, of half a million people living in limbo, with little to occupy their time or their minds. Walking through the camp in the late morning's dusty heat, the place felt deserted. Many had already retreated to their shelters to eat a meagre midday meal and chew on some *qat*, a mildly narcotic leaf, as the rest of the day drained away with their lives. I was concerned that, when they were eventually able to return to their ravaged country, if they ever did, they would have lost the impetus or the skills to rebuild their lives, so dependent had they become on aid from a largely unseeing world.

Back to Nairobi, it was then a 45-minute midnight flight to Burundi, a country which had shown a great deal of interest in the Federation's national society development working group. The national society, run by a young and inspirational leader called Anselme, had invited me to come and see what they were doing. I was mightily impressed. In a lush and hilly country of 8.5m people, physically about the size of Wales, the national society had recruited more than 300,000 volunteers in the space of eight years or so since the end of a 20-year civil war which had split the country into its three main ethnic groups of Hutu, Tutsi and Twa, and devastated the economy.

The national society had been a pillar of strength during the civil war, but as soon as the fighting stopped, the external funding had dried up and the local Red Cross had virtually collapsed. It wasn't until Anselme arrived on the scene in 2006 that the recovery had started. Thanks to great leadership, a hardworking management team and a strong sense of commitment, the national society was enabled to reach out across the ethnic divides and create a sense of community cohesion and 'One Red Cross'.

In the space of a two-day visit I met scores of volunteers, from all the main groups, happily distributing home-grown food to destitute neighbours, constructing a dam, growing and stockpiling food for emergencies, raising money from the sale of home-made charcoal briquettes, planting seeds and promoting healthcare and first aid. The breadth and diversity of this home-grown community activity was very exciting and had clearly been inspired by a feeling that they were working not just for the Burundi Red Cross, but more importantly for their neighbours and friends.

Anselme's problem, as was the case with so many other national societies in Africa, was that he was only covering about 10 per cent of his costs with local fundraising – for the rest, he had to hold out a begging bowl to wealthier parts of the Red Cross family, and this simply wasn't sustainable. We talked at length about membership fees, payment for services and basic fundraising techniques, and I encouraged him to send someone to Mark Astarita's annual international fundraising 'skill share'. I returned to the UK more convinced than ever of the necessity for the Federation to invest properly in mechanisms and a strategy to help all national societies at least aspire to fundraising self-sufficiency and real financial independence from those of us lucky enough to live and work in the prosperous parts of the world.

After a round of meetings in London and Geneva, I was soon away on my travels again, this time to Myanmar. The military junta, which had been in power since the 1960s, had recently been officially dissolved following a general election in 2010, and their high-profile 'hostage' Aung San Suu Kyi had been released, along with a number of other political prisoners. The country had suddenly become more accessible, and we had been invited to join a consortium of four national societies to work with the Myanmar Red Cross on one of the country's most serious healthcare and social issues – the high number of children who die under the age of five, nearly fifty in every thousand births. We were working in more than seventy villages in four remote regions of Myanmar, and I was there to sign the consortium agreement with the local Red Cross.

After the formal ceremony, accompanied as ever by the exchange of small gifts and followed by a press conference attended by every media organ in the country, there was a key meeting with the local DFID office which had, so far, been unwilling to help fund our efforts in the country. Then there was time for a quick whizz round Yangon and supper, before an early flight up-country to Mandalay, celebrated in the Kipling poem *The Road to Mandalay* and the Bob Hope film of the same name – which are just about all anyone knows about the country that used to be called Burma. From there, we had a magical five-hour drive through the hills overlooking the Irrawaddy river to Mogok, a quiet, charming, provincial capital where Kipling would have felt quite at home, even now. As we arrived, late in the afternoon, the small shops were closing and people were heading home for tea, mostly on foot or by bicycle.

We went straight to the Red Cross office, where we were met by the local manager, a dedicated, passionate and untiring volunteer, who seemed to be on every voluntary committee in town and who ran a small ruby mine in her spare time. I christened her Mrs de Beers, and we got on famously. The town was built on rubies and sapphires, a fact belied by the muddy streets and scruffy buildings, but we discovered that all the larger mines were owned by the military, which presumably explained why the wealth was not trickling down to the local population. The only place we saw any kind of ostentatious display was in the nearby Buddhist temple, on a hill at the edge of town, where every effigy of the Buddha was festooned in a dazzling array of sparklers.

Finding the small villages we were to visit the following morning would have been impossible without our guide, high up as they were in the lush green hills, past tea plantations, terraced rice-paddies and swollen streams. In the pouring rain, we felt like Victorian explorers ourselves, very conscious that the villages we were visiting had been almost completely left behind by the twenty-first century, and the one before, and that the inhabitants would have to cope alone with any and every crisis that came along.

And so it proved. The first village did have electricity, but only to the tiny Christian church and its adjoining hall where we were to meet. There was a primary school, too, with all the kids leaning out of the windows to see us arrive. But there was little else. We sat inside the dark village hall, talking to a group of mothers and babies, with a sprinkling of their menfolk, about what life was like in this incredibly remote community. They described their diet, just rice and a few vegetables, very bland and lacking in any variety.

'No meat?' I asked.

They fell about laughing.

'We hardly ever eat meat!'

There were no permanent jobs, just occasional temporary work in the fields or in the local mine. There was no clinic, doctor, nurse or midwife either – only the five volunteer community health-workers, and eventually the part-time assistant midwife who we were training. Many babies died before or as soon as they are born, because there was no one to attend their mothers before, during or after the process, and because no one can afford the taxi ride to hospital, an hour or more down the hill to Mogok

– if, that is, a message could be got to the taxi in time and the taxi could be persuaded to come out of Mogok at all.

We suggested a Q & A session about the programme, which prompted a few desultory questions, until one woman, braver than the others, stood up. There were smiles and some nudging and, from the grin on her face, it was clear that she was a bit of a local character.

Hands on hips, she looked me in the eye and asked, 'Why, actually are you here? Have you really come all this way just to help us?'

It was as if the very idea of help from outside was a complete novelty, something they could barely comprehend. I hardly knew where to start with the answer, but talked a bit about the UK, and charities, and then went on to describe the Red Cross and its work. There was a hush when I finished, and a few were dabbing away tears. It was an extraordinarily moving moment.

On our way to the next village we stopped at a little wayside café for a delicious bowl of pork, with pictures of Daw Suu, 'the Lady' as they call Aung San Suu Kyi, covering the wall behind the bar. We wondered what the security chap who had been following us all day made of this. We were taken on a tour of our second village and went first to the one-roomed school, for about a hundred 6- to 11-year-olds, who all tumbled out of the room in a rush as we arrived, on their way home at the end of the day. They stared at our strange white faces, then raced off shrieking with laughter. We followed them out and went on a little tour of the village.

The houses were tiny, each crammed with three generations plus often aunts and uncles as well. Birth control methods were not widely available or used. In one house we met a couple in their mid-forties who had had eleven children, plus two who had died; all were living in a space about 12ft square and cooking on an open fire, with a minuscule adjoining bedroom which I was invited to inspect. The eldest daughter, aged twelve, was washing the dishes ready for the next meal. Next door lived Pye Ma See, who was in bed. She had been lucky, just the week before, to survive the birth of her thirteenth child, having somehow made the journey of several miles on foot downhill to the nearest hospital, where she had needed eleven pints of blood. Her husband sat, quiet and bemused, by the small log burning on a fire in the corner.

'No', he said. 'We don't use any birth control.'

Our Myanmar Red Cross volunteer director, Madame de Beers, took us to a ruby mine on the way home, where the workforce, on a rickety scaffolding gantry, sifted through great piles of white stones pulled from a torrent of water gushing from the mountainside. With extraordinary dexterity they managed to separate out small rocks studded with small pinky-white gemstones, barely visible to the naked eye, from the mass of identical-looking lumps on the table in front of them, holding them up for inspection and applause from their neighbours, before tossing them into a scuffed yellow plastic bucket which held their 'catch' for the day. Then we trooped into the mine itself, via an opening in the hillside about 10ft high, and trudged along a series of dark tunnels blasted out of the mountain, not a pit-prop in sight, to the rock face itself where, in the ghostly yellow light produced by a few hanging light bulbs, we could just make out dynamiters preparing to place charges in holes drilled into the rock, heaps of spare explosive charges dotting the walls around.

Outside once more, we came upon a huge pile of spoil, with two hundred local scavengers picking over the rocks rejected by the paid workers on their scaffolding above, in the forlorn hope of finding a rough gem the latter might have missed. We did a bit of half-hearted negotiating for the tiny stones they had found and were selling at several hundred dollars apiece.

It was pouring with rain again the next day as we set off for another village meeting, this time in a tranquil Buddhist monastery. We sat in the teak assembly hall, with open windows on three sides looking out to the valley and hills around, sunlight now dappling the walls through the window spaces. A monk sat quietly to one side as we sat on the floor with the village mums and their children, drinking green tea and nibbling sweet jackfruit. The peaceful atmosphere belied the threat these villagers face from rival criminal gangs who come to demand protection money or cart the menfolk off to join their gang. A few of the men had joined our discussion, sitting off to one side and smoking, but listening intently enough to what we were talking about with the women. There was a hoot of delighted laughter from the women when I turned on the men and asked them what they thought their role was in 'this childbirth business'. After a little consultation and a bit of rueful grinning, they produced what they clearly hoped was a creditable stab at the answer, whilst their women grinned sceptically in their turn.

Then it was time to head to the airport for the flight back to Yangon, and on to visit the downtrodden and abused Rakhine in the west of the country, where inter-communal violence between ethnic Rakhine and Muslim communities had resulted in the displacement of over 125,000 people in recent months, most of whom were now living in segregated and inadequate camps. The Buddhist majority, resentful of the Muslims, had been showing increasing animosity towards anyone helping them, and Red Cross offices and staff had been threatened. We intended to set up a livelihoods programme in the camps, and the purpose of my visit, with our desk officers Inma and Razmi, was to look at the possibilities and talk to the authorities – only I never got there.

Sitting in the dismal little airport on a dark, rainy day, I got a call from Roger Smith.

'You'd better sit down,' he said. 'Charles is going.'

He was referring to Charles Allen, our new Chairman, who had joined us only eight months previously. He had been offered a peerage for his work on the management board of the Labour party and knew that, if he was going to accept the Labour whip, he would have to resign as chair of the Red Cross. I was completely flattened by this sad and unexpected news, since we had got on well. I was tired after what seemed like a relentlessly busy few years and dreaded the thought of starting again on the search for a new chair, so soon after finding, and now losing, the last one. My trip to the Rakhine would have taken another week, but I knew I had to return instead to London for the 'what now' discussions with the trustees. I cancelled my internal flight west, waved Inma and Razmi goodbye and flew instead to Yangon and then on, after a restless night, to Heathrow.

The search for Charles' successor started almost immediately, led by Paul Taylor, one of the two vice-chairs, a regular Red Cross volunteer and a safe pair of hands. This was the trustees' appointment, but Paul fully understood that a positive relationship between chair and chief executive was important for the whole organization and he made sure I was fully involved at every stage. We had a good field, with the trustees finally choosing David Bernstein, a former chair of Manchester City FC, the Football Association and several commercial companies. David was quietly-spoken and kindly but had a sharp sense of the commercial realities in the world in which charities operated, and I knew immediately that he would do the job well when he took over from Charles at the end of the year.

Meanwhile, the work went on, and I was scheduled to visit Orkney and the Western Isles, where we had a small but loyal volunteer base and an area director, Helen Bath, determined to develop more services in these remote islands. In conversations with staff, volunteers and local health officials both in Kirkwall and in Stornoway in the Outer Hebrides, I found myself reminded time and again of the villages I had so recently visited in Myanmar, where the same issues – of rural isolation, reducing or non-existent services, severe weather, thin support from the centre – had been the focus of our attention. The islands seemed in some ways as isolated as had the villages, and I wondered if the same system of community mobilizers was needed here too.

Soon after that, I was off to China and then North Korea for a week. I had formed in recent months a close working relationship with my counterpart in the Chinese Red Cross, Baige Zhao. She had become interested in the work I had been doing within the Federation on national society development and fundraising. She had a lively mind and an engaging style with a good sense of humour and, despite our massively different backgrounds, we enjoyed our talks. At the time, the Chinese Red Cross (which had strong links with the Chinese Communist Party) was beginning to develop a small portfolio of aid projects overseas, an extraordinary development in a country (and a Red Cross) that had always seemed so inward-looking, and we had found ourselves working alongside each other, including in North Korea, which Baige invited me to visit with her.

I arrived in time for a working dinner with Baige and her colleagues at the house of a famous eighteenth century Chinese author, beside a lake in the botanical gardens, where we talked of China ancient and modern, before our flight to Pyongyang the next morning. It was nine years since I had last visited, and the city had changed – it was much busier, with many more cars, and many more people out on the broad boulevards with their sweeping vistas and adoring statues to Kim Jong Il, who had rescued the country from its Japanese occupiers in 1945. It was hard to tell, in this inscrutable place, if the inhabitants scuttling to and fro were any happier or more prosperous, but the streets were spotless and the place had a more purposeful air than it had before.

We met up with three or four more other national society leaders in the capital, all of us working in the same 'Cooperation Agreement' partnership on disaster management and healthcare programmes with the efficiently-run North Korea Red Cross, and there to conduct the annual progress review. The Government's overriding priorities were independence, and security from the US-led invasion that was perceived to be imminent, rather than economic and social development; and the 'Great Leader' had been at pains to develop the ideal of self-reliance or *Juche* in his people – it was a case of 'needs must' given the poor state of the country's health and social services.

As we travelled to three of the local branches we were working in, through the hilly countryside, much of it uncultivated and deforested, and heard tales from our hosts of frequent flash-flooding during the bitter winters and early spring, of exhausted soil and the effect of sanctions biting deep, I had a sense of potential frustrated and talent wasted, in an endless struggle for bare subsistence. We went to one wide valley where a combination of upstream open-cast coal mining and massive soil erosion had created a desolate, dusty wilderness. Coal trucks pounded through fields of struggling maize, an opaque dirty yellow sun peering through the grit; and in the local Red Cross branch, the volunteers waited patiently for funds to become available so they could start trying to shore up the village's defences against the seasonal crashing of water from the surrounding hills that threatens each year to wash their meagre lives away.

In other branches we visited, prioritized for government and Red Cross action, an integrated programme of disaster preparedness and risk reduction measures (embankments, tree planting, early warning systems, etc.) coupled with health education, support to local clinics and improved water supply, had resulted in a much better environment. Enthusiastic (or well-drilled) volunteers proudly showed us their achievements, with before and after pictures and reams of statistics, before treating us to a picnic on a sunny hillside overlooking what had been a watery graveyard five years earlier.

We had invested £300,000 that year, out of hard-won general funds, in our programmes in North Korea, and we were hoping to persuade DFID to help us invest more, as I explained to a delighted British Ambassador, who said he had been trying to persuade his political masters to engage with the issue of humanitarian need in North Korea for some time, notwithstanding their justifiable concerns about nuclear weapons and human rights. The Red Cross was focussed on the humanitarian situation, and raising the money was difficult; North Korea was not at the top of anyone's list for generous donations.

I spent most of my time with Baige Zhao and our North Korean counterpart, Ri Ho Rim, in the black limo that had been provided by the national society for their special Chinese guest. Our discussions and arguments were wide-ranging and extremely direct.

'I recognize this place,' said Zhao. 'It's like China was thirty years ago.'

She identified deeply with the simple folk we met outside Pyongyang, having herself, as the daughter of a professor, been forced to spend five years working as a landless peasant during the Cultural Revolution.

'It made me strong, and helped me understand the needs of the people,' she said, and she referred constantly to the reservoirs of human capital she saw here, waiting to be unlocked, and expressed a determination to help the local national society with its existential struggles in the harsh environment it faced.

We argued about human rights and the freedom to think and learn and communicate, and I attempted to explain (if not defend) America's 'global policeman' role in the context of frequent sabre-rattling, or rather rocket-rattling, from North Korea. I argued that China could help North Korea best by persuading the DPRK government to 'back off' from its occasional warmongering rhetoric, in order to reduce the temperature of concern in Washington and other western capitals, and was surprised that Baige appeared to have some sympathy with this argument and intended to raise it with senior political contacts in Beijing. I have no idea who they were, or if she did, and of course there was no discernible result, but it was fascinating to see how a shared humanitarian perspective seemed to offer a route through even the most intractable political and philosophical differences.

Back in Pyongyang after three days in the field, we had a little time to relax and to enjoy a Korea versus the Rest volleyball tournament in a local park. It was 'Ancestor Day', when Koreans remember those who have gone before, and our friends had organized a hillside picnic for us, amongst countless local families at ease on the grass, often with a framed portrait of their ancestors with them on the rug. It was a charming sight and, as we all sat and enjoyed the gentle day, Koreans and Chinese and Norwegians and Brits, Sri Lankans and Swedes, a Canadian and a Finn, I reflected on the joys of international friendship, shared visions in the Red Cross and globalism, and the hope for the future that they inspired.

But Syria, where over 6m people had been displaced by the fighting, either internally or in neighbouring countries, was also a constant nagging concern. Food security was a huge issue, with economic activity in the country almost at a standstill, and food convoys, particularly to the rebel-held north of the country, becoming ever more dangerous. Thirty-four Syrian Arab Red Crescent volunteers had already been killed while on duty and many others had been injured or had simply disappeared; six ICRC staff had been abducted as well. We had raised over £4m but we needed much more, and fundraising was hampered by understandable confusion amongst the general public at the time about the complexities of the conflict and damaging press allegations that food aid was going direct to terrorist groups. Our Appeal after Typhoon Haiyan in the Philippines raised more in a month than we had for Syria in a year.

It was ironic and disturbing that food security was also becoming a real issue in the UK during this period, with an estimated 5.8m people struggling to afford basic food items, as the Government's 'austerity' response to the global financial crisis started to bite. I visited the offices and operations centre of the food bank charity FareShare and agreed that we would ask our volunteers to help persuade shoppers at Tesco stores throughout the country to donate food items for distribution to those who would otherwise go without in the run-up to Christmas. It was already clear that 'austerity' was going to be a very significant factor in our thinking about future strategy, with needs increasing and the resources to meet them going down. The likely strap line for the new strategy *'refusing to ignore people in crisis'* was beginning to seem both more apt and more challenging by the day.

The General Assembly in Sydney was a very strange and disorientating affair, not because there was anything particularly controversial to discuss from an operational point of view, but because of the internal politics. Not only did President Konoe face a tougher than expected battle against his South American challenger and his supporters, but I too became embroiled, despite my serious personal misgivings, in the election of a Vice President for Europe. There was only one candidate for this post when I arrived in Sydney, a very able lawyer from Italy called Francesco Rocca, much respected in his own country. However, there was widespread concern that there was only one candidate, and I came under great pressure to put my hat in the ring.

Our five-strong delegation to the Assembly, including our own Vice Chair Paul Taylor and international director David Peppiatt, were keen that I should stand, as was our outgoing Chairman Charles Allen when Paul consulted with him by phone. I spent a miserable and sleepless night debating with myself whether it was the 'right' thing to do in principle and whether, even if it was, I wanted to do it. It would clearly be good for the British Red Cross, and I felt sufficiently sure of my international contribution to believe that it might even be good for the Movement. It could also be important to have a strong set of Vice Presidents if Konoe was defeated by his challenger. But I had always felt uncomfortable about the 'internal politics' that played out in the Red Cross and other international institutions, and I felt particularly bad about challenging Rocca, who had been campaigning for months before the election. I was brought up, too, in the English system which said that paid staff couldn't be part of the governance of their own organization – although, in fact, that was no objection in this case because the Federation was not my employer, and several Board members were paid members of their own national societies.

I finally decided, with huge misgivings, to give it a go, provided there was clear evidence that I would have significant support amongst the electorate – all 190-odd other national societies. Paul and the team fanned out around the conference hall and in the coffee bars that morning and by lunchtime they were able to report that my candidacy would be greeted with enthusiasm. With the elections the very next day, we all set to work drafting my prospectus and starting the 'campaign' – and I sought out Rocca to give him the news in person. He was not pleased.

I must confess I felt distant and disengaged, but the team was fantastic and the campaign quickly gathered momentum and support. At the breakfast time round-up the next morning it was clear from what they had all heard that I actually stood a chance of being elected, which may have said more about this rather febrile election process than it did about me, but was nevertheless, and despite my misgivings, exciting to hear. The ballot started at 11.00 am, with countries being called out in alphabetical order and each 'Head of Delegation' filing into the booths in turn to vote, first for the President (Konoe won), and then later for the other positions.

Soon after 1.00 there was a hush and the total votes for each Vice-Presidential candidate were read out. Europe – it was a tie! I gasped, and felt slightly sick: it seemed barely possible to have garnered so many votes in 24 hours. There had never been a tie before, and no one was quite sure what to do – there was a huddle on stage, and then a further vote was announced for 2 o'clock. Panic ensued, as by this time many delegations had disappeared to the cafés and bars in and around the conference centre for lunch. We decided there was little to be done but await the outcome of the second vote, but the Italians were smarter, and better at the politics, and raced around corralling supporters and lobbying the waverers.

By 2 o'clock the hubbub around the voting area was intense and, as late lunchers sauntered back into the hall, the final result was announced – Rocca had won by a narrow eleven votes. I breathed a sigh, of both relief and disappointment, and raced down the rows of seats to be amongst the first to congratulate the victor – who went on to become an excellent President in 2017.

Chapter 15

My Last Year, 2014

Up Helly Aa – Philippines Cyclone

This was to be the worst year of my life; in many ways the end of my life, at least in the way that I had come to think of it.

But in January I had no inkling of what lay ahead. I was just tired. Too much travelling, too many things to do and to think about, three Chairs in as many years, a feeling of being spread too thin and that perhaps it was time to slow down. And I knew that was possible; I just wasn't sure how.

Although we had lost some key colleagues, I still had a great team, particularly with Mike Adamson holding down the important Managing Director of Operations slot, Roger Smith still steadily and comfortingly with me after over twenty years, and the sector's fundraising star Mark Astarita bringing in the money, recession notwithstanding – £156m of fundraised income in 2013 according to Mark's 'scores on the doors', a record. But my style had always been energetic, active, fully engaged and visible, and stepping back a bit to become more 'the elder statesman' (as someone had put it) wasn't really me. So what to do …?

I had an early New Year two-day meeting in Kuwait, where I was representing Dr Hany's Humanitarian Forum and making a keynote speech at a UN pledging conference for Syria; I described what I had seen on my visit there in graphic terms and told the story of the Syrian Arab Red Crescent volunteers, their fearful bravery and terrible losses. I met Ban Ki-Moon and most of the heads of UN agencies, and had useful lobbying sessions with John Kerry, US Secretary of State, and Kristalina Georgieva, who at that time was the EU Commissioner for International Cooperation and Development. It all felt a bit surreal.

Almost immediately afterwards, I had promised to visit the Shetlands and meet our volunteers up there for the extraordinary *Up Helly Aa* fire festival at the end of January, when the Red Cross was in charge of first aid. With large crowds waving flaming torches about and Viking warriors brandishing swords, it was likely to be a busy day. I flew in to Aberdeen, after a working lunch with President Konoe and his team on the Sunday, preparing for what was likely to be a difficult first full meeting of the Governing Board, and spent the day visiting our offices and projects in the city before hopping across to Lerwick for the big day. It was cold and damp, and I had developed a peculiar pain in my abdomen which, after a few hours of surreptitious fumbling, I discovered I could only alleviate by pressing on a particular spot through my trouser pocket – it was a hernia. But I had no time to get help – the town was already buzzing with excitement, and the Red Cross volunteers were in high spirits.

With good reason, for *Up Helly Aa* is quite something. Each year, a committee appoints some local character or worthy to be the 'Guizer Jarl', whose job it is to form a squad and then build the replica of the Viking galley that will form the centrepiece of the celebrations, plus all the Viking costumes for his men, each clad like a specific warrior hero. Meanwhile, no fewer than forty-six other squads are spending their long winter evenings kitting themselves out as warriors too – with the result that, when the day comes, half of Shetland (for all this is going on in other towns too) has been transformed into a Viking stronghold.

This year, the Guizer Jarl, Ivor Cluness, had chosen to dress as Ivar ('the Boneless') Ragnarsson, a Danish Viking chieftain who had to be carried into battle lying on a shield because he was missing some bones in his leg (hence the name), a disability which endeared him to us in the Red Cross and which he made up for by being reputedly one of the most cunning warriors who ever lived. In revenge for the murder of his father in a snake pit by the Geordies of that time in Northumbria, he led an invasion of East Anglia in 865 AD, marched north, captured the murderers of his dad and sentenced them to death by the 'Blood Eagle' method of cutting the ribs from the spine and drawing the lungs back through the opening. Clearly not a man to be messed with.

Our first view of Ivar's reincarnation and his gang was in the ornate Town Hall, after three hours of parading through the town with the Galley, including a formal reading of 'the Bill', a proclamation about the day's events pasted up at the Market Cross. We were in our seats in plenty of time, clutching 'a wee dram' which we were given on arrival and listening to lengthy speeches of welcome from the Mayor and other local celebrities. Then in they marched, Ivar the Jarl and his Squad, with suitably bloodthirsty shouts and aggressive gestures of sword and spear at anyone they recognized in the crowd, all garbed in magnificent helmets, breastplates and furs, clutching large shields and sporting bushy beards grown for the occasion. It really was quite an impressive sight, notwithstanding the slight disappointment caused by Ivar the Boneless's arrival walking on his own two pins, instead of being borne aloft on his shield as perhaps he should have been.

Once settled, there were more speeches, and then a rousing toast to the Guizer Jarl and his Squad, whereupon we downed the nicely warmed-up drams that we had been holding in our laps.

'And now,' cried the Mayor, 'it's time to hear the Guizer Jarl's Song!'

A frisson ran through the crowd, and I waited for some bloodcurdling tale of glorious rape and pillage from days gone by. The Squad sprang to their feet, lifted their spears high, and launched with a roar into – Van Morrison's *Brown-eyed Girl*. I looked around, expecting shouts of disapproval, or at the very least a stifled giggle or two, but no, there we all were, swaying in time, 'laughin' and a-runnin', skippin' and a-jumpin', like the good Vikings that we hoped to be.

The day passed quickly, following the Parade, visiting the various impressive exhibitions of Viking lore, customs and art, and of course talking to our amazing First Aid volunteers, out in all weathers and on their feet as usual, as good-humoured as ever and delighted to be able to dish out water, bandage scrapes, reunite little Vikings with their Mums, and generally keep everyone safe in their Red Cross overalls. As always, I felt incredibly proud of what they were doing.

By the evening, the mood was at fever pitch as we ate our meals in the various halls and hostelries that were hosting private parties, then gathered, thousands of us, behind the Squads and the beautifully-constructed Galley, Ivar the Boneless at its helm, waiting for the torches to be lit and the night-time procession to begin. Then we were off, winding through the streets of Lerwick, torches streaming in the stiffish breeze and sparks flying alarmingly above our heads, slowly and majestically towards the burning site, not far from the sea. There, surrounded by a vast mob of costumed warriors, spears aloft and torches held high, the Jarl stepped from his galley to a great cheer and, with a roar that filled the night, the Warriors all hurled their torches into the vessel, which they had spent months constructing, and watched for a minute or two as it filled with flames crackling into the sky, before launching into a strange wild lament, *The Norseman's Home*.

It had been a really remarkable day, daft at times, admittedly, but moving too in its celebration of courage and valour and heroes long dead and the laughter and light and gaiety it brought to the long Shetland winter.

The next day, I was due to see more of our work on the Islands, but by this time I was practically doubled over with the pain and discomfort of my stomach, and our local director, Helen Bath, took one look at me as I struggled round the town in her wake and bundled me off to the local hospital – they took one look and said 'Ah yes, a nasty hernia, you need to get that seen to – immediately.'

I returned to London and hospital, three hernia repairs, and then spent two weeks at home recuperating – and working on the detailed drafting of our new five-year strategy *Refusing to ignore people in crisis* with my 'chef de cabinet', Caroline Leighton. Goodness, we were thorough. I have the file in front of me now, or part of it – oversight by a programme board of both trustees and executives, several working groups, dozens of 'buzz' groups at local level, a full-scale review of *Saving Lives Changing Lives* and its implementation and impact, competitor and external environment analysis, piles of data, mapping exercises, pathfinder documents, input from Booz & Co (our pro bono management consultants), discussions with external interlocutors and 'critical friends' and partners, and an impressive amount of consultation and discussion, drafting and redrafting, over more than a year of feverish activity.

I remember thinking back to my first year as a CEO, at Macmillan Cancer Relief in 1995, when I proposed to my slightly old-fashioned management team that we undertake a similar (though far less strenuous) exercise.

'Oh', said one of them, a crestfallen look on his face, 'do we have to? Douglas [my predecessor] used to do all that' – probably on the back of the proverbial fag packet.

Fashions and fads change, and good planning was essential in a complex and multi-faceted international organization like the British Red Cross, with a turnover approaching £250m p.a. – almost all of it other people's money – and delivering, not commercial widgets but life-saving services, in a multiplicity of different, difficult and rapidly-changing contexts, and with an infinity of directions and priorities to choose from. I sometimes wondered if these lengthy planning exercises justified all the energy that went into them, but this time, planning as we were from a position of considerable strength, there was scope for real innovation and some 'revolutionary moments', as we called them.

There were risks, too, with a growing swell of public and media concern about charity fundraising, particularly the increase in asking for support 'face to face' (i.e. in the street) and 'door to door' (i.e. on the doorstep), aimed at recruiting large numbers of small-scale regular givers. We had been at the forefront of this trend, with a carefully-monitored and strictly-controlled campaign, sustained over many years, which had by this time brought us over 600,000 monthly donors, who not only tended to stay loyal for six years or more but often supported us in other ways or even remembered us in their wills. I had always had a horror of upsetting people who were kindly or generously disposed towards us, so we responded to the extremely small proportion of complainants quickly and in person, but other charities were perhaps not so scrupulous; the media noise was getting louder, and the possibility of restrictive legislation, which might have a dire effect on our income, was not to be ruled out.

At the same time we had identified the possibility of a funding gap two years on, when we were due to return to a break-even position after three or four years of extra investment in our services and infrastructure, thanks to some research and risk analysis which showed us that our reserves were a bit higher than they needed to be. Our cautious income projections during the strategy process highlighted the need for corrective action; we had done a lot of work on identifying where and how we could make the necessary savings and were proposing an immediate start. What we did not predict, with serious consequences for the organization, was the media storm that erupted after the death in 2015 of a generous charity donor called Olive Cooke, who was (wrongly as it turned out) alleged by an upset family member to have taken her own life as a result of being hounded by charities. The Government responded with swingeing new legal restrictions, resulting in very large drops in income for many charities, including our own.

Nevertheless, our strategy was still ambitious, with an intense and organization-wide focus on getting ever closer to the people who needed our help; another strong push towards advocating even more strongly on their behalf; increasing our investment in digital technology; promoting and encouraging ever more passionate volunteer and staff engagement with the cause – and all the while ensuring a 'smooth glide path' to the intended break-even over the course of the strategy. Throughout, the emphasis was on the 'difference we make', and on identifying very clear implementation plans, performance indicators and milestones. Twenty years previously, when I first stepped through the door of the Society's dusty old headquarters in Grosvenor Crescent, I would not have believed it possible that the organization could produce such a forward-looking, professional and inspiring document.

But before I was due to present it to the Trustees in early April, I had another overseas trip to make, to the Philippines, where Typhoon Haiyan had caused over 6,000 deaths in November 2013 and wrought billions of pounds worth of damage. Somewhat to our surprise, we had raised over £23m in our emergency appeal, and the Chairman of the Philippines Red Cross, a prominent public and political figure in the islands and a fellow Governing Board member, as well as being an old Red Cross friend, had invited me out to sign the MoU with him and see how they were proposing to spend the money. It meant a long trip, and I didn't really feel fully fit yet, but I didn't feel I could let him down, so I went anyway.

We had decided to work on Panay, one of the worst affected but remoter islands, about an hour's flight from the capital Manila, a classic paradise of palm-fringed sandy beaches and, thanks to the typhoon, a large area of devastation near the main town of Iloilo. We had agreed to build 3,000 new houses, to repair 8,000 damaged houses, to rebuild or repair a number of schools and clinics and to provide cash and other livelihoods support to 9,000 individuals. It was a complex operation, with the damaged and destroyed houses spread out over a wide area, dotted here and there in seven municipalities and more than a hundred remote fishing and/or farming villages and hamlets. I was worried that we had taken on too much.

But the beauty of the Philippines, with vibrant cities, fertile fields and seas, beautiful beaches and resourceful, welcoming and hard-working people, and the complete irrepressibility of the local Red Cross Chairman, Richard Gordon, soon reassured me. Gordon was every inch the popular vote-winning politician, whether it was schmoozing the local Governor; persuading mayors to drive for hours to meet him; carousing with a friendly rags-to-riches restaurateur; grasping hands to shake and posing for photos left and right; dreaming up ever more ambitious schemes for his teams to implement; dishing out prizes at a municipal family day; quoting Shakespeare or Bogart; carolling *As Time Goes By* or even his own Red Cross song as we sped through the lanes in an open-topped Jeep; or commentating on his own 'Son et Lumière'. He was exhausting, probably maddening to work with – and enormous fun.

The visit to the small fishing village of Ajuy was typical. Our convoy of Red Cross vehicles and camera crews swept into the village in the blistering late morning sun. It was really no more than a collection of ramshackle huts and houses propping each other up in a small jungle clearing and surrounded by drying salt-water fish ponds and great thickets of bamboo. Gordon leapt from the Jeep like a film star and headed straight for the nearest gathering of slightly watchful villagers, all clearly perplexed by the circus that had suddenly descended upon them. His boisterous hugs and handshakes produced a show of wan enthusiasm from the group, who evidently had only a vague idea of who he was. I wondered quite what he would do next.

But then the moment was saved by the official welcoming committee, led by a great laughing sparky dynamo of a woman, who swept forward from the shelter of a nearby awning surrounded by dozens of small children (many of them, it transpired, her own) and bore us off on a grand tour of her tragically wrecked village.

The damage was epic for such a meagre community. The shattered dwellings the villagers were so willing to show us around, so proud of and so keen to have repaired, were so basic that we would hesitate to use them at home for garden tools or old flower pots. We tottered into one shack, reeling from the heat and shocked that these people had managed to survive in this condition since November, and I noticed an incongruous-looking picture of a smart young man in graduate robes pinned on the wall.

'That's our boy,' said his thin shy and tired mother.

His father, a bit older, unsmiling, solemn and silent, took it down and they stood together clutching the photo as Gordon's cameramen clicked away. She looked at me quietly.

'He's a criminologist,' she whispered, 'just graduated. He paid for himself, you know, all through school and college. Selling ice cream.'

A fleeting smile fluttered wistfully across her face, her thoughts far away in Manila with her son.

We met several other families with similar tales of courage and enterprise over an astonishing lunchtime spread of mackerel, marlin, snails, oysters, shrimp and crabs, pulled from the sea in our honour an hour or two earlier. You had to be hopeful for a country where such fortitude, determination and generosity were a way of life.

I had to hasten back to London for a Board meeting to present the draft strategy; it was enthusiastically, almost rapturously, received, and I then spent a quiet day in the office, before a trip to Poole with the Finance Director Rohan and my chef de cabinet to visit the Royal National Lifeboat Institution, where another old friend, the former Royal Navy submarine commander Paul Boissier, had been putting his organization through the same kind of exercise to boost agility, efficiency and cost-savings as we were ourselves considering. It was a grey, dull day, though full of interest despite waves of jet lag, and I was glad to get back to Suffolk for the weekend and have a good sleep.

At 7.20 the next morning, the phone rang.

Chapter 16

The End

It was our eldest son Edward, panic in his voice.

'Dad, it's Alex, he's missing.'

It took me a while to understand what he was saying. Alex was our middle boy, a tall, bright, happy, sporty, successful young executive in the City. It seemed that Ed had been telephoned earlier that morning by Alex's distraught girlfriend, who had in turn been phoned by the police. Alex's jacket, with his mobile and wallet in a pocket, had been found on Tower Bridge late the previous night. Of Alex himself there was no sign.

I was about to call the police myself, when Alex's girlfriend herself rang, in tears. They had been out in a bar for a Friday night drink with colleagues after work. She and Alex had argued, and then he had left. They had exchanged angry text messages, and she had decided to go home to her mum's.

The police, when I rang them, could tell me little more, save that they had been looking for him all night, including in the Thames, but had found nothing. We decided to return to our flat in the Barbican to await events. We were both panic-stricken.

As soon as we arrived, the police asked us to attend at Bishopsgate Police Station, from where the search was being conducted. Alex's brothers, meanwhile, and many friends had been out patrolling the Thames all morning.

At the station, the police were solemn. From CCTV cameras and witness statements, they believed that Alex had jumped from the bridge at around 10.30 pm. He had not been seen since. In the gentlest way, they explained that the tide at that time had been going out fast, and that the likelihood was that Alex had been swept away with it.

'Mr Young, I must tell you that very few survive in those circumstances. I'm so sorry.'

Numb, we returned to the flat. There was quite a gathering there, what with our other two boys and a posse of friends, plus Alex's girlfriend and her mother. We talked fitfully, in quiet murmurs; there was little to say, and they all went home, leaving us in the flat with our thoughts.

For a week there was no news. We went back to Suffolk, then returned to London after a day or so, unable to settle. I walked on my own to the bridge, late at night, and stared down from the steel and granite rampart into the inky-black water.

It was not until the next weekend, back in Suffolk and after morning service in our village church, that we heard any more. As we sat drinking coffee at home, the doorbell rang. There were two officers on the doorstep. We sat down. Alex's body had been found, in the waters around Tower Bridge, late the previous evening, and identified from dental records. He had been dead for several days.

This book is not the place for a detailed account of what happened next – the post mortem and police investigation; the memorial service, with 600 of his friends in attendance, and burial in the village churchyard, a few hundred yards from our family home; the flood of messages from around the world; the hours of CCTV from the bar and the bridge to be watched and dissected, ready for the inquest; the incredible kindness throughout of DC Nick Wilson, who was in charge of Alex's case – none of it brought him back, nor explained why a young man at the top of his game, with hundreds of friends and no history whatsoever of mental illness or even significant unhappiness, with his life before him, should have jumped to his death, with clear deliberation and, so the witnesses said, a smile on his face. We will never know.

In the days immediately after we heard the news, two acts of kindness stand out particularly – the letter and bouquet from Prince Charles that arrived the next day, and the call I received a couple of days later from Paul Boissier at the RNLI, the colleague I had been visiting on the day Alex disappeared.

After the usual condolences, Paul said, 'Nick, there's something I must tell you. I was on my live feed from our boat on the Thames that night, as they spent hours searching for your son. I didn't know, at the time, that it was him, of course, but I want you to know that they arrived on the scene incredibly quickly and did absolutely everything they could have done to find him.'

David Bernstein, the Chairman, and all my friends at the Red Cross were brilliant. I was given unlimited leave of absence and had long talks with David about my eventual return. But I knew it was hopeless. There was simply no way I could have left my darling wife Heli alone, to fly off to another conflict or disaster area, and within a few weeks I announced that I was stepping down.

But there was still plenty to do. It was agreed that I would work part-time until the end of August, to clear my desk and effect a smooth handover to Mike Adamson, who was to be acting CEO until the formal process to find my successor could be put in place. There was also another Buckingham Palace Garden Party to arrange.

Some time previously, Prince Charles had offered to host another Garden Party for the Red Cross, to celebrate the Movement's 150th anniversary – but also partly in recompense for the washout of our last Garden Party in 2008. Planning was already well in hand, the invitations to volunteers, supporters, colleagues and partners all over the world had gone out, and we had a grand occasion planned, with a Red Cross conference the morning before and a glittery Red Cross Red Crescent dinner in Whitehall's Banqueting Hall for our international guests in the evening. It was to be my last hurrah and, whilst I wasn't sure I could rise to the occasion, I knew I had to, and wanted to.

It was indeed a splendid day, dry, hot and sunny with a carnival atmosphere and everyone, from the Prince down, in good form. The conference in Westminster attracted a great deal of interest, with its theme of current threats to humanitarian aid workers. I was asked to give the keynote address and I talked about our emblem, 'the sign of hope in a crisis', that surely everyone caught up in a struggle for life will look for and long to see.' But, I went on:

> That emblem is more than just a logo on a flag, or a design painted on the side of a clinic or Land Cruiser. For us, it is all that protects us on the field of battle; it is the only shield we carry, the sign that means 'don't shoot, we're here to help' – or should do. For in today's world, humanitarians venturing onto battlefields are all too often seen as a legitimate target for political capital, or warnings to others, or as a means of frightening off those who may get in the way of military or political objectives.

The Garden Party was as magical as they always are, with everyone in their summery best dress, and the Prince and other members of the Royal Family, all of us melting in the heat, talking and being charming to everyone to whom they were introduced. There wasn't a plastic poncho or a rain hat in sight, and it was all just perfect.

Then in the evening came the dinner where, surrounded by so many of my friends in the Movement from all over the world, I made one of my trademark tours of the room, microphone in hand, to introduce and interview the real stars of the show, humanitarian warrior colleagues from around the world. Then it was time to say goodbye as, with a catch in my voice and tears in my eyes, I tried to explain what they and the Red Cross meant to me, and to give thanks. They all rose as I sat down, and I can hear the clapping still.

Chapter 17

Conclusion

I hardly know what to say. The Red Cross meant more to me than anything else in life, apart from my beloved wife and family, and leaving it was hard. It was not a job, or a succession of days in the office, as I have tried to show, but a vocation, and a privileged one at that, in which you get a chance to work with passionate and caring people, making a difference in lives across the planet and engaging with some of the most difficult and devastating issues of our time.

The volunteers and staff of the British Red Cross had shown me nothing but friendship, and loyal and talented support, for thirteen years as their Chief Executive, and it is to them that I owe my gratitude for putting up with me all that time, and even occasionally agreeing with what I did and wanted them to do. I enjoyed (pretty much) every minute of it. Together, we turned a bit of a basket case, deep in a crisis of confidence and financial control, into one of the most successful and admired charities in the country, ready to take on any crisis or emergency, secure in the knowledge that it would do its best and do it well. As it has continued to do, across the world or around the corner, even during the recent difficult times of pandemic and lockdown.

I admire it from afar, and miss it still, that certain sign of hope in a crisis.

Index